Australian Good Birding Guide: Tasmania

Ted and Alex Wnorowski

Published by
Ted and Alex Wnorowski

ISBN N°: 978-0-6480104-6-3

Published in October 2017

by Ted and Alex Wnorowski
Gladstone
Queensland
Australia
Mob.   0432 422 862
Email: awnorowski100@gmail.com
Website: https://www.australian-good-birding-guide.com/

Subjects: Birdwatching – Australia
          Birdwatching - Guidebooks

Front cover: Green Rosella, Tasmanian endemic
Back cover: Horizontally: Bar-tailed Godwits roosting in Orielton Lagoon
             Vertically: Tasmanian Native-hen, White-fronted Chat, Black-faced Cormorant, Cape Barren Goose
Spine: Scaly-breasted Lorrikeet

All photographs in the book by Alex Wnorowski

Printed by Lightning Source®

Table of Contents

Introduction

According to the statistics published by Geoscience Australia, the tiny State of Tasmania occupies 0.9% of the surface area of Australia (68,400 square kilometres). Population of the State capital Hobart is 229,000 while the whole of Tasmania has 517,000 inhabitants as per 2016 census.

Located southernmost off the Australian mainland, Tasmania has nothing to protect it from the freezing breath of Antarctica so the island, standing a lone sentinel duty in the icy Southern Ocean, can be bitterly cold and wet. Even in summer the temperatures rarely climb above "mild". Despite its challenging climate, this small, unbelievably picturesque land is however a tourist magnet and a favourite destination of many a birdwatcher.

The Tasmanian landscapes have been shaped by the previous ice ages. Many areas are still very difficult to access, representing the true "wilderness" which is fast disappearing elsewhere under the pressure of human expansion. Flora diversity on the island is remarkable, and includes some of the most ancient plant species on Earth and a high proportion of endemic plants. Matched to that unique environment, Tasmanian fauna is highly diversified and endemic. The island has acted as a refuge for several wildlife species that are now extinct on the mainland.

Although the State birdlist stands only at around 260 species, with 200 being regularly recorded, you'll find here a dozen of endemic bird species that cannot be seen anywhere else. Moreover, most of these endemic birds are quite abundant and easy to find in Tasmania. On the list of endemics are: Forty-spotted Pardalote, Tasmania Scrubwren, Tasmanian Thornbill, Scrubtit, Tasmanian Native-hen, Dusky Robin, Green Rosella, Yellow-throated Honeyeater, Strong-billed Honeyeater, Black-headed Honeyeater, Yellow Wattlebird and Black Currawong. Two species of rare, critically endangered parrots breed on the island (so called breeding endemics); these are Orange-bellied Parrot and Swift Parrot. Tasmanian Morepork, newly elevated to a species level, is found mostly in Tasmania but is not strictly endemic as some birds have recently been found on the mainland.

Some species which occur both on the mainland Australia and in Tasmania have often developed Tasmania-specific phases, races or subspecies, for example Australian Magpie, Wedge-tailed Eagle, Azure Kingfisher and Brown Quail.

Only white phase of Grey Goshawk occurs in Tasmania.

Bushfires and sudden weather changes are the main natural hazards while exploring the birdwatching destinations. For National Park closures, changed conditions and fire hazards, check the page http://www.parks.tas.gov.au/index.aspx?base=7785 and the local Park's website.

Vehicle entry fees apply at most of Tasmanian national parks and reserves. This cost can be reduced by buying an annual pass from the Parks and Wildlife Services website here: http://www.parks.tas.gov.au/index.aspx?base=914. The pass does not cover any fees payable for overnight camping; these are extra.

Do not drive anywhere on roads marked "Closed". If you get bogged and require towing from a closed road, you'll pay a hefty penalty for that on top of your towing fees. If you lit a fire (even in a portable butane gas stove) when a total fire ban is imposed, you'll face significant fines and, more importantly, risk causing a bushfire. The fire ban warnings are *NOT* displayed in the National Parks, you do need to check the relevant website.

Nomenclature used in this chapter follows the *Systematics and Taxonomy of Australian Birds* by Les Christidis and Walter E. Boles, CSIRO Publishing, 2008, unless newer changes to taxonomy have been introduced (Birdlife's *Working List of Australian Birds* v2.1, October 2016). Nomenclature of seabirds follows the *Field Guide to New Zealand Seabirds* by Brian Parkinson, New Holland Publishers, 2000.

Tasmania

Tasmania has been divided in this book into regions. The approximate geographical locations of these regions are marked on the State map below, with hyperlinks to the detailed birding information available in the ebook edition.

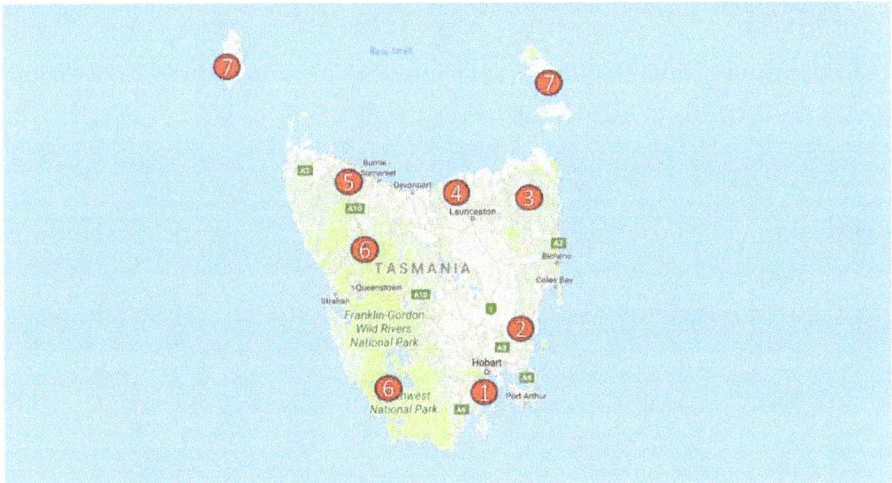

Expect the unexpected

More than 260 bird species have been recorded in the wild in Tasmania and on the nearby islands. Out of them, 182 species are recorded regularly, the rest are vagrants. Most of the vagrants come from the Australian mainland and usually are found first in the northern part of Tasmania. There are also some escapees from the aviaries, bird parks and farms that are slowly building up their numbers.

Some species are self-introduced – the most successful example is Cattle Egret. It started to appear in Tasmania in small wintering flocks in 1980' and now flocks of over 100 birds are regularly found in places such as Burnie, St. Helens, Queechy Lake (Launceston), etc.

Some other interesting reports of vagrant / blown away / self-introduced birds include:

- Stubble Quail – St. Helens, May 2007 (but plenty on King Island)
- Straw-necked Ibis – Launceston, March 2009
- Magpie Goose - Bridgewater on Derwent River, September 2009
- Willie Wagtail – Bruny Island, December 2009
- Red-backed Kingfisher – Bicheno, July 2010
- Indian Mynah – this bird is not welcome in Tasmania but sneaks in by ferry and was found in Devonport (February - May 2011)
- Buff-banded Rail – Ulverstone, March 2011
- Brown Booby – Fortescue Bay, April 2011
- White-throated Treecreeper – Burnie, June 2011
- Wandering Whistling-Duck - Lake Dulverton, November 2011
- Spangled Drongo – St Helens, May 2013
- Gentoo Penguin – Fortescue Bay, May 2013
- Red-kneed Dotterel – Strachan, June 2013
- Australian Darter – Interlaken, February 2014
- Straw-necked Ibis – Port Sorell, July 2013; Smithton, August 2016
- White-necked Heron – Henderson Lagoon, May 2014; Somerset, April 2017
- White-winged Triller - Maria Island (Frenchs Farm), December 2014
- Forest Kingfisher – Wynyard, June 2015
- Fiordland Penguin, Bicheno Beach, July 2015
- Pied Stilt – Tamar Island Wetlands, September 2015
- Banded Stilt – Ansons Bay, February 2016; Lauderdale, August 2016; Marion Bay, September 2016
- Rose-crowned Fruit-Dove –Devonport, April 2016; Snug Tiers, January 2017
- Great Frigatebird – St Helens, June 2016
- Lesser Frigatebird – St Helens, June 2016
- Franklin's Gull – Strachan, August 2016

- Stubble Quail – Campbell Town, August 2016
- Snares Penguin – Tasman National Park, September 2016
- New Zealand Scaup – Goulds Lagoon, 2016
- White-headed Pigeon – Devonport, February 2017
- Olive-backed Oriole – Moulting Lagoon, March 2017
- Sacred Kingfisher – Wynyard, April 2017.

Sacred Kingfisher is one of the unexpected finds in Tasmania

Many rarities can be expected during pelagic trips. Thousands of seabirds pass Tasmania's shores on their migrations. Some breed on the coastal islands. There are always some unusual birds among them. As an example, Eaglehawk Nest pelagic trips reported:

- Great Shearwater - April 2012
- Stejneger's Petrel – December 2014
- Little Shearwater – January 2016
- Arctic Tern – May 2016
- Antarctic Tern – October 2016
- Buller's Shearwater – January 2017
- Grey Petrel – May 2017
- Blue Petrel – May 2017.

Over 30 bird species were introduced to the wild by man. Most of them survived and built viable populations while the status of some of them is still uncertain. If you find any, you may wonder whether these are aviary escapees or wild population. Examples include:

- Common Pheasant (Ring-necked Pheasant). There are numerous records from areas north of Hobart, including Sorell, Copping, Forcett, Seven Mile Beach and Marion Bay. Usually males are seen. We saw two males and one female in November 2011 in a pine forest near Seven Mile Beach.
- Indian Peafowl. These birds are regularly found in the Cataract Gorge in Launceston, they have been here for about 100 years. Elsewhere, you may encounter farm escapees as these birds are often kept for ornamental reasons. "Tickable" populations are established on King Island and Flinders Island.
- Barbary Dove. A small group can regularly be seen on the wires and in bushes in Richmond near Sorell as you enter the township. We saw 5 birds sitting on the wires near the river in November 2010.

Some of the introduced species seem to be currently taking over Tasmania. Among them are:

- Rainbow Lorikeet. Flocks of up to 30 birds have been recorded in Ulverstone, Devonport, Burnie, Hobart and Taroona and sightings seem to be on the increase.
- Long-billed Corella. Regularly reported from the Sorell area.
- Superb Lyrebird. This species was deliberately introduced in 1930' to two small pockets near the Hastings Caves. It has now spread into the whole south-west wilderness area of Tasmania. These amazing birds are capable of incorporating calls of different other birds to their songs. We were surprised to hear a Whipbird call near the road to Hasting Caves – that was a lyrebird. It could not have heard a Whipbird itself – this sound must have been brought from the mainland by the first lyrebirds nearly 70 years ago – the population still remembers it! We also observed the same bird to use the local Green Rosella and Crescent Honeyeater's call so the repertoire has been updated over the years!

Search also for very rare birds in Tasmania. There is more to them than just the famous Orange-bellied Parrot, Swift Parrot, Forty-spotted Pardalote and the Tasmanian subspecies of Wedge-tailed Eagle. Therefore, be on a lookout for:

- Azure Kingfisher. Approximately 250 birds of the Tasmanian subspecies remain in Tasmania, most often found on Gorgon and Arthur Rivers. Recently, a good place to spot this rare subspecies seems to be on the Inglis River Walk near Wynyard.

- Grey Goshawk (white form morphology). Only 110 breeding pairs are left in Tasmania. The bird is easily noticeable due to its white plumage but remember that the total numbers are frightfully low. It is still being killed by farmers.
- Painted Button-quail. Small numbers are regularly seen in Meehan Ranges and Risdon Brook Reserve, both in the Hobart area.
- Spotted Quail-thrush. Difficult to see but you can expect them in a forest in the St. Helens area.
- Nankeen Night-Heron. Small numbers breed in the Launceston area (Queechy Lake, Tamar Island Wetlands).
- Australasian Bittern. Very rare everywhere. Good places to try to find them are Queechy Lake in Launceston and Windmill Swamp in St. Helens.

Hobart and Surrounds

Hobart is the capital city of the Tasmanian State and the main gateway to the island. It is the place of breathtaking beauty and of significant historic interest. It was one of the first European settlements in early 1800' and a big penal colony. Several convict-built stone buildings dating back to this early period are still in use in town today.

The most prominent geographical features that contribute to Hobart's splendour are River Derwent, Mt Wellington and of course the Storm Bay that Hobart wraps itself around.

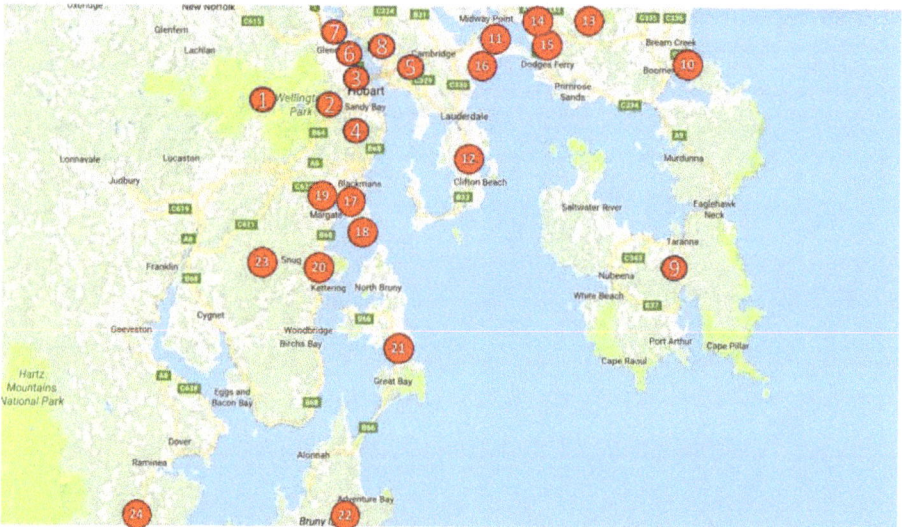

1	Mt Wellington	13	Woodvine Nature Reserve
2	Waterworks Reserve	14	Townsend Lagoon, Lewisham
3	Queens Domain & Botanical Gardens	15	Blue Lagoon, Dodges Ferry
4	Mt Nelson and Truganini Reserve	16	Pittwater Rd, Seven Mile Beach
5	Meehan Ranges	17	Peter Murrell Reserve
6	Goulds Lagoon Sanctuary	18	Tinderbox Peninsula
7	Murphys Flat Wetlands, Granton	19	Dru Point, Margate
8	Gage Brook Wetlands	20	Oyster Cove (Putalina IPA)
9	Tasman National Park	21	Bruny Island
10	Marion Bay	22	South Bruny National Park
11	Pitt Water and Orielton Lagoon	23	Snug Tiers Recreation Area
12	South Arm Peninsula	24	Hastings Caves State Reserve

Mt Wellington

A wilderness experience in the city – Mt Wellington is a mighty mountain that dominates the Hobartian landscape. Towering 1,271m above the sea level, it provides a schoolbook demonstration of vertical habitat stratification. The impressive dolerite pinnacles known as Organ Pipes are the main feature of the mountain.

Mt Wellington exerts a strong influence over the city weather. Even in summer its peak may be covered by snow. A sealed 20km-long Pinnacle Rd leads to the summit. It winds itself through the wet sclerophyll forest and patches of rainforest growing on the lower slopes of the mountain until it reaches subalpine and alpine vegetation at the higher elevations. The mountain slopes are criss-crossed with many walking tracks and fire trails. A lookout on the summit offers simply magnificent panoramic views from the top, just don't forget to take your warmest clothes with you – it's bitterly cold up there even in the middle of summer.

Mt Wellington is part of the Mt Wellington Park that extends westwards for 30km and covers 18,000ha, one of the biggest Tasmanian parks, located right in the middle of State Capital.

Mt Wellington is easily accessible from the City by car, bus or on foot. By car, take Davey St (A6) westward from the City and continue to Huon Rd (B64). If you turn right into Pillinger Dr (C616) just before Tree Fern, it will take you to the top of the mountain (changing name to Pinnacle Rd on its way). However, the entry to the Wellington Park's birdwatching heaven is from the Tree Fern village, a bit further on along the main road. We recommend a walk on the Fern Glade Tk, with an entrance located behind a quaint, little old church. Go uphill at least a couple of kilometres through the magical temperate rainforest full of water-dripping ferns and mosses. After that, drive back to Pillinger Dr and Pinnacle Rd and go to the top of the mountain, stopping at different altitudes to observe the birdlife changing along with the vegetation zones.

Parking is available at Fern Tree, The Springs and on the summit. Limited parking is available at other points along Pinnacle Rd. Facilities located in Fern Tree (close to Fern Glade Tk) include picnic tables, barbecues, shops and the tavern. At The Springs you'll find a picnic shelter, wood barbecues and several walking tracks. At Halls Saddle off Pipeline Tk, a picnic shelter and wood barbecues are provided. A good map of the area is provided in the bushwalking brochure downloadable here: https://www.wellingtonpark.org.au/assets/WP_Walk_Info_Sheet-2014-Web_kunanyi_revised140819.pdf.

About 90 bird species have been recorded in the Park. **Key species** are Scrubtit, Tasmanian Thornbill and Pink Robin. Other birds of interest include Black Currawong, Tasmanian Scrubwren, Bassian Thrush, Green Rosella, Wedge-tailed Eagle and Grey Goshawk.

Fern Glade Track

This short walk is one of the best tracks for Tasmanian endemics, found mostly at the bottom of the track. If you then take a walk to The Springs, both tracks will form a 3.8km loop that will take half a day to complete.

The ornamental start of the Fern Glade Track

At Fern Glade Tk, we located the Tasmanian Scrubwren's nest with three chicks just near the church at the entry to the track. Scrubtit was foraging in a tree, going down on a tree trunk like a Sittella, collecting insects for two youngsters begging on a branch. Grey Goshawk showed itself far in the gully; it was so white that we took it first for one of Sulphur-crested Cockatoos flying around. Bassian Thrush is common on the forest floor, look for them near the church. Pink Robin and Dusky Robin can be located easily in the ferns along the track. Pink Robins are tame and unafraid. Other bush birds, such as Tasmanian Thornbill, Green Rosella and Scrubtit are common here.

Fern Tree village proved to be a good birding site. Honeyeaters (Yellow-throated Honeyeater, Black-headed Honeyeater, Strong-billed Honeyeater, Eastern Spinebill, Yellow Wattlebird and Little Wattlebird) were common, feeding in the flowering eucalyptus trees. A flock of Rainbow Lorikeets, rare in Tasmania, landed on a gum tree while we enjoyed a cold drink on the local tavern's veranda. Horsfield's Bronze-Cuckoo was shouting loudly from a small bush near the church. In a tree nearby, Grey Goshawk was trying to look inconspicuous – an impossible task with its white plumage. Later we also found Tawny Frogmouth roosting in a tree in the playground of a small park.

Other birds in the area included Shining-Bronze-cuckoo, Scarlet Robin, Musk Lorikeet, Black Currawong, Golden Whistler and plenty of Striated Pardalotes.

Pipeline Track

Pipeline Tk runs along the foothill of Mt Wellington along Huon Rd (B64), connecting the Waterworks Reserve with Fern Tree. Where Pipeline Tk crosses Chimney Pot Hill Rd, Halls Saddle is located, offering a picnic shelter for a rest.

A section of the track between the Waterworks Reserve and Halls Saddle runs mostly through the dry sclerophyll forest. Grey Currawongs are very common here and their 'clink-clink' call can be heard the whole day round. Other birds include Yellow-throated Honeyeater, Strong-billed Honeyeater, Black-headed Honeyeater, Pallid Cuckoo, Shining Bronze-cuckoo, Brown Thornbill, Spotted Pardalote, Striated Pardalote and Black-faced Cuckoo-shrike. In Halls Saddle, Bassian Thrush usually quietly stands in the bushes behind the barbecue.

Scarlet Robin

A section between Halls Saddle and Fern Tree runs mostly through a dense wet forest with the shrubby understory. Bassian Thrush an Olive Whistler are common here. A good birding spot is located around the old pipelines in the gully. Look there for Pink Robin, Tasmanian Thornbill, Shining Bronze-cuckoo, Golden Whistler, Crested Honeyeater and Black Currawong.

The area from the point where the track crosses Clegg Rd up to the Silver Falls is fantastic for Scrubtits. Look also for Pink Robin, Scarlet Robin, Olive Whistler, Tasmanian Morepork and Grey Goshawk.

Pinnacle Road

About 1.5km past the houses on Pillinger Dr you'll come across a sharp U-shaped curve known as Shoobridge Bend. A small carpark is located on the left, provided for the access to a short loop through the forest, with connections to other tracks up and down the mountain. Hollows in large stringybark gums growing here are being used for nesting by Swift Parrots and Green Rosellas. Also, Tasmanian Moreporks make use of these hollows. Tasmanian Thornbills, Striated Pardalotes and Scarlet Robins are very common here. Other birds in the area include Golden Whistler, Dusky Robin, Grey Shrike-thrush, Yellow-tailed Black-Cockatoo and Sulphur-crested Cockatoo.

Another 1.5km uphill from the Shoobridge Bend on Pinnacle Rd, at The Springs picnic site, the Scrubtits are extremely common and tame. If you are lucky, you may find Black Currawong among very common Grey Currawongs. Crescent Honeyeater, New Holland Honeyeater, Eastern Spinebill, Scarlet Robin, Golden Whistler, Forest Raven and Satin Flycatcher can also be found in this area.

Next, you'll see the Big Bend on Pinnacle Rd about 2km before the summit. The heath around the Big Bend is good for Striated Fieldwren.

The birds that are the most visible at the very top and the most audible through the howling wind are Flame Robins. If you look carefully, you will also find Olive Whistlers in the low alpine heath cover. We also watched a pair of Wedge-tailed Eagles soaring through the thinned air. In summer, flocks of White-throated Needletails are often seen flying over the summit.

Stunted vegetation at the top of Mt Wellington

Waterworks Reserve

The Reserve is located at the foot of Mt Wellington, 4km from Hobart CBD. The Waterworks were constructed in 1860' to collect water flowing in the creeks on the higher slopes of Mt Wellington. The Reserve comprises a water reservoir and areas of dry sclerophyll eucalyptus forest.

Coming back from Mt. Wellington, turn left from Huon Rd (B64) into Chimney Pot Hill Rd. The road name changes to Ridgeway Rd and later to Waterworks Rd. The reservoir is on the left. From Hobart, take Davey St (B64), drive 2.3km then turn left into Lynton Av. After 200m make a right turn into Waterworks Rd. The reserve is 1.5km along this road on the right.

You'll find here several carparks, barbecues and shelters. It is a very popular picnic spot for Hobart dwellers. Cars may enter daily from 8:30 am to 4:15pm. Otherwise walk through the turnstile adjacent to the main gate. A network of walking tracks meanders around the two reservoirs and uphill into bushland of Ridgeway towards the slopes of Mt Wellington. A map is included in the site brochure, downloadable from the City of Hobart's website here: https://www.hobartcity.com.au/Community/Parks-reserves-and-sporting-facilities/Find-a-park-or-sportsground/Waterworks-reserve.

Over 80 bird species have been recorded in the Reserve. **Key species** are Masked Owl and Satin Flycatcher. Other birds of interest include Tasmanian Morepork, Tawny Frogmouth, Australian Owlet-nightjar, Bassian Thrush, robins, cuckoos and honeyeaters.

Come here for spotlighting. This is the best location for Masked Owl in the Hobart area. Look in the bush behind the playground. Australian Owlet-nightjar can be found there, too. They have also been recorded in the bush at the south side of the bottom reservoir and the north side of the top reservoir. Tawny Frogmouth usually hunts insects near the lamp posts beside the bottom reservoir. A pair is regularly found roosting during the day near site #9. Tasmanian Morepork often calls from the hills.

Waterworks Reserve is a good place for Satin Flycatcher. Look for them in the bush behind the playground. A pair was found nesting near site #9.

Take a walk around the reservoir, in particular around the top reservoir. You may include a side trip along Circular Tk. On the water, you will find grebes (Australasian Grebe and Hoary-headed Grebe), Great Cormorant, gulls (Kelp Gull, Silver Gull and Pacific Gull) and ducks such as Hardhead, Chestnut Teal, Mallard and Australian Shelduck. A small flock of Australian Wood Ducks is regularly seen here. The park's population of Kelp Gulls is large; they often gather in large flocks (80-200 birds) on the water or on lawns.

Tasmanian Native-hen is found in the Waterworks Reserve in good numbers

Bush birds in the reserve include Green Rosella, Yellow-throated Honeyeater, Strong-billed Honeyeater, Black-headed Honeyeater, Tasmanian Scrubwren and Black Currawong. Dusky Robin is very abundant on the grassy areas south of the top reservoir. Tasmanian Native-hen, Beautiful Firetail, Bassian Thrush, Pink Robin and Scarlett Robin are regularly reported from the grounds. The reserve is also good for pigeons (Common Bronzewing, Brush Bronzewing and Spotted Dove) and cuckoos in summer (Shining Bronze-Cuckoo, Horsfield's Bronze-Cuckoo, Fan-tailed Cuckoo and Pallid Cuckoo).

The site is home to a large flock (60+ birds) of Sulphur-crested Cockatoos. They roost in the tall trees near the water.

The bush along Sandy Bay Rivulet near Gentle Annie Tk is worth checking. Bassian Thrush, Olive Whistler and plenty Brush Bronzewings and cuckoos can be found there.

Queens Domain and Botanical Gardens

This 13.5ha urban park, locally known as the Domain, is a small hilly area of bushland along the River Derwent by the Tasman Bridge just 2km northeast of the CBD. On the side of a hill, framed by the river, sit the Royal Tasmanian Botanical Gardens and the Government House. The gardens were established in 1818 as the gardens for the Government House so most of the plants are exotic but still attract a good selection of native birds. The northwest face of the hill that is covered with open grassy woodland is the Domain part of the site.

To get there, take Tasman Hwy (A3) north, then just past the Aquatic Centre on the left turn into Lower Domain Rd. Botanical Gardens are on your right, the Domain is on the left. Facilities in the gardens include carpark, Visitor Centre, shops and a restaurant. In the Domain, there are picnic areas, barbecues and walking tracks.

About 60 bird species have been recorded here. **Key species** are Painted Button-quail (rare), Swift Parrot, Eastern Rosella and Musk Lorikeet. Other birds of interest include Australian Magpie, Brown Thornbill, Tree Martin, Laughing Kookaburra, Peregrine Falcon and the honeyeaters.

The Gardens attract a variety of native and introduced common species. Among the all year-round residents are Yellow Wattlebird, Little Wattlebird, Yellow-throated Honeyeater, Eastern Spinebill, Yellow-rumped Thornbill, Bassian Thrush and Laughing Kookaburra. Summer visitors include Swift Parrot, Tree Martin, Welcome Swallow and Black-faced Cuckoo-shrike.

Painted Button-quails are rare but can be found in the northern part of the Domain, rushing through short grass at the edge of dense bushland.

Tasmanian subspecies of Australian Magpie, resident in the Gardens

On the lawns, you may usually find good numbers of Eastern Rosellas and Green Rosellas and families of Tasmanian Native-hens. Flocks of Musk Lorikeets will be in the trees. Look also for Dusky Robin, Scarlet Robin and Golden Whistler. On a small lake, there will be Australian Pelicans, Black Swans, Northern Mallards and gulls. Mallard hybridises so intensely with Pacific Black Duck here that we were unable to find a single pure Black Duck on the lake.

A breeding colony of Silver Gulls is located on the old railway track. The birds nest on and in between the sleepers.

The most common species in the Domain's native bushland include Brown Thornbill, Crescent Honeyeater, Black-headed Honeyeater, Little Wattlebird, Noisy Miner and Grey Currawong.

Many raptor species may be encountered in the area, in the middle of a State capital, such as Wedge-tailed Eagle, Peregrine Falcon, Grey Goshawk, Brown Goshawk, Brown Falcon, Australian Hobby and occasionally Tasmanian Morepork.

Mt Nelson and Truganini Reserve

In the past, the 352m high Mt Nelson was the location of signal stations. In the early 19th century they linked Hobart with Port Arthur and announced the arrival of boats in Storm Bay. Now it is a popular tourist attraction with an excellent lookout, picnic area, historic buildings, a restaurant and an environmental reserve, just 10min from the CBD. From the Lookout, you'll have sweeping views of Hobart, Storm Bay and Derwent estuary. It's been rated by some the second-best view after Mt Wellington.

On the southeastern side of Mt Nelson, from the summit to the Lower Sandy Bay, a 65ha Truganini Reserve is located. A 2km Truganini Tk runs along Cartwright Creek, climbing up from Sandy Bay Rd to Mt Nelson Signal Station. The first 1km of the track is wet sclerophyll forest full of tree ferns and mosses, later giving way to dry sclerophyll forest dominated by Tasmanian blue gums with the understory of dense shrubs.

To get there, take Sandy Bay Rd (B68) from the CBD as far as West Point Casino, then turn right into Nelson Rd which will take you to the summit over a very bendy route. You can also catch a bus to Mt Nelson from Franklin Square. To walk the Truganini Tk from the bottom end, turn off Sandy Bay Rd in Taroona near the bus stop No. 32.

Over 70 species are on the Mt Nelson's birdlist. The **key species** is Masked Owl. It is a very good site for all of the Tasmanian endemics. Even Forty-Spotted Pardalote is sporadically recorded.

Masked Owl can be found roosting half-way through the Truganini Tk. In the upper part of the track near the Signal Station, Swift Parrots appear regularly in summer in the blue gums. Fan-tailed Cuckoo and Pallid Cuckoo are common in summer. Look also for Satin Flycatcher, Green Rosella, Brown Thornbill, Dusky Robin, Crescent Honeyeater, Yellow-throated Honeyeater, Black-headed Honeyeater and Yellow Wattlebird.

In the wet gullies at the bottom part of the track, you may come across Satin Flycatcher, Brush Bronzewing, Pink Robin, Olive Whistler, Tasmanian Thornbill, Tasmanian Scrubwren, Silvereye, Crescent Honeyeater, Bassian Thrush and Golden Whistler. Beautiful Firetails can be found in a tea tree scrub near Cartwright Reserve.

Among the raptors, Brown Goshawk is most frequently found in the Reserve. Sporadically, Wedge-tiled Eagle and Collared Sparrowhawk can appear. Nocturnal birds beside Masked Owl also include Tasmanian Morepork and Tawny Frogmouth.

Juvenile Tawny Frogmouth

Meehan Ranges

Meehan Ranges Nature Recreation Area is located northeast of Hobart in the suburb of Clarence. It consists of a series of steep hills running parallel to River Derwent.

A 2,700ha conservation area is situated at the Red Gate section of the Range. The land is protected from development due to its conservation status. Vegetation in the Range is mainly dry sclerophyll forest which makes it prone to bushfires. Several severe fires went through the area in the last 25 years.

The area is very popular with Tasmanian birdwatchers thanks to a small resident population of Painted Button-quails.

From the city, take Tasman Hwy (A3) towards the Hobart Airport, then take the second turnoff to Cambridge Rd (B31/C328), turning immediately west (left) into Belbins Rd; the Reserve gate will be in 300 metres. Birding is conducted along Stringy Bark Gully Tk, 6km one way, that runs mostly along the Barilla Rivulet through dry sclerophyll forest, with magnificent views. The bad news is that then you have to walk 6km back to your car...

The Reserve is used heavily by the mountain bikers. A maze of unmarked mountain bike tracks criss-crosses the area so don't lose your way.

Over 70 bird species are on the site's birdlist. **Key species** are Painted Button-quail, Swift Parrot and Blue-winged Parrot. Other birds of interest include Tasmanian Morepork, Brown Thornbill, Satin Flycatcher, Dusky Woodswallow, Scarlet Robin, Dusky Robin, Yellow-throated Honeyeater, Strong-billed Honeyeater and Beautiful Firetail. Among the rarities are Peregrine Falcon and Masked Owl.

Painted Button-quails are regularly found in the vicinity of a small waterhole along Stringy Bark Gully Tk. Masked Owl can be found in the trees 50m west of the waterhole. In the bush around the waterhole you may come across robins (Scarlett Robin, Flame Robin and Dusky Robin), thornbills (Brown Thornbill, Yellow-rumped Thornbill) and honeyeaters (Yellow-throated Honeyeater, Strong-billed Honeyeater, Crescent Honeyeater, Black-headed Honeyeater, Eastern Spinebill and Yellow Wattlebird).

Near the entrance gate, a few Tasmanian Native-hens and Blue-billed Parrots can be found. Olive Whistlers live in dense vegetation along Barilla Creek, 500m from the carpark. In this area you may also encounter Beautiful Firetail, Grey Currawong, Satin Flycatcher and Tasmanian Scrubwren.

Brown Goshawk is often found along the track. Whenever you see a stand of Tasmanian blue gums, look for Swift Parrots which live here in summer.

Other birds that may be found during this walk include Brush Bronzewing, Common Bronzewing, Green Rosella, Sulphur-crested Cockatoo, Black Currawong, Spotted Pardalote and Striated Pardalote. Watch for a pair of Wedge-tailed Eagles in the sky. You may also get Brown Falcon and Peregrine Falcon.

Goulds Lagoon Sanctuary

This ephemeral freshwater lagoon, very popular with birdwatchers, is part of the magnificent wetland habitat of River Derwent. The site is located just half an hour drive northwest of Hobart. This small area is very important for breeding, resting and feeding for many waterbirds, in particular for crakes and rails. The site was declared a sanctuary as early as 1938 by its owner, Arthur Gould.

The site is located on the south side of the River Derwent, opposite Bridgewater. To get there from Hobart, take Brooker Hwy (1) to Granton on the west side of the river. Get off the highway near Granton and head back southeast on the Main Road towards the Austins Ferry village. After 3km you'll see the lagoon on your right; turn off to a small carpark. Alternatively, approach the site from the east side of the river on East Derwent Hwy (B32), cross the bridge to Granton and head back southeast on the Main Road. A walkway runs around the lagoon with interpretative signage, sections of boardwalk, a viewing platform and a bird hide.

Over 100 bird species have been recorded here. **Key species** are Australian Spotted Crake, Baillon's Crake, Lewin's Rail, Latham's Snipe and Freckled Duck. Other birds of interest include Australasian Shoveler, Hardhead, Dusky Moorhen and Little Grassbird. The area is well-known for vagrant sightings. Rarities found here include Little Ringed Plover, Pink-eared Duck, Great Crested Grebe, Rainbow Lorikeet, Black-tailed Native-hen, Magpie Goose and New Zealand Scaup.

The lagoon is best for birding in early summer when water is receding exposing a muddy margin. Crakes are easy to watch then as they like to come out onto the mud, particularly in the area adjacent to the walkway just before the bird hide. Latham's Snipes are present in good numbers around the lagoon every summer. A small flock of Freckled Ducks has made home in the lagoon since 2012 and their numbers seem to be slowly creeping up. Dusky Moorhen breeds in the lagoon.

At times, the lagoon may be completely covered by the waterfowl. Eurasian Coots, Grey Teals and Chestnut Teals are usually the most numerous. A wailing call of Little Grassbird can be heard around the lagoon. In summer, you may also find here Australian Reed-Warbler, otherwise rare in Tasmania.

There should be plenty of honeyeaters in the surrounding bush, in particular you may hear the belching call of Yellow Wattlebird. Look also for Pallid Cuckoo, Dusky Woodswallow, Scarlet Robin, Yellow-tailed Black-Cockatoo, Caspian Tern and Kelp Gull. Flocks of Sulphur-crested Cockatoos often roost around the lagoon.

Eight raptor species have been recorded at this site. Seen most often is Swamp Harrier but you may also find Grey Goshawk, Brown Goshawk, White-bellied Sea-Eagle, Brown Falcon and Wedge-tailed Eagle.

Murphys Flat Wetlands, Granton

River Derwent widens west of Granton forming fantastic wetlands between Granton and New Norfolk. Extensive areas of reed beds can be found on the banks of the river on both sides. On the southern shore besides the Lyell Hwy, Murhpys Flat Conservation Area, a popular birding spot, is located. It covers 66ha of reed beds, marshes, underwater vegetation and tidal flats where a variety of birds breed and feed.

To get there, drive from Granton along Lyell Hwy (A10). The site is located midway between Granton and New Norfolk, close to the entrance of Pipeline Fire Tk. Site coordinates are 42.44.47 S and 147.10.40 E.

About 100 bird species have been recorded in Murphys Flat Wetlands. **Key species** are Australasian Bittern, Australian Spotted Crake, Lewin's Rail, Dusky Moorhen and Musk Duck. Other birds of interest include Black Swan, Chestnut Teal, Australasian Shoveler, Eastern Great Egret, Little Grassbird and Australian Reed-Warbler. Rare species include Blue-billed Duck and Baillon's Crake.

This is a very good area to try to get an Australasian Bittern. Most often it is observed flying or roosting on the northern side of the River Derwent.

Waterbirds congregate here in huge numbers. Counts of just Eurasian Coots sometimes reach 1,500 birds. Hundreds of Black Swans, Chestnut Teals, Purple Swamphens and Pacific Black Ducks frequent the area. A good population of Musk Ducks and Australasian Shovelers lives in the swamp. Dusky Moorhens breed there. You may also find a few Grey Teals, Hardheads, Hoary-headed Grebes and Great Crested Grebes as well as an occasional Australian Pelican.

We observed good numbers of Northern Mallards and hybrids of Mallards with Pacific Black Ducks. This hybridization occurs along the whole course of the River Derwent. This easy cross-species breeding is a significant threat to the native Pacific Black Duck whose future looks bleak if not addressed. In New Zealand, Pacific Black Duck (called Grey Duck there) has nearly been wiped out due to cross-breeding with Mallard and only a few pure-bred populations can now be found in remote locations such as East Cape.

Little Grassbird and Australian Reed-Warbler can be found in the reeds. Swamp Harrier breeds in the swamp and can often be seen patrolling the area. Bush birds to be found at this site include Brush Bronzewing, New Holland Honeyeater, Crescent Honeyeater,

Horsfield's Bronze-cuckoo, Musk Lorikeet, Eastern Rosella, Noisy Miner and Little Wattlebird.

Other birds of Murphys Flat Wetlands include Eastern Great Egret, Little Egret, Hoary-headed Grebe, Tasmanian Native-hen and Kelp Gull. Latham's Snipe has also been found in the area.

Eastern Great Egret

Gage Brook Wetlands

Gage Brook Wetlands are situated along the northern side of East Derwent Hwy (B32) on the northern side of Derwent River just before the Gagebrook village. If you got to the roundabout in the village, you went too far, turn around and go back about 400m. The wetland can be reached on foot from the highway, as we recommend, as it may not be well visible from the road. Approximate site coordinates are 42.45.22S and 147.16.21E.

Small flocks of Pied Stilts are regularly found there. They are very rare in Tasmania although in recent years their reporting seems to be on the rise. This small wetland can also produce a good selection of ducks including Australasian Shoveler, Hardhead, Grey Teal, Australian Shelduck and, occasionally, Blue-billed Duck. The wailing calls of Little Grassbird can be heard from the vegetation. Large flocks (100-200 birds) of Sulphur-crested Cockatoos often choose to roost in the trees. Other birds recorded at Gage Brook Wetlands include Black-fronted Dotterel, Crescent Honeyeater, Grey Butcherbird, Hoary-headed Grebe, Tasmanian Native-Hen and Brown Falcon.

Tasman National Park

Tasman Peninsula protrudes south on the eastern side of the Storm Bay, opposite Hobart. Access is easy via Arthur Hwy (A9). The whole Peninsula is a good place for many Tasmanian endemic bird species, shorebirds and seabirds. It's a must for a short-term visitor who cannot spend much time travelling to more remote locations. As most of the land is a national park or a reserve, all sites located on Tasman and Forestier Peninsulas will be described under the chapter heading of Tasman National Park.

The area features two narrow isthmuses, Dunnalley and Eaglehawk Neck. The former connects the Forestier Peninsula with the mainland and the latter connect Tasman Peninsula with Forestier Peninsula. The isthmuses currently play an important role in the regulation of Tasmanian devil population, aimed at separation of the healthy groups from the animals infected with the deadly facial tumour virus.

The Park covers 10,700ha. It comprises three large separate parcels of land as well as several small state reserves and historic sites:

- First block is situated on the eastern side of Forestier Peninsula, from Dunnalley Isthmus down to Osprey Point. This block is rarely visited.
- Second block wraps itself around the southeastern coast of Tasman Peninsula from Pirates Bay to Cape Pillar and includes several small islands such as Tasman Island and Hippolyte Rocks.
- Third block (Cape Raoul section) starts at the western entrance to Port Arthur and follows the coast to Storm Bay including Cape Raoul.
- The small reserves include Tessellated Pavement State Reserve, Eaglehawk Neck Historic Site and Port Arthur Historic Site.

Besides the well-known convict history of Port Arthur, Tasman National Park is renowned for its striking coastal panorama, in particular for its 300m-high cliffs, sea caves, blowholes, coastal arches, etc. Tasmania hard volcanic dolerite resisted erosion and its columns form the iconic and dramatic coastal cliffs. Arguably, some most stunning coastal scenery of Tasmania can be found here.

The wet and dry sclerophyll forest and coastal heath dominate the Park. Extensive heathland and coastal scrub can be found at Cape Pillar, Cape Hauy and Cape Raoul. There are also smaller areas of dune vegetation, wetlands and saltmarshes and small patches of rainforest and subalpine scrub.

Dramatic dolerite cliffs of Tasman Peninsula

Several wildlife-watching boats operate from Tasman Peninsula, offering an opportunity to see seabirds, whales, dolphins, seals, as well as to enjoy the spectacular scenery of the peninsula cliffs. Regular pelagic trips are available from Eaglehawk Neck (see below for details).

To get to the National Park, follow Arthur Hwy (A9) from Sorell, 27km northeast of Hobart. Several access roads lead to different areas of the Park.

- To the northern end of the Tasman Peninsula turn off Arthur Hwy (A9) into Blowhole Rd (C338) just past Eaglehawk Neck. This road will take you to Tasman Arch and Devil's Kitchen. Along Blowhole Rd, a signposted gravel road (Waterfall Bay Rd) to the right leads to Waterfall Bay. This road provides access to Tasman Tk southwards or to Tasman Arch to the north.
- To reach the southern area of the Park, continue on Arthur Hwy (A9) towards Port Arthur. Turn left into Fortescue Rd (C344) 6km past Taranna. Drive 12km on a dirt road which provides access to the Fortescue Bay Campground and to the walking track to Cape Hauy, Canoe Bay and Cape Pillar. Otherwise, turn off A9 in Port Arthur into Safety Cove Rd (C347) to Crescent Bay.
- The western part of the Park can be reached via Stormlea Rd off Nubeena Rd (B37) past Nubeena.

Facilities around Tasman Peninsula include a plethora of walking tracks and the Park's only campground in Fortescue Bay. Fuel and plenty of accommodation and food options can be found in Port Arthur and Nubeena. Facilities in the Cape Raoul section are limited to walking tracks and a carpark at the end of Stormlea Rd.

Over 120 bird species have been recorded in the Tasman National Park. **Key species** are Swift Parrot, Little Penguin, Peregrine Falcon and White-bellied Sea-Eagle. Other species of interest include Cape Barren Goose, Satin Flycatcher, Bassian Thrush, Brown Thornbill, Tasmanian Thornbill, Wedge-tailed Eagle, seabirds and honeyeaters. Among the rarities are Snares Penguin and Gentoo Penguin. 11 out of 12 endemic birds are found in the Park, the only one out is Forty-spotted Pardalote.

There are several Little Penguin colonies in the Park. They can be watched coming onshore at night at Pirates Bay and Fortescue Bay. The Park is the stronghold of Peregrine Falcon and White-bellied Sea-Eagle; both species breed in the Park. One of the recent surveys counted over 20 nests (collectively for both raptors).

Many seabirds nest on Hippolyte Rocks, Tasman Island and the rock tacks around the Peninsula. These include Short-tailed Shearwater, Sooty Shearwater, Fairy Prion, Black-faced Cormorant, Pacific Gull, Kelp Gull, Silver Gull and Caspian Tern.

Eaglehawk Neck Pelagic Trips

Eaglehawk Neck Pelagics are the only trips that regularly sail to the shelf off the east coast of Tasmania. St Helens pelagics have been discontinued.

The best pelagic tours from Eaglehawk Neck are organised three times a year by Rohan Clarke (rohan@wildlifeimages.com.au) under the auspices of Birdlife Australia. The recent trips were organised in January, July and September 2017. Information on the 2017 programme is presented here: http://birding-aus.org/pelagic-trips-off-eaglehawk-neck-tas-in-2017/. The 2018 programme was not yet available at the time of this book going to print.

The boat departs from a jetty at Eaglehawk Neck, just off Arthur Hwy (A9). A full-day trip will let you tap into the knowledge of experienced seabirders that are always on the boat. Up to 40 seabird species (20-25 on average) have been observed during a single trip. A wide selection of South Ocean seabirds as well as many vagrants from all over the world may be encountered. You'll need to book a place as the tours are high in demand.

In total, over 100 species have been recorded. Winter pelagic trips up to September are good for albatrosses. Most common are Shy Albatross, Indian Yellow-nosed Albatross, Buller's Albatross, Black-browed Albatross, Northern Royal Albatross, Southern Royal Albatross, Gibson Wandering Albatross, Antipodean Wandering Albatross and Snowy

Wandering Albatross. The rarities include Grey-headed Albatross, Salvin's Albatross, Chatham Albatross and Light-mantled Sooty Albatross. Summer brings plenty of shearwaters, with the common species including Short-tailed Shearwater, Fluttering Shearwater, Hutton's Shearwater and Sooty Shearwater. Rarer records include Buller's Shearwater, Little Shearwater, Flesh-footed Shearwater, Great Shearwater and Wedge-tailed Shearwater.

A wide range of petrels can be sighted on the pelagic trips. The most common are White-chinned Petrel, Great-winged Petrel, Soft-plumaged Petrel, Grey-faced Petrel, Common Diving-Petrel and Cape Petrel (winter and spring only). Less frequent and very rare records include Stejneger's Petrel, Blue Petrel, Grey Petrel, Cook's Petrel, Westland Petrel, Kermadec Petrel, White-necked Petrel, White-headed Petrel, Gould's Petrel, Mottled Petrel and Providence Petrel. Four species of prions (Fairy Prion, Antarctic Prion, Slender-billed Prion and Salvin's Prion) are common; occasionally Broad-billed Prion is recorded. Storm-Petrels are abundant, particularly White-faced Storm-Petrel, Wilson's Storm-Petrel and Grey-backed Storm-Petrel. Occasionally, Black-bellied Storm-Petrel, Southern Giant-Petrel and Northern Giant-Petrel are encountered. One trip record exists to date of European Storm-Petrel.

Skuas and Jaegers are frequently found on the trips at various times of the year. The records include Arctic Jaeger, Pomarine Jaeger, Long-tailed Jaeger, Brown Skua and sometimes South Polar Skua. Occasionally found are Southern Fulmar, Arctic Tern, Antarctic Tern and Brown Booby.

Closer to the shore, cormorants (Black-faced Cormorant, Little Pied Cormorant, Little Black Cormorant, Great Cormorant), gulls (Silver Gull, Pacific Gull, sometimes Kelp Gull), Crested Tern and Australian Pelican can be observed all year round. White-bellied Sea-Eagles are also regularly seen in the area.

If the Eaglehawk Neck pelagic trip is not your option, the next best thing is a 3-hour eco-tour along the coast by Tasman Island Cruises (https://www.tasmancruises.com.au/) or other coastal touring companies. There are two departure points, Eaglehawk Neck or Port Arthur, depending on the sea conditions. The trip provides excellent views of ocean-sculpted arches, blowholes and islands, created by relentless pounding of the waves. The waters off the Tasman National Park are teeming with marine wildlife feeding on schools of fish.

We took a 3-hour eco-trip cruise in November and saw whales, seals, dolphins, albatrosses, penguins and rafts of pelagic seabirds. The rock stacks and cliffs of Tasman Peninsula provide nesting areas for large colonies of Silver Gulls, Pacific Gulls and Kelp Gulls. Surprisingly, Tree Martins were also breeding on the cliffs. White-bellied Sea-Eagles perched in leafless trees on the cliffs and Peregrine Falcons were nesting on a rocky shelf.

Australasian Gannets and Black-faced Cormorants were feeding in the waters close to the shore.

Shearwaters and petrels formed huge rafts on the water – each raft was a good pointer to look for the whales as the birds and whales are partial to the same schools of fish. Among the hundreds of shearwaters in the rafts were Grey Petrels, White-headed Petrels, Cape Petrels, Hutton's Shearwaters, Sooty Shearwaters and Light-mantled Sooty Albatrosses. Some serious feeding frenzy was demonstrated!

Shearwaters and other seabirds are sometimes seen hunting with whales

Eaglehawk Neck

This is the first worthwhile stop on Arthur Hwy (A9) south of Sorell, often done when arriving for a boat trip. Eaglehawk Neck is a narrow isthmus connecting Tasman Peninsula to the mainland. In colonial times, the isthmus was guarded by ferocious dogs intended to ensure no convicts escaped the Port Arthur penal settlement. Now the area is popular with tourists drawn here by the impressive coastal rock formations of the Devils Kitchen, Tasman Arch and the Blowhole. These can be reached via Blowhole Rd (C338).

Hooded Plovers and Australian Pied Oystercatchers often roost in the Pirates Bay near the Blowhole and are easy to find there. Honeyeaters, thornbills, pardalotes and robins are common in the surrounding woodland and bushes. Look for Tasmanian Scrubwren, Tasmanian Thornbill, Dusky Robin and Black-headed Honeyeater. There are isolated reports that Forty-spotted Pardalote visits this area. Black Currawongs are really tame –

we observed one stealing fries from a visitor's picnic basket in the carpark. Scarlet Robins and Forest Ravens were nearby. In September 2016, Snares Penguin was recorded on the Blowhole rocks.

Tasmanian Morepork often roost in the bushes near the Tasman Arch. Flame Robin, Tree Martin, Yellow-throated Honeyeater and Tasmanian Thornbill are common near the Arch.

The Devil's Kitchen lookout in bad weather allows for viewing of Shy Albatross, Black-browed Albatross, Campbell's Albatross, Little Penguin and Australasian Gannet. Sooty Oystercatcher may be present on the rocks. Peregrine Falcon is often seen flying over the cliffs. Crescent Honeyeaters and Strong-billed Honeyeaters are very common. Other birds here include Eastern Spinebill, Beautiful Firetail, Dusky Robin, Flame Robin, Scarlet Robin and Brown Thornbill.

Tasmanian Devil Unzoo, Taranna

The Tasmanian Devil Unzoo is located south of Eaglehawk Neck, at 5990 Arthur Hwy (A9) in Taranna, on the right side of the road going south. For opening times see their website at https://tasmaniandevilunzoo.com.au/. It is the closest place to Hobart where Cape Barren Geese can be seen in good numbers. We observed a flock of nearly 200 birds grazing on the grass in a paddock near the Unzoo's entrance. The site itself is worth visiting to appreciate the conservation efforts undertaken there. It is also an excellent spot for many endemic species. The Park feeds their animals and the wild birds sneak in to share the table.

Green Rosellas come to bird feeders in the Unzoo, purposefully put up to attract them

Small birds such as Tasmanian Thornbill, Brown Thornbill, Yellow-rumped Thornbill and Tasmanian Scrubwren are very common to the area. Honeyeaters (Yellow-throated Honeyeater, Strong-billed Honeyeater, Black-headed Honeyeater and Yellow Wattlebird) are plentiful; look for them feeding in the gum trees. All four cuckoos that occur in Tasmania (Pallid Cuckoo, Fan-tailed Cuckoo, Shining Bronze-Cuckoo and Horsfield's Bronze-Cuckoo) are calling constantly during the summer season.

Not surprisingly, the large numbers of birds around the Unzoo attract birds of prey. Look for Grey Goshawk, Brown Goshawk, Peregrine Falcon, Swamp Harrier and even Wedge-tailed Eagle.

Fortescue Bay

Midway between Taranna and Port Arthur, turn into Fortescue Rd (C344) and drive 12km to the Fortescue Bay Campground. The road and campground give access to Cape Pillar and Cape Hauy walking tracks. The south end of the famous Tasman Tk is here.

The stands of Tasmanian blue gums on the foreshore of Fortescue Bay are magnet for Swift Parrots; they breed there. Little Penguins come onshore in the evening. On the way to their burrows they'd move in between the tents. In May 2013, a single Gentoo Penguin was observed walking about 50m from the campground. It spent there a few hours and then disappeared. This was the 6th record of this species in the whole Tasmania.

Birds common around the campground include Tasmanian Scrubwren, Green Rosella, Yellow-tailed Black-Cockatoo, Black Currawong, Yellow Wattlebird, Crescent Honeyeater, New Holland Honeyeater and Strong-billed Honeyeater. In the bush near Cape Hauy, look for Satin Flycatcher, Olive Whistler, Bassian Thrush, Tasmanian Thornbill, Shining Bronze-cuckoo and Tasmanian Native-hen. The Peregrine Falcon's nest is located on the cliff not far from the lookout.

Tasmanian Morepork and Masked Owl are regularly heard from the campsite. Peregrine Falcon and White-bellied Sea-Eagle put in a daily appearance, flying over the cliffs.

On the beaches, Hooded Plover, Bar-tailed Godwit and both oystercatchers have been recorded. The rare Fairy Tern was observed flying along the cliffs.

Port Arthur

Port Arthur, in the 1800' the largest penal station in the country, today is an open-air museum and one of most significant European heritage areas. It is also the place for the birds. You will be welcomed by the resident pair of White-bellied Sea-Eagles, roosting in the tall bare trees, and by the oystercatchers on the beach. Cape Barren Geese forage in the museum grounds, not fazed at all by the milling crowds. We also saw a flock of about 30 Australian Wood Ducks, a rarity in Tasmania, grazing on the lawn. Right behind the geese and ducks, scattered groups of parrots can often be seen feeding on the lawns. These include Green Rosellas, Eastern Rosellas, Blue-winged Parrots, Galahs and Sulphur-crested Cockatoos. Yellow-tailed Black-Cockatoos are frequent visitors within the museum grounds; Musk Lorikeet can also be found there.

Swift Parrots breed in Port Arthur – look for them in the trees in the nearby caravan park.

Flocks of White-throated Needletails can be seen circling overhead in summer. They are usually accompanied by large numbers of Welcome Swallows and Tree Martins.

The surrounding bushland and woods are full of honeyeaters, including Yellow-throated Honeyeater, New Holland Honeyeater, Eastern Spinebill and Noisy Miner. Brush Bronzewing, Satin Flycatcher, Brown Thornbill and Tasmanian Thornbill may also be found in the scrub.

Usually 1-2 Musk Ducks can be found in the harbour. Caspian Terns may be flying overhead.

A pair of Masked Owls utilises a tree hollow near the carpark. A spotlighting exercise may also reveal the presence of Tasmanian Morepork and Tawny Frogmouth.

Crescent Bay

To get there, take Safety Cove Rd (C347) from Arthur Hwy (A9) past the Historic Site in Port Arthur, drive nearly to the end, then turn to Dog Bark Wk. The bush along Dog Bark Wk is good for Scrubtit. On the beach, Hooded Plover, Australian Pied Oystercatcher and all three gull species are always there.

Australian Pied Oystercatcher is common around the Tasmanian coast

Cape Raoul Section

From Nubeena Rd (B37) turn south into Stormlea Rd and drive to a carpark at the end of the road. From there, take a walk to Cape Raoul. Common birds on the track include Tasmanian Thornbill, Olive Whistler, Golden Whistler, Black Currawong, Green Rosella, Scarlet Robin, Dusky Robin, Flame Robin, Beautiful Firetail and Tasmanian Native-hen.

If you reach the end of the track at Cape Raoul, look down from the cliffs – Australian fur seals are usually there. Look for Sooty Oystercatchers on the rocks and Peregrine Falcon and White-bellied Sea-Eagle flying along the cliffs.

White Beach Road, Nubeena

White Beach Rd is a scenic drive along a picturesque, coastal scrub-covered bay, located between two small coastal villages, Nubeena and White Beach. The site is easily accessible from Nubeena Rd (B37). You have an off-chance of finding Ground Parrot here but at least should be plenty of Beautiful Firetails in the heathland. Swift Parrot visits in summer, in some years in good numbers.

Other birds of interest in this location include Brush Bronzewing, Australian Pied Oystercatcher, Sooty Oystercatcher, Pallid Cuckoo, Fan-tailed Cuckoo and honeyeaters

(Black-headed Honeyeater, Yellow-throated Honeyeater, New Holland Honeyeater, Little Wattlebird and Yellow Wattlebird).

On the way from Port Arthur to Nubeena, on a small pond off Nubeena Rd we recorded a pair of Musk Ducks and a Swamp Harrier circling over the water.

Lime Bay State Reserve

This beautiful, 1,300ha Reserve features two sheltered beaches, Sloping Lagoon and a network of trails through the area. Vegetation is mostly heath and open eucalypt forest. A historical mining site from the convict times is preserved on site.

The Reserve is located at the northernmost tip of Tasman Peninsula. To get there, turn off Nubeena Rd (B37) onto Saltwater River Rd (C341) and drive north along the coast to the campground in Coal Mine Rd.

Over 70 bird species have been recorded here. **Key species** are Painted Button-quail and Hooded Plover. Other birds of interest include Beautiful Firetail, Flame Robin, Scarlet Robin, Dusky Robin, White-fronted Chat and Brush Bronzewing. Among the rarities is Forty Spotted Pardalote. A colony of Forty Spotted Pardalote existed on the historic mine site until 1990'. The manna gum habitat deteriorated and the birds have disappeared. Since then, only sporadic records of these birds exist. Painted Button-quails live in the Reserve but are difficult to find. In December 2016, a small flock of six birds was observed feeding in the litter near the campground.

It is an excellent place for Flame Robin which occurs in high numbers around the Sloping Lagoon especially when it is nearly dry. We also saw good numbers of Crescent Honeyeaters, Black-headed Honeyeaters, Yellow Wattlebirds and Musk Lorikeets in the flowering banksias and eucalyptus woodland around the campground. During the night, Tasmanian Morepork and Masked Owl can be heard or seen.

Check out the track running between Lime Bay Beach and Lagoon Beach along the Sloping Lagoon. Birds here include White-fronted Chat, Beautiful Firetail, Tasmanian Scrubwren, Brown Thornbill, Dusky Woodswallow, Satin Flycatcher, Flame Robin, Black Currawong and Tasmanian Native-hen. There are always some waterbirds in the lagoon such as Black Swan, Chestnut Teal and Hoary-headed Grebe. On Lagoon Beach you may get Hooded Plover, Red-capped Plover, Sooty Oystercatcher and Australian Pied Oystercatcher. Check the Hog Island from the beach where usually three gull species and Black-faced Cormorants are present. Occasionally, White-bellied Sea-Eagle is consuming its prey on the rocks.

Marion Bay

Marion Bay is a large bay located on the east coast of Tasmania just north of the Tasman Peninsula. 580ha of beaches and mudflats around the southwestern side of Marion Bay were identified by Birdlife International as a Key Biodiversity Area (KBA). The KBA includes intertidal mudflats off Porpoise Hole, the Long Spit Nature Reserve, Two Mile Beach and part of Marion Bay Beach. This is an essential habitat for the local and migratory shorebirds.

A small settlement of Marion Bay located on Bay Rd consists of a huddle of beach shacks erected on coastal dunes near the tidal mudflats.

To get there, take Arthur Hwy (A9) from Sorell, then turn into Marion Bay Rd (C337) to Marion Bay. A carpark is located at the end of Marion Bay Rd, with a viewing platform on the dunes, visible from afar and serving as an orientation landmark for people wandering in the vast areas of heath. On the spit, you'll find a private Marion Bay Reserve.

Over 90 bird species have been recorded in Marion Bay. The **key species** is Hooded Plover. 17 wader species are on the site's birdlist including rarities such as Banded Stilt, Whimbrel, Red Knot and Ruddy Turnstone. Other birds of interest include Brown Quail, Little Grassbird, White-fronted Chat, Little Egret, Cattle Egret and Eastern Great Egret. Among rare birds are Forty-spotted Pardalote, Royal Spoonbill and Cape Barren Goose.

Whimbrel

Good birdwatching can be found along the Long Spit to Marion Narrows. Check the area around the viewing platform and the mouth of Bream Creek. This is a good spot for waders, usually you can get Red-necked Stint, Bar-tailed Godwit, Double-banded Plover (in winter), Sooty Oystercatcher and Australian Pied Oystercatcher. Also recorded in this area were Red Knot and Whimbrel. Beaches here have a good population of Hooded Plovers; flocks of up to 20 birds have been counted. Other waders on the beach include Ruddy Turnstone and Red-capped Plover.

On the track along the spit you'll see plenty of White-fronted Chats. Be on a lookout for Horsfield's Bronze-cuckoo, Pallid Cuckoo, Brown Quail, Tasmanian Scrubwren, Little Grassbird, Australasian Pipit, Scarlet Robin and Swamp Harrier. Check the mudflats along Bay Rd for waders such as Common Greenshank, Sharp-tailed Sandpiper and Curlew Sandpiper. Banded Stilts have been reported a few times from this site. Little Egrets regularly hunt for fish in the Porpoise Hole. On the water in the Hole you may get some waterbirds including Black Swan, Australian Shelduck, Grey Teal and sometimes Musk Duck.

Check the tree and bushes along Bay Rd in Marion Bay. Swift Parrot, Musk Lorikeet, Green Rosella, Grey Currawong, Little Wattlebird, Yellow Wattlebird and Yellow-throated Honeyeater can be found there. Occasionally, a small flock of Forty-spotted Pardalotes feeds in the manna gums, probably during temporary dispersal from Maria Island.

Pitt Water and Orielton Lagoon

Orielton Lagoon and the Pitt Water Nature Reserve are one of the most visited birdwatching sites in Tasmania thanks to the richness of waders and waterbirds and a convenient location close to the Hobart Airport. The Pitt Water Nature Reserve is part of the Ramsar site that covers approximately 3,300ha and consists of five discrete areas: Orielton Lagoon, Barilla Bay, upper Pitt Water, Woody Island and Barren Island.

Orielton Lagoon comprises an estuarine system with a large area of saltmarsh. The estuary offers a diversity of habitats creating a species-rich environment. The site has large areas of tidal mudflats and sandflats. Restricted tide inflow through the mouth leaves extensive areas exposed and suitable for foraging by the wading birds. It is an important feeding and breeding site for Australian Pied Oystercatcher and many seabirds including terns (Crested Tern, Caspian Tern) and gulls (Pacific Gull, Kelp Gull, Silver Gull).

The site is located about 10km north of the Hobart Airport, accessed via Tasman Hwy (A3). The Sorell Causeway is crossing the lagoon via Midway Point, reaching Sorell on the other side. Access is restricted; viewing spots include Cemetery Point on the eastern side of the Lagoon, Shark Point Rd on the northern side, outfall works at Midway Point on the western side and Henry St and Stores Ln in Sorell from the east. You can also watch the birds directly from the Causeway as a small parking area is provided. There is also a cycle lane that may be used by pedestrian traffic. See map in the Pitt Water Nature Reserve brochure downloadable here: http://www.parks.tas.gov.au/file.aspx?id=11639.

Over 130 bird species have been recorded here. **Key species** are Great Crested Grebe, Musk Duck and Royal Spoonbill. Over 30 wader species are on the site's birdlist including such fantastic rarities as Common Sandpiper, Pectoral Sandpiper, Buff-breasted Sandpiper, Ruff, Black-tailed Godwit, Hudsonian Godwit, Little Stint, Grey Plover, Grey-tailed Tattler, Red Knot and Great Knot. Other species of interest include Australasian Shoveler, Little Egret and Cape Barren Goose.

Royal Spoonbill and Little Pied Cormorant roosting in a tree

Several shorebirds breed in the Pitt Water Nature Reserve and Orielton Lagoon. As per survey of 2013, nests of Kelp Gulls (300), Silver Gulls (400), Australian Pied Oystercatchers (64), Sooty Oystercatchers (4), Red-capped Plovers (10) and Caspian Terns (3) were found.

Sorell Causeway

This site is particularly good at low tide when the shorebirds are feeding on the mudflats on both sites of the causeway. Common species include Eastern Curlew, Common Greenshank, Bar-tailed Godwit and Red-necked Stint in summer. Occasionally you may get Whimbrel, Great Knot, Curlew Sandpiper, Sharp-tailed Sandpiper and Pacific Golden Plover.

On a small rocky island called Suzie Islet, Great Cormorants, Black-faced Cormorants, Little Pied Cormorants and Caspian Terns often roost in good numbers. It is also a favourite roosting site for Royal Spoonbills and Australian Pelicans. Common Sandpipers are regularly recorded roosting on various pieces of the causeway structure protruding from the water.

Musk Ducks and Great Crested Grebes can easily be located from the causeway. Up to 20 Musk Ducks may be on the water, we saw eight from the causeway. Other waterfowl here includes Chestnut Teal, Black Swan and Hoary-headed Grebe.

Waterview Bird Sanctuary

The site can be accessed via Stores Ln in Sorell, turning off from Tasman Hwy (A3). You'll see a gate at the end of the lane between two large industrial buildings. Walk through the gate to the water. A flat island covered in samphire is situated close to the shore. Alternatively, continue from Stores Ln to Gibblin Dr to the end of the road where on the right is a vacant block of land (as of 2017) giving access to the water and allowing views of the island.

An island in Orielton Lagoon, visible from Stores Ln and Gibblin Dr

During our visit, Chestnut Teals, Grey Teals, Hardheads, Kelp Gulls, Pacific Golden Plovers and Curlew Sandpipers were roosting in samphire on the island. Australian Spotted Crake put on a short appearance at the south end of the island. A raft of about 20 Hoary-headed Grebes hunted fish in the water. On the shore side were plenty Tasmanian Native-hens squeezing under the gate in and out of the Sanctuary enclosure. A pair of Black-fronted Dotterels were feeding at the edge of the water. Common Greenshank, Red-necked Stint and Little Egret are regularly recorded at this site.

In the gums near the end of Stores Ln, look for Musk Lorikeet, Striated Pardalote, Little Wattlebird and Yellow-throated Honeyeater. Look for White-fronted Chat in the saltmarshes.

Cemetery Point

From Tasman Hwy (A3) in Sorell turn north onto Nash St, cross Forcett St, take William St and then turn left into Henry St. Park your car near the cemetery. You'll find access to the water from Forcett St and Henry St, and a neatly mowed track is provided behind the cemetery. From here you can observe Musk Ducks and Great Crested Grebes on the water.

Pacific Golden Plovers like to roost in the samphire in front of the cemetery. Usually, there are also Red-necked Stints, Sooty Oystercatchers and Australian Pied Oystercatchers. The latter breed in the area.

Brown Quails are common around the cemetery, often seen on the lawns. Tasmanian Morepork roosts in the macrocarpa trees. Other birds in this area include Eastern Rosella, Musk Lorikeet, Noisy Miner, Brown Thornbill, Tasmanian Scrubwren, Forest Raven, Eurasian Skylark, Grey Butcherbird and Little Egret.

Greenshank Bay

Access to the site is from Tasman Hwy (A3). At Midway Point turn north onto Penna Rd, then take Fenton St to the right to get to Lake Vue Pde, changing its name to the Esplanade. Drive to the end of the road at a golf course.

Stop on Lake Vue Pde near a small wastewater treatment plant (visible below). Walk on the south side of the plant to a sandspit. Check the ponds – usually Musk Duck, Chestnut Teal and cormorants can be found here. Waders often roost on the spit. The regulars there include Bar-tailed Godwits, Common Greenshanks and Australian Pied Oystercatchers. Occasionally, Red Knot or Black-tailed Godwit are recorded.

Drive to the end of the Esplanade - a major roosting and feeding site for the waders is located in Greenshank Bay. Access from the road has recently been restricted due to urban development. Try to scan the area from the available vantage points on the Esplanade. Alternatively, drive back to get to the golf course via Penna Rd and ask permission to wander around.

We found a large flock of Bar-tailed Godwits and Australian Pied Oystercatchers roosting in the bay on the outgoing tide. There were about 20 Common Greenshanks and one Little Egret among them.

The golf course proved to be a parrot heaven, they were everywhere. Small flocks of 5-20 Long-billed Corellas, Little Corellas, Galahs and Eastern Rosellas moved from tree to tree. There were also small numbers of Sulphur-crested Cockatoos, Yellow-tailed Black-Cockatoos, Green Rosellas and Musk Lorikeets. A single Rainbow Lorikeet was hanging out with the group of Musk Lorikeets. Other bush birds included Little Wattlebird, Yellow Wattlebird, Crescent Honeyeater and Noisy Miner. Feeding on the lawn were Tasmanian Native-hens and Cape Barren Geese.

Swift Parrot and Blue-winged Parrot were also recorded at this golf course.

In bad weather, Pacific Golden Plovers which usually roost at the Cemetery Point, move to the other side of the bay to roost at the edge of the golf course. Black-fronted Dotterels are often found feeding at the edges of small ponds on the links.

Penna Settling Ponds

From Tasman Hwy (A3) turn north onto Penna Rd at Midway Point and drive until you get to the intersection with Shark Point Rd. The ponds are on your left in the corner of these two roads. Access is not permitted but you may find good vantage points along the road to be able to scan the ponds. Typically, a large concentration of waterfowl on the water can be expected. Among common ducks there should be Musk Ducks and occasionally Blue-billed Ducks and Pink-eared Ducks. The regulars include Australasian Shoveler, Australian Shelduck and large numbers of Hoary-headed Grebes.

Check the property fences for the presence of Scarlet Robin and Flame Robin. In the gums in the shelter belt along Penna St, Musk Lorikeet, Little Wattlebird, Brown Thornbill and Grey Butcherbird may often be found.

Shark Point Road Marshes

From Tasman Hwy (A3) turn north onto Penna Rd at Midway Point, then turn right at the intersection with Shark Point Rd (Settling Ponds are on the other side). There are extensive mudflats in the area where Frogmore Creek and Orielton Rivulet enter the Orielton Lagoon. A large colony of Kelp Gulls (about 300 nests) is located here. Pacific Golden Plovers often roost here and Eastern Curlews feed on the mudflats.

Pacific Golden Plover

We flushed six Blue-winged Parrots from the samphire and three Latham's Snipes from the wetland vegetation. Other birds at this site included Red-capped Plover, Eurasian Skylark, Australasian Pipit, Flame Robin and White-fronted Chat.

South Arm Peninsula

South Arm Peninsula forms an eastern bank of the lower Derwent estuary. South Arm Rd (B33) runs through the Peninsula passing Lauderdale, Pipe Clay Lagoon, Calverts Lagoon and South Arm on its way. The Peninsula is a very good place for shorebirds, right on the Hobart's doorstep. In spite of the residential encroachment and constant human pressure, large areas of valuable wetlands still remain with not much interference from humans, dogs, traffic, etc. Access to the sites described below is from South Arm Rd.

Over 120 species are on the site's birdlist. **Key species** are Hooded Plover, Double-banded Plover (in winter), Australian Pied Oystercatcher and Sharp-tailed Sandpiper. Other birds of interest include Brown Quail, Short-tailed Shearwater, White-fronted Chat, Black-fronted Dotterel and Pink Robin. Among the rarities are Common Sandpiper, Banded Stilt, Pied Stilt, Whimbrel, Hudsonian Godwit, Red Knot and Zebra Finch.

Ralphs Bay Conservation Area

The site is located near Lauderdale south of Orielton Lagoon on the southeast side of Derwent Estuary, 12km from Hobart CBD. This shallow bay is sheltered by the spit of South Arm and Opossum Bay. The extensive mudflats in the bay are very important for migratory and local waders and the area has been identified as South Arm Key Biodiversity Area due to the fact that 5% of Australian Pied Oystercatcher population (400 birds) spend their winter there. The area was subject to a long battle with a local developer who attempted to build a canal housing estate on the mudflats (the main canal was actually dug out). The battle was won in 2010 and 170ha conservation area was created.

To get there, drive along the coast on South Arm Rd (B33) in Lauderdale and start birdwatching from a small carpark at the northern end of Ralphs Bay. At high tide the waders usually roost on Lauderdale Spit, at low tide look for them scattered on the mudflats. The waders here include Red-necked Stint, Red-capped Plover, Hooded Plover, Double-banded Plover (in winter), Bar-tailed Godwit, Common Greenshank, Eastern Curlew, Sooty Oystercatcher and Australian Pied Oystercatcher. Common Sandpiper was reported a few times, always from the same spot (the stony banks of the Lauderdale Canal). In July 2016, 23 Banded Stilts appeared in the bay to spend a few months there.

A good selection of raptors can be found around the area including Swamp Harrier, Australian Hobby, Brown Falcon, Wedge-tailed Eagle and White-bellied Sea-Eagle.

Clear Lagoon, Sandford

Past the spit in Lauderdale turn off South Arm Rd (B33) into Forest Hill Rd and drive approximately 1km down the road. The lagoon is on the right side of the road. Walk through the gate. When there is water in the lagoon, it is a good site for shorebirds and waterbirds.

When we visited the place, there was a raft of Grey Teals in the shallow water. We also saw a pair of Black Swans with cygnets and a small flock of Australian Shelducks and Australasian Shovelers. Good numbers of White-faced Herons were scattered around the lagoon. At the water edge were eight Black-fronted Dotterels. Small numbers of Sharp-tailed Sandpipers are regularly reported from this site.

In the surrounding bush and swampy areas, we found White-fronted Chat, Australasian Pipit, Flame Robin, Shining Bronze-cuckoo, Common Bronzewing and Brown Falcon.

Pipe Clay Lagoon

Return from the Clear Lagoon to South Arm Rd (B33), turn south and continue through Sandford, then turn into Cremorne Av. Next, turn right into Pipe Clay Esplanade. The high tide is the best time to observe the birds along the shore. There will be large numbers of shorebirds standing on the lawns at the water edge including Bar-tailed Godwit, Sooty Oystercatcher, Australian Pied Oystercatcher, Red-capped Plover and plenty of gulls and terns. A crowd of up to 200 Australian Pied Oystercatchers often roosts on the lawn. Peregrine Falcon and White-bellied Sea-Eagle often hand around this area.

To access the south end of the lagoon, go back to South Arm Rd (B33) and drive south. Turn into Clinton Beach Rd then turn left to Bicheno St. This is the part of the lagoon where Double-banded Plover and Red-necked Stint can be found. Curlew Sandpiper occasionally visit this spot.

Further down Bicheno St turn right into Cape Deslacs Tk to get to the Cape Deslacs Nature Reserve. From a carpark take a 10min walk to the viewing platform located in the middle of the Short-tailed Shearwater rookery. At dusk thousands of birds come back from a day of fishing to their burrows. A longer track through the reserve gives a chance to find Pink Robin, Scarlet Robin, White-fronted Chat, New Holland Honeyeater, Musk Lorikeet, Golden Whistler and Brown Thornbill.

Calverts Lagoon

Further south on South Arm Rd (B33), you'll arrive at Calverts Lagoon. Park at the gate and walk a short distance to the lagoon. Hooded Plover and Red-capped Plover can usually be found on the beach but when the lagoon is drying out they move over to the lagoon side.

This is a good spot for Sharp-tailed Sandpipers that occur here in small numbers but on a regular basis.

When the Clear Lagoon dries up, this lagoon takes over the waterfowl load and becomes inundated with Grey Teals and Black Swans.

An inspection of a bushland in the area may produce eight honeyeater species, four cuckoo species, Green Rosella, Musk Lorikeet, Scarlet Robin, Flame Robin, Golden Whistler, Dusky Woodswallow, Australian Owlet-nightjar and Tawny Frogmouth.

Goat's Bluff

On South Arm Rd (B33) past Calverts Lagoon you'll find a terrific lookout on your left. The lookout panorama includes Betsey Island and Black Jack Rock. The lookout is poorly signposted; when you see a turnoff to a track on your right next to a sign 'South Arm Recreational Area', the turnoff to the Lookout comes very shortly. If you turn off into a road with steep descent, you've gone too far.

Betsey Island in front of the lookout is home to 75,000 pairs of Little Penguins. We observed Forest Ravens investigating the area and possibly entering the burrows in search of an egg or a small chick.

On the rocks near the lookout there were Black-faced Cormorant, Crested Tern, Kelp Gull, Australasian Gannet and Sooty Oystercatcher.

Kelp Gull with a juvenile

In the bush on the hill behind the Bluff we found Shining Bronze-cuckoos, Golden Whistler, Flame Robin, Yellow-tailed Black-Cockatoo, Brown Thornbill, Little Wattlebird, Crescent Honeyeater and Eastern Spinebill.

Brown Quail and Grey Goshawk have also been reported from this site. Great Frigatebird was recorded here in December 2016.

Woodvine Nature Reserve

A 377ha Woodvine Nature Reserve is located approximately 45km northeast of Hobart. The property was donated to the Crown by Mr. Ernie Shaw in 1998. This is a green island of native vegetation, contrasting with grazing land around. The dominant plant communities are black peppermint forest and heathy swamp gum woodland with areas of native grasses, sedgeland and buttongrass swamp.

Access is via Delmore Rd (C333) past Forcett (on Arthur Hwy, A9). Turn right soon onto unsealed White Hill Rd which will take you to the Reserve. The Shaw family homestead is now a historical site.

Over 50 bird species have been recorded in the Reserve. The buttongrass swamp is favoured by Southern Emu-wren and Beautiful Firetail. This site is one of the Hobart locations where Southern emu-wren can be spotted with a relative ease. Stands of Tasmanian blue gums and swamp gums are suitable for Swift Parrot's foraging and nesting.

On the lower paddocks, you can spot good numbers of Scarlett Robins, Dusky Robins and Superb Fairy-wrens. If you walk along the ridgeline track you can get honeyeaters (Strong-billed Honeyeater, Yellow-throated Honeyeater, New Holland Honeyeater, Crescent Honeyeater, Black-headed Honeyeater, Eastern Spinebill, Little Wattlebird and Yellow Wattlebird). Common Bronzewing can be observed on the forest floor. A resident pair of Wedge-tailed Eagle often circles overhead.

Townsend Lagoon, Lewisham

This small lagoon is worth checking out when you are on your way to Blue Lagoon at Dodges Ferry. To get there, from Arthur Hwy (A9) past Sorell turn south onto Lewisham Scenic Dr (C340). The lagoon is located at the corner of Quarry Rd and Lewisham Scenic Dr just before Clarks Bay.

This is a good place for Australian Spotted Crake, Latham's Snipe and Black-fronted Dotterel. Hoary-headed Grebes regularly breed here. On the water, you may see Chestnut Teals, Grey Teals and Black Swans.

Other birds in the area include Eastern Great Egret, Cattle Egret, Tasmanian Native-hen, Purple Swamphen, Pallid Cuckoo and Musk Lorikeet.

Blue Lagoon, Dodges Ferry

This small freshwater lagoon is situated at Dodges Ferry, a coastal township south of Sorell. To get there, from Tasman Hwy (A3) past Sorell turn south on Old Forcett Rd (C334) to Dodges Ferry. Continue on Carlton Beach Rd when in town. The lagoon is on the corner of Carlton Beach Rd and Tiger Head Rd. Access is from Kannah St.

Over 50 species are on the site's birdlist. **Key species** are Spotless Crake and Rainbow Lorikeet. Other birds of interest include Australasian Shoveler, Musk Lorikeet, Eastern Rosella, Yellow-throated Honeyeater and Eastern Spinebill.

This is the best site to find Spotless Crake near Hobart. The birds breed in the bulrushes that surround the lagoon. We observed a bird darting across a gap in the bulrushes.

This is also good place for parrots that roam the park surrounding the lagoon. Among them are Yellow-tailed Black-Cockatoos, Galahs, Green Rosellas, Eastern Rosellas and Musk Lorikeets. A small population (up to 25 birds) of Rainbow Lorikeets come to roost in trees in the park every evening.

Other birds at this site include Hoary-headed Grebe, Brown Thornbill, Pallid Cuckoo, White-throated Needletail and Swamp Harrier.

Pittwater Road, Seven Mile Beach

This short side road off Tasman Hwy (A3) near the Hobart Airport, leading to the Seven Mile Beach township, is worth exploring. On both sides, there are a variety of habitats including eucalyptus woodland, pine forest, wetland and coastal dunes.

In *The complete guide to finding the birds of Australia*, published in 1996, Richard and Sarah Thomas described the Masked Owl location in Pittwater Road 400m from the turnoff from Tasman Hwy in a hollow of an old gum tree, 150m from the road. We visited the site at dusk in March 2017 – a Masked Owl was still living there, in the very same place, after over 20 years! We also found a Grey Goshawk near the owl's tree.

The surrounding eucalyptus forest proved to be very good for parrots. Three breeding hollows were occupied by Yellow-tailed Black-Cockatoos. The area was also good for Musk Lorikeet, Green Rosella and Eastern Rosella. A breeding pair of Laughing Kookaburras had their nest in another tree hollow nearby. Feeding on the flowering gum trees, honeyeaters were plentiful (Yellow-throated Honeyeater, Crescent Honeyeater, Little Wattlebird, Yellow Wattlebird and Noisy Miner). Common Bronzewings were easy to find on the forest floor.

Eastern Rosellas

Large flocks of Tasmanian Native-hens were feeding alongside the red-bellied pademelons (Tasmanian wallabies) on the farmland along the road. Mixed with them on the pasture were Galahs and Sulphur-crested Cockatoos. A small flock of Brown Quails flushed from the wet grass.

Brown Falcon perched on the power line while Swamp Harrier was annoying the Tasmanian Native-hens.

The pine forest yielded large numbers of Forest Ravens and Grey Currawongs. Scarlet Robins and Brown Thornbills kept to the forest edge. To our surprise, we found two male Common (Ring-necked) Pheasants on the road to Five Mile Beach.

White-fronted Chats were popping up in the coastal vegetation and Beautiful Firetails were easy to spot in the coastal grasses. Beach and bay waters were packed with cormorants (Great Cormorant, Black-faced Cormorant, Little Black Cormorant, Little Pied Cormorant) and gulls (Pacific Gull, Silver Gull, Kelp Gull), with Kelp Gull in dominant numbers. Australian Pied Oystercatcher, Sooty Oystercatcher and Eastern Curlew were numerous along the Seven Mile Beach.

Peter Murrell Reserve

Peter Murrell Reserve is the best-kept secret of Hobart's birdwatching community, being the easiest place to find the very rare Forty-spotted Pardalote on the Tasmanian mainland. Sadly, the Reserve is under threat from development – new residential suburbs and industrial areas are mushrooming around. This rare refuge of Forty-spotted Pardalote in Hobart does not seem to have a chance.

The Reserve is located in Huntingfield south of Kingston, at the base of Tinderbox Peninsula, about 20min drive south of Hobart. Take the Southern Outlet (A6) to Blackmans Bay and continue along Channel Hwy (B68) until you pass the Australian Antarctic Division Office on your left. Go straight at the roundabout (while the Blackmans Bay traffic turns left) and turn left into Huntingfield Av about 50m past the roundabout and drive until you'll see the sign for the Reserve (past the Vodafone call centre).

We drove to the end of Huntingfield Av and were welcomed by a flock of 100+ Blue-winged Parrots on a paddock adjacent to the Reserve. Dusky Robin was sitting on the fence wire. Yellow-throated Honeyeaters, Black-headed Honeyeaters, New Holland Honeyeaters and Yellow Wattlebirds were feeding on the gum trees planted along Huntingfield Av.

Our bushwalk started in the early morning at two small dams. We were lucky to catch a glimpse of the platypus in the water. Along the edge of dam's vegetation, Spotless Crake sneaked out to feed. We heard an unmistakable wailing call of Little Grassbirds around the dam. After 10 minutes of wandering around the dams, we located three Forty-spotted Pardalotes mid-high in the gum trees near the dam. There were also plenty of other pardalotes in the Reserve (Striated and Spotted Pardalote).

Some other Tasmanian endemic species are also relatively easy to find in the Reserve including Tasmanian Thornbill, Tasmanian Native-hen, Green Rosella and Black Currawong.

There were a few ducks on the water including Chestnut Teal and Northern Mallard. Tawny Frogmouth was nesting near the dam. Four Brown Quails were feeding at the grassy edge of the Reserve while several Australasian Pipits stood in a grassless paddock. A large flock of Yellow-rumped Thornbills mixed with Common Greenfinches and European Goldfinches was foraging on fallen grass seeds. Six Yellow-tailed Black-Cockatoos were systematically moving through the bush.

New Holland Honeyeater, Little Wattlebird, Golden Whistler, Eastern Rosella and Grey Currawong were everywhere in the Reserve. Cuckoos (Horsfield's Bronze-Cuckoo, Shining Bronze-Cuckoo, Pallid Cuckoo and Fan-tailed Cuckoo) were plentiful and very vocal in different parts of the Reserve.

A pair of Wedge-tailed Eagles were soaring over the Reserve. You may also find here Swamp Harrier, Brown Goshawk, Grey Goshawk, Peregrine Falcon and Brown Falcon.

Other species of interest that were reported from the Reserve include Dusky Woodswallow, Common Bronzewing, Brush Bronzewing, Satin Flycatcher and Crescent Honeyeater.

Alternative Entry to the Reserve

Another entry point to Peter Murrell's Reserve is from Howden Rd (C626) – drive along Channel Hwy (B68) past Huntingfield and turn left past the golf course. Forty-spotted Pardalotes are known to come here from Bruny Island. After searching through many white peppermint eucalyptus trees (manna gums), we located two birds.

At this location, there were plenty of other endemics including Dusky Robin and Tasmanian Scrubwren. Particularly active were Black-headed Honeyeaters, New Holland Honeyeaters and Crescent Honeyeaters. Two Swift Parrots were calling from the top of a gum tree near the main road.

Scarlet Robins were very common and a few Flame Robins and Pink Robins also came out of the bushes.

Tinderbox Peninsula

The site is located 20km south of Hobart. A quiet road goes around the peninsula, mostly between private properties. A forested ridge runs in the middle. A small Tinderbox Hills Reserve is established on the ridge where small numbers of Forty-spotted Pardalotes can be found. Adjacent to the southeast tip of the peninsula is Tinderbox Marine Nature Reserve with a lookout at Piersons Point. This lookout is situated directly opposite Dennes Point on Bruny Island where the largest colony of Forty-spotted Pardalotes is located.

From Hobart, there are two main routes to get there:
- Take Southern Outlet (A6) from Hobart to Kingston. At the roundabout in Kingston take Channel Hwy (B68) and continue for 4km, then take a left turn onto Howden Rd (C623). Turn south (right) into Tinderbox Rd (C624) to make a circular trip around the peninsula.
- Alternatively, at the roundabout in Kingston take the second exit into Algona Rd from A6 and then turn right into Roslyn Av (C623) in Blackmans Bay. Veer left into Tinderbox Rd (C624).

There are no facilities on the peninsula except for the lookout 6km south of Blackmans Bay.

Over 70 bird species have been recorded in the area. **Key species** are Forty-spotted Pardalote, Swift Parrot and Blue-winged Parrot. Other birds of interest include Brush Bronzewing, Satin Flycatcher, Brown Thornbill, Black-headed Honeyeater, Beautiful Firetail and Pallid Cuckoo Among the rarities are Lewin's Rail and Rainbow Lorikeet.

The best place to find Forty-spotted Pardalote is among the manna gums (white gums) near the tennis court at Piersons Point. They can also be found in the hills.

Piersons Point

The site is located opposite Mount Louis Rd, the site coordinates are 43.03.12 S and 147.20.87 E.

Following the post-breeding dispersal, some of the Bruny Island's Forty-spotted Pardalotes may stay at Piersons Point.

Blue-winged Parrots can often be seen here feeding in small flocks in the grassy areas. You will find here all four species of cuckoos occurring in Tasmania, very vocal in summer. In particular, Pallid Cuckoo can be found in good numbers. There are plenty of Brown Thornbills, Beautiful Firetails, Black-headed Honeyeaters, Yellow-throated Honeyeaters and New Holland Honeyeaters in the surrounding bush. Wedge-tailed Eagles are often flying over the peninsula.

Other birds found in the area include Laughing Kookaburra, Grey Currawong, Common Bronzewing, Dusky Woodswallow, Scarlet Robin and Satin Flycatcher.

New Holland Honeyeater

Tinderbox Jetty

The jetty is located in the southeast section of Tinderbox Rd. A narrow public road leads to the jetty.

The surrounding scrub is fantastic for Swift Parrots in summer. On the shore, look for Black-faced Cormorant, Kelp Gull and Australian Pied Oystercatcher.

Not far from the jetty turnoff, an ephemeral wetland is located where Lewin's Rail was found a few times.

Tinderbox Hills Reserve

The best way to explore this Reserve is via a 3.6km return Tinderbox Hills Tk that runs on top of the ridge. Access to this track is from a carpark located at the end of Estuary Dr off Brightwater Rd (C623).

Check the manna gums for Forty-spotted Pardalotes. Common birds here include Grey Shrike-thrush, Green Rosella, Yellow Wattlebird, Yellow-throated Honeyeater and Black-headed Honeyeater. Look also for Satin Flycatcher, Dusky Robin, Grey Butcherbird, Golden Whistler, Dusky Woodswallow and Brown Goshawk. Brush Bronzewing was found on the track. Swamp Harrier regularly patrols the hills.

Dru Point, Margate

To get there, take Southern Outlet (A6) from Hobart to Margate. In Margate, turn left into Beach Rd, then take left into the Esplanade. At the end of the road turn left into Dru Point Rd which will take you through the Dru Point Bicentennial Park. You will find here a network of tracks and two very interesting sewage ponds.

The **key species** is Swift Parrot, found in the park regularly when the Tasmanian blue gums are in bloom.

On the ponds there are always huge numbers of birds, mostly Silver Gulls and Kelp Gulls. There may also be some Musk Ducks, Northern Mallards, Grey Teals, Hardheads, Hoary-headed Grebes and occasionally a few Australasian Grebes.

This is one of Hobart's sites where Rainbow Lorikeet has taken permanent residence and started breeding. There is also a variety of other parrots here such as Musk Lorikeet, Eastern Rosella, Green Rosella, Galah, Long-billed Corella and Yellow-tailed Black-Cockatoo.

Other common birds in the Park include Brown Thornbill, Striated Pardalote, Black-headed Honeyeater, Silvereye, Pallid Cuckoo, Dusky Woodswallow, Scarlet Robin and Dusky Robin.

Oyster Cove (Putalina IPA)

The village is located on Channel Hwy (B68) north of Kettering. Turn into Manuka Rd and after a few kilometres, at the corner of Manuka Rd and Old Station Rd, you will find the sign for Putalina IPA (Indigenous Protected Area).

The **key species** here is Lewin's Rail. The foreshore of the area is the only reliable spot for Lewin's Rail in Tasmania. They may be found foraging on the exposed mud in the creek at mid and low tide. Often can be seen with chicks.

Nearly all Tasmania endemic bird species can be found within the IPA including the endangered Forty-spotted Pardalote. The one out is Scrubtit.

The shore is good for Australian Pied Oystercatcher, Sooty Oystercatcher, Black-faced Cormorant, Pacific Gull, Kelp Gull, Crested Tern, Grey Teal, Chestnut Teal, Great Egret and Hoary-headed Grebe.

Pacific Gull

Tasmanian Native-hens may be walking with their chicks along Manuka Rd. Robins are plentiful, Dusky Robin and Scarlet Robin breed in the area but you can also find Flame Robin and Pink Robin here. There is an abundance of Green Rosellas. Swift Parrots visit the site.

Other notable birds in Oyster Cove include Dusky Woodswallow, Olive Whistler, Beautiful Firetail, Brush Bronzewing, Bassian Thrush, Pallid Cuckoo, Crescent Honeyeater, New Holland Honeyeater, Wedge-tailed Eagle and Grey Goshawk.

Bruny Island

Bruny Island is located on the southeast coast of Tasmania 30km south of Hobart. It is separated from the mainland by the narrow D'Entrecasteaux Channel. The island 50km long, actually comprising two islands, North and South Bruny, joined by a very narrow strip of land called The Neck.

This location is special, with the abundant wildlife and stunning clifftop views. With a bit of luck, you can get all 12 endemic Tasmanian species on the island and also many of the other Tasmanian natives. The island is very important for Forty-spotted Pardalote, with a major population located here. Another significant population of Forty-spotted Pardalotes lives on Maria Island.

Vegetation of the island consists mostly of cleared grazing land, dry eucalypt forest, coastal heathland and woodland as well as areas of wet eucalypt forest between Lunawanna and Cloudy Bay. The dry sclerophyll forest dominated by manna gums grows mostly on North Bruny – this is the habitat critical for the survival of Forty-spotted Pardalote.

Coastal woodland of Bruny Island

Access from Hobart is via Southern Outlet (A6) to Kettering, approximately 45min drive. The car ferry company at Kettering provides several crossings daily. See the timetable and pricing at http://brunyislandferry.com.au/bruny-island-ferry-timetable/. The trip across the straits takes only 15min. Try to avoid weekends as the place is a favourite Hobartian getaway so the island can get crowded and you may waste a lot of precious birdwatching time queuing for a ferry.

You'll find a network of sealed roads around the island, with Bruny Island Main Rd running north-south through the whole island. Accommodation choices range from campgrounds to holiday homes. A campsite is located at the southern end of The Neck. Adventure Bay has two caravan parks and the only fuel on the island. There is a small general store in Adventure Bay and also in Lunawanna. At several places you will find a café, a restaurant or another eatery (these may be closed out of season). There are also many carparks, picnic tables and walking trails scattered throughout the island. The area is famous for its gourmet food farms. Try the local cheese, berries, oysters or wine.

Over 140 bird species have been recorded on Bruny Island, a very respectable number for the cold region of Tasmania. Our birdlist on the island in November was 87 species. **Keys species** are Forty-spotted Pardalote and Scrubtit. Other birds of interest include Blue-winged Parrot, Swift Parrot, Tawny-crowned Honeyeater, Hooded Plover, Pink Robin, Bassian Thrush, Olive Whistler, Satin Flycatcher, Brown Quail, Little Penguin and Short-tailed Shearwater. Among the rarities are Cape Barren Goose, Lewin's Rail, Ground Parrot, Painted Button-quail, Banded Stilt, Australasian Bittern, Southern Emu-wren, Fiordland Penguin, Snares Penguin and White-necked Heron.

Nature lovers will also rejoice in other plentiful wildlife such as fur seals, whales, dolphins, wallabies, pademelons, echidnas, etc.

The range of self-introduced parrots from mainland Tasmania, some just visiting, some staying longer and trying to establish a population, includes Rainbow Lorikeet, Musk Lorikeet, Sulphur-crested Cockatoo, Long-billed Corella, Galah and Easter Rosella.

The endangered endemic Forty-spotted Pardalote is Bruny Island's star attraction but two other pardalote species (Striated Pardalote and Spotted Pardalote) are very common there and it will take careful checking to identify the rare one. The Forty-spotted Pardalote occurs mostly on North Bruny. The birds can be found the easiest at the following accessible locations:

- Dennes Point (near the old quarry)
- Dennes Hill Nature Reserve, also known as Waterview Hill. Check around the base of the hill.
- Missionary Rd, a 500m stretch from junction with Lennon Rd and also further down after crossing the creek in McCrackens Gully
- Great Bay – near the rest area north of the township
- Cape Queen Elizabeth Tk – bush surrounding a dry lagoon near the Big Lagoon
- Apollo Bay Rd and Mulcahys Rd near the ferry (occasional sightings)
- South Bruny National Park, South Bruny – small numbers, difficult access
- If you fail to see the birds in one of the above places, go and stay at Inala Country Accommodation. Sightings are guaranteed as the birds breed in the nest boxes there.

Good birdwatching starts even before the ferry gets to the island. As our ferry cast off in Kettering, we saw three Pallid Cuckoos chasing each other on the power lines. Black-faced Cormorants passed the ferry on their way towards Bruny Island. You may also encounter Shy Albatross, Short-tailed Shearwater or White-bellied Sea-Eagle.

Apollo Bay

This spot is located south of the Roberts Point ferry terminal. Take Apollo Bay Rd to the bay. Forty-spotted Pardalotes can occasionally be found in Apollo Bay Rd and Mulcahys Rd. Painted Button-quail had been recorded a few times from this area. Common species in the bushland include Black-headed Honeyeater, Crescent Honeyeater, Dusky Robin, Striated Pardalote, Tree Martin and occasionally Satin Flycatcher and Swift Parrot.

Tree Martin

Missionary Road

Missionary Rd veers north from Lennon Rd (B66) and leads along the coast to Barnes Bay. This is an excellent area for Forty-spotted Pardalote which can be found along a 500m stretch of the road starting at the junction with Lennon Rd and along the creek. However, check any stand of manna gums on your way.

Blue-winged Parrots are common, often seen feeding in wheat fields or grassland or perching on the power lines. In a similar habitat look also for White-fronted Chat, Scarlet Robin, Dusky Robin, Dusky Woodswallow, Brush Bronzewing and Beautiful Firetail.

In the McCrackens Gully there are plenty of Brown Thornbills and Green Rosellas. Four species of cuckoos can be found here.

Dennes Point

This site is located at the north end of Bruny Island Main Rd (numbered in this section C625). It's a good idea to stop near The Lookout accommodation to see Tree Martins and take in the magnificent views.

Near the Dennes Point jetty, just past the Jetty Café, there were plentiful New Holland Honeyeaters, a few Crescent Honeyeaters and three Forty-spotted Pardalotes on a flowering gum tree. A small flock of Galahs was flying over the Café. White-fronted Chats were present in the dune vegetation.

At the corner of Nebraska Rd and Sports Rd we sighted eight Common Bronzewings. Pallid Cuckoo was calling from the power lines. At night, hooting of Masked Owl and Tasmanian Morepork can be heard from the hills. Two Tawny Frogmouths were catching insects around a lamp post on Nebraska Rd.

In trees along the beach we saw plenty of Striated and Spotted Pardalotes which kept us busy trying to find Forty-spotted among them. We were not successful on this occasion.

Old Quarry

The site is located 3.5km south of Dennes Point on the west side of Bruny Island Main Rd (C625). GPS coordinates are 43.05.32 S and 147.21.31 E. This is an excellent place for Forty-spotted Pardalotes; 10-20 birds have been counted in the area. Other birds here include Tree Martin, Dusky Robin, Brown Thornbill and Yellow-throated Honeyeater.

Dennes Hill Nature Reserve

The site, also called Waterview Hill, is located near the Old Quarry. Forty-spotted Pardalotes can be found at the base of the hill, one of the biggest colonies of these birds on the island is located here. Moreover, Swift Parrots are regularly found here and honeyeaters are common. Look also for the other pardalotes, Dusky Robin, Scarlet Robin, Dusky Woodswallow, Common Bronzewing, Brown Thornbill and Grey Butcherbird.

Lennon Road T-junction

About 0.5km north from the turnoff from Lennon Rd into Bruny Island Main Rd (C625), in the gum trees near the 'North Bruny Disposal Site' sign, there were three Forty-spotted Pardalotes. Further along, just before the turnoff to Barnes Bay, the forest was teeming with birdlife, including three endemic honeyeaters (Yellow-throated Honeyeater, Black-headed Honeyeater and Strong-billed Honeyeater), abundant Brown

Thornbills and Tasmanian Thornbills as well as Green Rosellas, Yellow Wattlebirds, Striated Pardalotes and Spotted Pardalotes. Also along this road we found eight Tasmanian Scrubwrens.

Whaymans Road

From Bruny Island Main Rd (B66) turn west into Whaymans Rd, you'll be driving through the farmland. Later take any available track leading south to the bay. We found a large flock of Common Bronzewings (about 40 birds) along the road. A couple of Brown Quails flushed from the roadside grass. On the farmland, we recorded Flame Robin, Australasian Pipit, Scarlet Robin, Yellow-rumped Thornbill, Blue-winged Parrot and plenty of White-fronted Chats and Green Rosellas. Two Eastern Rosellas were perched on a fence.

Cape Barren Goose was recorded from this area a couple of times.

Great Bay

The village of Great Bay is located on Bruny Island Main Rd (B66) about 5km south of the turnoff to the ferry.

Bush around the rest area north of Great Bay is a very reliable site for Forty-spotted Pardalote. We also found there a raucous pair of Satin Flycatchers. Flocks of 10-40 of Blue-winged Parrots are regularly seen along the road.

Bar-tailed Godwit, note the remains of its breeding plumage

During our visit, there were waders on the sand bar (Bar-tailed Godwits, Australian Pied Oystercatchers, Sooty Oystercatchers and one Red Knot). This site is known for its large congregations of Australian Pied Oystercatchers (up to 150 birds). Also, Kelp Gulls have been recorded in large flocks of 100-300 birds. In winter, Double-banded Plovers visit here.

The swampy area on the left had plenty Tawny-crowned Honeyeaters and New Holland Honeyeaters as well as a few Crescent Honeyeaters and White-fronted Chats.

Past the Great Bay village, there were hundreds Dusky Woodswallows and several Dusky Robins and Yellow-throated Honeyeaters in the banksias. The bushland was alive with cuckoos calling; look and listen for all four of them - Horsfield's Bronze-Cuckoo, Shining Bronze-Cuckoo, Pallid Cuckoo and Fan-tailed Cuckoo.

Cape Queen Elizabeth Track

This 12km return track is a great Bruny Island's day walk. Its start is just 2km north of the Little Penguin rookery on The Neck. The track runs along the Island Scenic Flights, after 2km reaching the Big Lagoon with beach access, then carrying on to Cape Queen Elizabeth.

This walk is another site on the island good to look for Forty-spotted Pardalote. The birds are resident in the bushland growing at the edge of a small, usually dry lagoon about 1.5km from the entry to the track. Among the weeds around this dry lagoon should also be plenty of White-fronted Chats, Australasian Pipits and Beautiful Firetails.

Flocks of Blue-winged Parrots can be found in the paddocks at the start of the track.

Big Lagoon is a very good spot for Musk Duck which is resident in this place. Other waterbirds here include Black Swan, Chestnut Teal, Grey Teal and Australian Shelduck. Small numbers of Curlew Sandpipers and Red-capped Plovers often feed on the mudflats. Occasionally, Latham's Snipe can be seen on the flooded paddocks. In winter, Double-banded Plover is commonly found in the area.

If you side-step to the beach, you may see Hooded Plovers; flocks of up to 15 birds have been recorded. Both Oystercatchers should also be present.

If you continue further on along the track, look for Dusky Robin, Pink Robin, Olive Whistler, Brush Bronzewing, Bassian Thrush, New Holland Honeyeater and Yellow-throated Honeyeater.

The Neck Rookery

At the narrow strip of land leading to the South Bruny, called The Neck, a penguin and shearwater rookery is situated. Little Penguins and Short-tailed Shearwater have their burrows here and from August till February rear their young. 240,000 pairs of shearwaters and several hundred pairs of penguins breed here. Public is allowed to watch the penguin parade at dusk from the boardwalk and the hide (no flashlights; torches have to be covered with red cellophane). If you come during the day, just look at the burrows and smell the characteristic odour of a seabird colony.

Short-tailed Shearwater burrows on The Neck, Bruny Island

Scan the coastline from Hummock Steps for Hooded Plover, both Oystercatchers and Red-capped Plover. In May 2013 a group of Banded Stilts landed here to feed along the shore. The Steps are also useful for watching the land birds that fly along the isthmus from one part of the island to the other. We saw flocks of Swift Parrots, Green Rosellas and three Forty-spotted Pardalotes. Two Satin Flycatchers were flying near the penguin colony carpark and Peregrine Falcon was circling over the dunes.

The Neck Campground

The site is located on the south end of The Neck off Bruny Island Main Rd (B66) in a very nice bush setting. Swift Parrots are regular visitors here. Sporadic records exist of Forty-spotted Pardalote sightings.

In the bush near the campsite look for Bassian Thrush, Olive Whistler, Scarlet Robin, Beautiful Firetail, Green Rosella and Yellow-tailed Black-Cockatoo. Very tame around the picnic tables are Common Bronzewings and Tasmanian Scrubwrens. This is a good spot for cuckoos, all four are calling loud in summer.

On the beach you will find Hooded Plovers, Australian Pied Oystercatchers and occasionally Bar-tailed Godwits.

Adventure Bay

Continuing south, we turned left into Adventure Bay Rd (C630). In the mature gums just before the Adventure Bay village, we found numerous Black-headed Honeyeaters and Strong-billed Honeyeaters, a breeding colony of Tree Martins and some very accessible Tasmanian Scrubwrens. Opposite the Adventure Bay Coastal Reserve, we got some Beautiful Firetails.

Adventure Bay is a stronghold of Swift Parrot. There were four of them at the Captain Cook Tourist Park. Moreover, Flame Robins are very common in the tourist park.

At a sandbar at the mouth of Captain Cook Creek we found three species of gulls (Silver, Pacific, Kelp), Crested Terns and Caspian Terns. At the Bruny Island Cruises' office were many Scrubtits, Tasmanian Scrubwrens and a White-bellied Sea-Eagle. On the beach at the Penguin on Bruny café were two Hooded Plovers and a pair of Australian Pied Oystercatchers with two chicks. In March 2010, a Fiordland Penguin marched onto the on the beach near Two Tree Point and was resting there for several days.

Bruny Island Cruises are award-winning coastal-viewing trips to admire the rugged beauty of South Bruny coastline, whales, dolphins and seabirds. For prices and timetables check their website at https://www.brunycruises.com.au/. Although the cruises are not focused on birdwatching, there is a good chance to spot Short-tailed Shearwater, Sooty Shearwater, Hutton's Shearwater, Shy Albatross, Buller's Albatross, Indian Yellow-nosed Albatross, Southern and Northern Giant-Petrel, Common Diving-Petrel, White-faced Storm-Petrel, Little Penguin, Black-faced Cormorant and raptors such as White-bellied Sea-Eagle and Peregrine Falcon. Short-tailed Shearwaters can occur in huge numbers if the boat comes across a shoal of fish.

Just east of Adventure Bay village, a detached section of South Bruny National Park is located on Fluted Cape. See the description of this site in the next chapter.

Mavista Nature Walk

This is a 30min-long, beautiful walking trail by a rainforest stream to a waterfall. The site is located near Adventure Bay. Take Coolangatta Rd (C629) from Adventure Bay Rd, then turn into Resolution Rd. The start of the walk is off this road, signposted. You'll find here a small carpark and shelter.

Mavista Nature Walk features towering stringybark and blackwood trees. The understory is made of magnificent tree ferns. The walk is fantastic for the wet forest species. We saw several Scrubtits in the undergrowth along the stream. There were also plenty of Grey Currawongs, Black Currawongs, Silvereyes, Tasmanian Scrubwrens, Tasmanian Thornbills and Pink Robins. We also came across Satin Flycatcher, Olive Whistler, Bassian Thrush, Green Rosella, Shining Bronze-cuckoo and Dusky Robin. We sighted eight Swift Parrots there.

Bruny Island State Forest

Unless you are on a bus or tow a caravan, take a steep and winding unsealed Coolangatta Rd (C629) running through the wet Bruny Island State Forest. We drove along this road between Adventure Bay and Lunawanna, stopping at the carpark of Mt Mangana Forest Reserve where we walked a short section of Mt Mangana Tk. We got plenty of Pink Robins, Tasmanian Thornbills, Tasmanian Scrubwrens and a few Olive Whistlers. There were also Yellow-throated Honeyeaters, Strong-billed Honeyeaters, Crescent Honeyeaters and Golden Whistlers. Black Currawongs were abundant and vocal, flying between the trees.

Further down the road we stopped at the Clemmets Mill carpark. This was a marvellous place for Scrubtit, Pink Robin and Olive Whistler. We also got Yellow-tailed black-Cockatoo and Collared Sparrowhawk there.

Simpson Bay

At the north end of the road on the west coast, our short detour from Bruny Island Main Rd (B66) onto Simpsons Bay Rd (C628) to Simpson Bay produced sightings of a White-bellied Sea-Eagle, some Tasmanian Scrubwrens, Dusky Robins, Flame Robins, Scarlett Robins, Beautiful Firetails, Brush Bronzewings and Common Bronzewings. Green Rosella was very common. Two Swift Parrots were sitting in a gum tree.

Simpson Bay area is also known for occasional occurrence of Forty-spotted Pardalotes.

Alonnah

This small village is located on the west coast of South Bruny where Bruny Island Main Rd (B66) reaches the coast.

We walked Sheepwash Tk – to get there from Alonnah, drive Pontoon Rd to the jetty where you'll find a carpark and the track along the coast. Near the jetty we saw Chestnut Teals, plenty of Black Swans, Kelp Gulls and a pair of Australian Pied Oystercatchers with a chick.

Our findings along the Sheepwash Tk included Yellow Wattlebird, Black-headed Honeyeater, Yellow-throated Honeyeater and Dusky Robin. Tasmanian Native-hens were everywhere. We also found Green Rosella, Flame Robin and Scarlet Robin. Dusky Woodswallow was sitting in a hollow of a large tree limb. Swamp Harrier was patrolling over the area. Swift Parrots are often found feeding along this track.
Tawny Frogmouths regularly nest near the cemetery.

We also checked the wooded areas south of Alonnah where we found Scrubtit, Blue-winged Parrot, Shining Bronze-cuckoo and Yellow Wattlebird.

Yellow Wattlebird

Daniels Bay

The site is located near Lunawanna at the south end of Bruny Island Main Rd (B66).

In the wetland near the estuary Lewin's Rails were found several times. During our stay we found Eastern Great Egret, Sooty Oystercatcher and a few hundreds of Silver Gulls.

Inala Cottages

Just south of Lunawanna in Cloudy Bay Rd (C644) just past Wrights Rd, Inala Cottages are located that are favourite of birdwatchers who wish to stay overnight on the island. For bookings visit http://www.inalanaturetours.com.au/ , tel. (03) 6293 1217.

The site's birdlist has over 110 species. Day and night guided nature tours are available or you may wander around by yourself. This 200ha 'Land for Wildlife' private property, covered in 80% by native vegetation, is home to several threatened species and all of the Tasmanian endemic birds, including one of the largest colonies of Forty-spotted Pardalotes. Nest boxes that have been provided to them are used gladly and the birds can be easily watched and photographed from an observation tower.

Another bird you can count on here is Grey Goshawk. The white birds are quite visible in the bush. It is also a very good place for Scrubtit, Satin Flycatcher and Brown Quail.

In one part of the walk, called Robin Glade, you may come across four robins (Pink, Scarlet, Flame and Dusky Robin). At night you could see Masked Owl, Tawny Frogmouth and Tasmanian Morepork, as well as many native marsupials as the Australian fauna is typically nocturnal.

South Bruny National Park

The South Bruny National Park is located at the south tip of Bruny Island. The Park encompasses all of the coastline and some of the hinterland between Cape Fluted and southern part of Taylors Bay. The land section of the Park includes Cape Fluted, Cloudy Bay and Labillardiere Peninsula with Cape Bruny. Many islands such as Partridge Island, Penguin Island etc. are also part of the Park. Much of the coast comprises towering cliffs, long sandy beaches, shearwater and penguin rookeries and a large area of kelp underwater gardens. The Labillardiere Peninsula is covered mostly by coastal heath with small patches of rainforest among the heath.

Access from Hobart is via Southern Outlet (A6) to Kettering, approximately 45min drive. The car ferry company at Kettering provided 9-11 crossings daily. See the timetable and pricing at http://brunyislandferry.com.au/bruny-island-ferry-timetable/. The trip across the straits takes only 15 minutes. Upon disembarking at the Roberts Point ferry terminal, proceed east on Lennon Rd (B66) and continue south on Bruny Island Main Rd (B66). Allow at least 1.5hrs to reach different locations in the Park. The most direct route to Cloudy Bay is via Alonnah and Lunawanna. In Lunawanna, take Cloudy Bay Rd (C644). To get to Labillardiere Peninsula, from Lunawanna take Lighthouse Rd (C629) to Cape Bruny. Just before getting to Cape Bruny, you can turn right into Old Jetty Rd to get to the Jetty Campground. Old Jetty Rd gives also access to Labillardiere Peninsula Tk. Both Cloudy Bay and Labillardiere Peninsula are very remote so arrive with food, water, fuel and other supplies with plenty to spare. Small shops are located at Lunawanna and Adventure Bay. The latter has also the island's only fuel. To help with navigation see a basic map in the Park brochure downloadable here:
http://www.parks.tas.gov.au/file.aspx?id=19053.

There are three bush camping areas in the Park, located at Cloudy Bay Rd (near Cloudy Beach), Cloudy Corner (3km down Cloudy Beach Tk from the previous site) and Jetty Campground on Labillardiere Peninsula. Facilities are basic and no drinking water is available. The choice of walks includes short walks, long walks and very long walks.

Over 120 species are on the Park's birdlist. **Keys species** are Forty-spotted Pardalote (difficult to find here), Tawny-crowned Honeyeater, Swift Parrot, Hooded Plover and Olive Whistler. Other birds of interest include Satin Flycatcher, Beautiful Firetail, Tasmanian Morepork, Bassian Thrush, Striated Fieldwren, Scrubtit (rare), Brown Quail, Grey Goshawk and seabirds. Rare species include Ground Parrot, Cape Barren Goose, Rainbow Lorikeet, Dusky Moorhen and Latham's Snipe.

Fluted Cape

This is the northern, separate part of the National Park. Fluted Cape flanks the Adventure Bay from the east. To get there, from Adventure Bay village continue on Adventure Bay Rd (C63) past the Bruny Island Cruises. Find the entry to Grass Point Tk near a boat ramp, a part of a 5km return Fluted Cape Walk running along the cliffs of the Cape. Extensive areas of heathland can be found on the Cape.

Grass Point Tk offers good vantage points to watch the seabirds. Large rafts of Australasian Gannets and Short-tailed Shearwaters may be seen from the cliffs. Look also for Shy Albatross, Black-browed Albatross, Northern Giant-Petrel, Fluttering Shearwater, Sooty Shearwater, Little Penguin, White-faced Storm-Petrel and Black-faced Cormorant. Penguin Island opposite Fluted Cape offers nesting grounds for thousands of seabirds. In the vicinity of this colony resides a well-known pair of White-bellied Sea-Eagles which specialises in penguin hunting. Many reports exist about a Sea-Eagle carrying a Little Penguin from rock to rock.

Swift Parrots breed here and are often seen in the Park. This is one of the best places on the island to find Satin Flycatcher. Sheoak thickets near the Grass Point are good for Beautiful Firetails.

Common birds on the track include Striated Pardalote, Dusky Robin, Crescent Honeyeater, Yellow-throated Honeyeater, Strong-billed Honeyeater and Black-headed Honeyeater. Look also for Black Currawong, Bassian Thrush, Green Rosella, Brown Thornbill and Hooded Plover.

Cloudy Bay

To get there, from Bruny Island Main Rd (B66) in Lunawanna take Cloudy Bay Rd (C644).

We explored the area around the Sheepwash Creek mouth and took a walk on a boardwalk to the middle beach. In the carpark, we found a small flock of Brown Quails, feeding quietly by the roadside. Near the carpark we also came across White-fronted Chats, Olive Whistler, Scarlet Robin and Yellow-rumped Thornbill. Shorebirds in the mouth of the creek included Australian Pied Oystercatcher, Sooty Oystercatcher, Kelp Gull, Caspian Tern and Red-capped Plover. There are also records of Sanderling and Grey-tailed Tattler from this location.

Grey-tailed Tattler in breeding plumage

On the middle beach we encountered a nice flock of eight Hooded Plovers.

The walking track and boardwalk yielded Bassian Thrush, Tasmanian Scrubwren, Black Currawong, New Holland Honeyeater, Yellow Wattlebird and Tasmanian Native-hen.

A White-bellied Sea-Eagle's nest is visible from the track. Swamp Harrier was flying over the dunes. Records of Whistling Kite, rare in the region, exists for this site.

Cape Bruny

To get there, from Bruny Island Main Rd (B66) in Lunawanna take Lighthouse Rd (C629) towards the Cape Bruny Lighthouse.

Driving south on Lighthouse Rd, at an intersection with Sharps Rd we found Crescent Honeyeaters. A 100m further down, the gum-lined road teemed with Tasmanian Thornbills, Tasmanian Scrubwrens, Dusky Robins, Dusky Woodswallows and Australasian Pipits. There were also Swift Parrots, Scarlet Robins, Pink Robins, Strong-billed Honeyeaters and Black-headed Honeyeaters.

Further south at Cloudy Bay Lagoon, expect to see Australian Pelicans and four cormorant species including Black-faced Cormorant. Scattered in the bush on both sides of the road, active shearwater burrows are hidden. Hooded Plover breeds in the area. There was a small flock of Red-capped Plovers, Australian Pied Oystercatchers, Caspian Terns and several Bar-tailed Godwits on the beach as well as plenty of Black Swans. A few Pacific Gulls were standing on the beach; these breed here.

Past the Cloudy Bay Lagoon, Inlet Beach is located; we found Hooded Plover on this beach. In the bush were Tasmanian Thornbill, Tasmanian Scrubwren, Dusky Robin, Satin Flycatcher and Horsfield's Bronze-cuckoo. A flock of Strong-billed Honeyeaters was very visible.

When you get to the National Park, pull over in the area where you need to pay the fee. We found three Swift Parrots, Black Currawong and Brown Falcon there. Honeyeaters were everywhere, mostly Crescent Honeyeaters, New Holland Honeyeaters and Strong-billed Honeyeaters. Tasmanian Thornbills were fossicking for insects in the damp vegetation below the road. Tawny-crowned Honeyeaters were singing in the heath. We also found Striated Fieldwren, Silvereye and Grey Fantail. Pallid Cuckoo was calling from a tree.

We drove to the lighthouse at the end of the road. In the grass near a cottage was a group of Brown Quails feeding in the open. Plenty of Beautiful Firetails were hopping around on the ground. There were also Brush Bronzewings, Australasian Pipits, White-fronted Chats, Flame Robins, Dusky Robins and Silvereyes. The heath expanse on Cape Bruny is the best place for Tawny-crowned Honeyeaters in the Park.

This area is a stronghold for Swift Parrots. Flocks of 80 birds have been recorded.

Cape Bruny is a good place for observing seabirds. Continued streams of Short-tailed Shearwaters can often be watched as they fly along the Cape. Other seabirds here include Shy Albatross, Buller's Albatross, Pacific Gull, Australasian Gannet, Crested Tern and White-fronted Tern (rare).

A good selection of raptors included White-bellied Sea-Eagle carrying some nesting material, Brown Falcon, Swamp Harrier and Collared Sparrowhawk.

Jetty Beach Campground

Take Lighthouse Rd (C629) to Cape Bruny. Just before getting there, turn right into Old Jetty Rd to get to the Jetty Campground. Please note that the only signage at the intersection points out to the Labillardiere Walking Track.

The area around the camp is good for Olive Whistler, Bassian Thrush, Satin Flycatcher, Dusky Robin, Horsfield's Bronze-cuckoo and Tasmanian Morepork. In the nearby heath will be plenty of Tawny-crowned Honeyeaters. The most common honeyeater in the camping area is Strong-billed Honeyeater.

On the beach near old ferry look for Hooded Plover, Australian Pied Oystercatcher, Sooty Oystercatcher, Black-faced Cormorant and Little Black Cormorant.

Labillardiere Peninsula Circuits

You can choose to take a 90min circuit or 14km track running along the whole peninsula which may take you the whole day. You will be walking in the most remote corner of Bruny Island. The walk will take you through the costal heathland and patches of dry sclerophyll forest. The entrance is midway in Old Jetty Rd, well-signposted and with a carpark provided.

The circuit runs mostly in short heath which allows good views of the beaches, sea and coastal islands. In the heath, you will have a chance of a Ground Parrot sighting although they occur here in low numbers. Other birds on the track include Olive Whistler, Beautiful Firetail, Brush Bronzewing, Tawny-crowned Honeyeater, Eastern Spinebill, Brown Thornbill, Brown Quail, Tasmanian Scrubwren, Dusky Robin, Golden Whistler and Swamp Harrier. In summer, flocks of White-throated Needletails can be seen in the sky.

Hooded Plover may occasionally be found on the beaches.

In the northernmost part of the walk, Partridge Island is located just offshore. This island protects the largest remaining colony of Forty-spotted Pardalotes. Access is only allowed for research.

Snug Tiers Nature Recreation Area

This 5,600ha conservation/recreation area is located 8km west of Snug and 25km south of Hobart. Snug Tiers are covered by the dry sclerophyll forest and contain extensive areas of buttongrass on top of the range. The 30m-high Snug Falls are the main landscape feature and the main tourist attraction in the area. A 2km Snug Falls Tk descends to a beautiful, cool gully below the Snug Falls. This walk takes you first through the dry sclerophyll forest. Down in the gully you'll find the rainforest with ferns and mosses, rocky outcrops and small caves.

Over 80 species are on the site's birdlist. **Key species** are Scrubtit, Ground Parrot and Southern Emu-wren. Other birds of interest include Swift Parrot, Pink Robin, Olive Whistler, Bassian Thrush, Tasmanian Thornbill and White-throated Needletail. Fork-tailed Swift has been occasionally recorded here.

Snug Falls

To get to Snug Falls, take Channel Hwy (B68) to Snug. Turn west onto Snug Tiers Rd in Snug and continue for 4km until you reach the fork in the road. Take the left fork, an unsealed Snug Falls Rd, and follow it to a well-signposted parking area.

Shining Bronze-cuckoo and Pallid Cuckoo may be calling in the carpark. Forest Ravens will be walking around. Brush Bronzewing and Common Bronzewing may also be found here. Beautiful Firetails are everywhere. Honeyeaters are plentiful, look for Strong-billed Honeyeater, Yellow-throated Honeyeater, New Holland Honeyeater, Crescent Honeyeater, Black-headed Honeyeater, Eastern Spinebill and Yellow Wattlebird.

Take a walk down a fern-lined gully at the base of the waterfall for a chance to see many of the Tasmanian endemics, in particular Tasmanian Thornbill, Tasmanian Scrubwren, Black Currawong and Green Rosella. Robins will prance around you including Pink Robin, Flame Robin and Dusky Robin. Pink Robins are quite tame here. On the top of the track you may spot Bassian Thrush. Olive Whistler and Golden Whistler can also be found in this area.

In summer, White-throated Needletails will be flying overhead, look for an occasional Fork-tailed Swift among them.

Forest Raven, a common bird Tasmania

Buttongrass Plains

To get to the buttongrass plains in the Snug Tiers Nature Recreation Area, drive Channel Hwy (B68) just to Margate and in Margate turn into Van Moreys Rd past the BP station. Drive approximately 10km to the carpark. The last 2.5km is rough, 4WD only. A dense network of 4WD tracks covers the area, it is a 4-wheel driver paradise. It is also easy to become lost here; be very careful.

We walked through the wet buttongrass plain and later investigated a few of the bush tracks. Ground Parrots, Striated Fieldwrens and Southern Emu-wrens were quite easy to find in buttongrass. We also flushed a few Latham's Snipes. A small flock of Blue-winged Parrots was foraging in the swamp.

In the bush, we found Brush Bronzewing, Olive Whistler, Yellow-tailed Black-Cockatoo, New Holland Honeyeater (plenty), Crescent Honeyeater, Tasmanian Thornbill, Golden Whistler, Beautiful Firetail and Brown Falcon.

Hastings Caves State Reserve

The amazing Hasting Caves are situated 125km southwest of Hobart, it's a 2hr drive. This is the place for people keen to see Superb Lyrebird in Tasmania.

The Reserve offers the visitors a variety of experiences including relaxing in the waters of the thermal springs and cave exploration. A birdwatcher may find little time left for birdwatching with all these non-birding temptations.

The site is reached via Huon Hwy (A6). The destination is well-signposted past Geeveston. Just north of Southport turn into Hastings Caves Rd (C635), a well-maintained gravel road which will take you to the Visitor Centre and the thermal pool. The biggest cave, Newdegate Cave, is located 5km further down the road.

Facilities on site include a carpark, Visitor Centre, swimming pool, café, picnic area and several walking tracks. The main vegetation type is wet sclerophyll forest.

Just 40 species are on the Reserve's birdlist (seems that not much time is spent here birdwatching). You'll find here a selection of wet forest species such as Scrubtit, Tasmanian Thornbill, Satin Flycatcher, Golden Whistler, Olive Whistler, Bassian Thrush and Pink Robin.

Superb Lyrebirds can often be seen dashing across the road connecting Thermal Springs with Hasting Caves.

Near the Visitor Centre, look for Green Rosella, Flame Robin, Black Currawong and Bassian Thrush. Welcome Swallows have built their nests under the eaves of the Visitor Centre. Dusky Woodswallows often perch on the power lines.

A good place for Scrubtit, Tasmanian Thornbill and Superb Lyrebird is the area near the Newdegate Cave.

Honeyeaters found in the Reserve include Yellow-throated Honeyeater, Strong-billed Honeyeater, Crescent Honeyeater, Yellow Wattlebird and Eastern Spinebill. Good numbers of Black Currawongs, Forest Ravens and Tasmanian Native-hens have been recorded.

Mid-East Coast

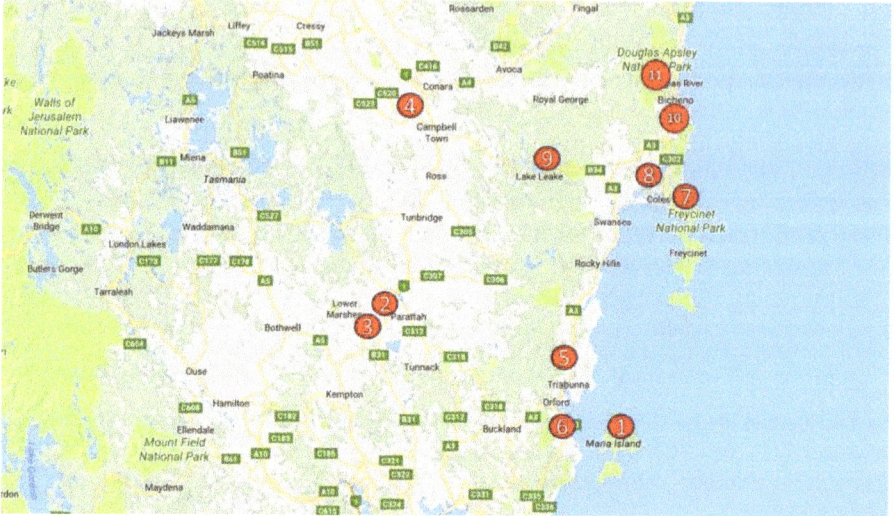

1	Maria Island National Park
2	Lake Dulverton Conservation Area
3	Ellesmere Dam
4	Midlands Area
5	Rostrevor Lagoon
6	Wielangta Forest
7	Freycinet National Park
8	Moulting Lagoon
9	Lake Leake
10	Bicheno
11	Douglas-Apsley National Park

Maria Island National Park

Located just a 30min ferry ride from the township of Triabunna on the mid-east coast of Tasmania, the entire Maria Island is protected by its National Park status. Triabunna is situated on Tasman Hwy (A3), about 90km (1.5hrs) from Hobart and 2.5hrs from Launceston. A basic locality map is included in the Park's brochure, downloadable here: http://www.parks.tas.gov.au/file.aspx?id=19045.

Maria Island is a very important birdwatching destination. Over 130 bird species are found on the island which is one of the best birdwatching places in Tasmania and perhaps the best place in Tasmania for the forest birds. Maria Island is home to all 12 bird species that are endemic to Tasmania (11 are common and Scrubtit is rare and difficult to find). Also breeding endemics (Swift Parrot and Tasmanian Morepork) occur here in good numbers. There is enough time during a day trip to find most of the endemic birds.

Maria Island is a special place for everyone, not only for the bird-crazy people. There are historic ruins, beautiful bays, rugged cliffs and fantastic, quite tame wildlife. The National Park was declared in 1972 to maintain an insurance population of the wildlife threatened with extinction on the Tasmanian mainland. Several species including Cape Barren Goose, Tasmanian Native-hen, Forester kangaroo and Tasmanian bettong were relocated to the island. The latest arrival is Tasmanian devil – a tumour-free population has been established in 2005 to safeguard against the facial cancer disease that is decimating the devils in mainland Tasmania. This will help to save this fascinating species whose survival in the wild is uncertain.

Maria Island stretches about 20km north-south and at the widest place east-west spans about 13km. The highest point is Mt Maria at 710m. The island consists of two parts joined by a narrow isthmus. A wide range of habitats includes large areas of grassland heavily grazes by the kangaroos and wombats and open woodland dominated by the Tasmanian blue gum, manna gum, peppermint and stringybark. There are also creeks, small patches of wetlands, beaches and coastal heath environment.

Access is possible only by the passenger ferry (unless you hire a boat or a charter plane). In summer, the ferry leaves from the jetty in Triabunna daily at 9am and the last return trip is at 5pm from Darlington. In the winter season the ferry runs on selected days only. The current (2017) operator is called Encounter Maria Island. Check their website at https://encountermaria.com.au/ for the current schedule and prices. There are no shops on the island – bring your own food!

Basic accommodation can be booked in the old penitentiary in Darlington. Bunk beds are provided, you must have your own bedding, food, lighting, pots and plates. Gas stoves are provided in the camp kitchen. Contact the East Coast Information Centre for booking on (03) 6256 4772 or get more info online at https://eastcoasttasmania.com/operator/maria-island-penitentiary-accommodation-maria-island-tasmania/.

Camping is allowed in designated places – Darlington, Frenchs Farm and Encampment Cove. No advanced bookings are required, pay your camping fees on arrival. Facilities in the campsites include gas barbecues, picnic shelters, drinking water and toilets. Coin-operated showers are provided at Darlington Penitentiary.

There is no vehicular traffic on the island except for the National Park vehicles. Bicycles can be used on the main roads but not on the beaches and walking tracks. A network of well-signposted walking tracks criss-crosses the area. Before embarking on a trek, go to the Visitor Centre in the Old Commissariat Store near the jetty and collect laminated copes of site maps with track descriptions. Remember to drop the maps back to the Store before leaving the island.

You will not miss spotting Cape Barren Goose or Tasmanian Native-hen, they will be the first birds to catch your eye on arrival and will accompany your during the whole time of exploration.

The **key attraction** is the endangered Forty-spotted Pardalote. Maria Island is the second-best place to see it in Tasmania, after Bruny Island. Look for them in the manna gums, also called white gums. The birds feed on the crystallised sugary fluid (manna) exuded by the manna gum. These trees have a smooth grey-yellowish trunk and shed bark from their upper branches. The bark dangles from the forks in long ribbons. The colonies of Forty-spotted Pardalote are easy to find on Reservoir Circuit (near the Reservoir and along Bernacchis Creek), a 2hr round trek west from Darlington. They are also present around Counsel Creek, 2km south of Darlington. Another good place for them is in the manna gums and sheoaks around Frenchs Farm. Look also for them on the track between Frenchs Farm and Encampment Cove as well as further down, in the northern section of the isthmus. There is also a chance of finding them on Painted Cliffs Tk.

Black-headed Honeyeater and Strong-billed Honeyeater can be easily located in the canopy of stringybark gums where they often feed in large groups. In the grassland, flocks of White-fronted Chats, Yellow-rumped Thornbills or Black Currawongs are often seen. Hooded Plover, another endangered species found on Maria Island, breeds on Darlington Beach near the jetty, Hopground Beach near the Painted Cliffs and on Ocean Beach. A colony of Little Penguins is located in Haunted Bay at the southern end of the island (practically not accessible).

Bird species occurring regularly but requiring some effort to locate include Beautiful Firetail, Brush Bronzewing, Olive Whistler, Satin Flycatcher and Bassian Thrush. A list of rare species found on the island is still growing and includes White-winged Triller, Tawny-crowned Honeyeater, White-throated Needletail, Cattle Egret, Little Corella, Sulphur-crested Cockatoo, Common Sandpiper, Fairy Tern and Nankeen Kestrel.

Triabunna

If you are staying overnight in Triabunna to be ready for the ferry in the morning, check the gardens, estuary and paddocks around the town - you may get some good finds there. While waiting for the ferry to Maria Island, we spotted Swift Parrot feeding with the group of Musk Lorikeets in the small gums next to the marina.

In the estuary at the end of Franklin Rd, waterbirds often congregate in large numbers. Our findings included Masked Lapwing (100+), Australasian Shoveler (15) and Hoary-headed Grebe (20). Walking along the Esplanade we came across large numbers of Little Pied Cormorants with a few Little Black Cormorants and Black-faced Cormorants in the mix, perched in a dead tree opposite the Police Station. Australian Pied Oystercatchers and Pacific Gulls were roosting on the lawn near the Police Station. A single Blue-billed Duck was sitting in a crowd of teals on a partially submerged overturned tree.

Little Wattlebird in the Triabunna Caravan Park

In the township, besides the masses of common introduced birds, we found Little Wattlebird, Tasmanian Native-hen, Musk Lorikeet, Brush Bronzewing and Yellow-throated Honeyeater. Tawny Frogmouth was hunting insect in the caravan park in the evening. We also heard Tasmanian Morepork and Masked Owl at night from the forest near Tasman Hwy.

Check the paddocks north of the township, there are records of Banded Plover (December 2016), Cape Barren Goose and Cattle Egret from there.

Ferry Passage

Seabirds on our half an hour ferry trip to Maria Island included Black-faced Cormorant, Black-browed Albatross, Shy Albatross, Short-tailed Shearwater, Fluttering Shearwater, Little Penguin, Australasian Gannet, Pacific Gull and Crested Tern.

You may also see dolphins, whales and seals.

Darlington Bay Beach

On our arrival, the jetty was covered in Black-faced Cormorants, gulls and terns. A welcoming committee of Cape Barren Geese flew over from the hills and landed on the beach, honking. That turned our attention to the beach where we quickly located a pair of Hooded Plovers, just there, about 50m from the ferry.

A couple of Laughing Kookaburras and Australian Magpies were hopping around, busy picking large brown beetles scattered densely on the sand. Other birds on the beach included Australian Pied Oystercatcher, Sooty Oystercatcher and Pacific Gull. Chestnut Teals with ducklings were feeding in a canal near the jetty. White-bellied Sea-Eagle was soaring over the jetty.

On the grassy hill behind the Old Commissariat Store, a large flock of White-fronted Chats foraged in the grass. We also recorded Tasmania Native-hen, Yellow-rumped Thornbill, Scarlet Robin, Australasian Pipit and Eurasian Skylark. Kangaroos were everywhere.

This was rich pickings just for the landing area on Maria Island and we did not even start exploring yet!

We went back to this area in the late afternoon to catch a ferry back to Triabunna. A dark, noisy cloud of Common Starlings flew over from the mainland and completely covered the coastal scrub near the beach for an overnight roost.

Cape Barren Geese on Darlington Bay Beach with a photobombing
Hooded Plover in the foreground

Darlington

The map of the Darlington area can be downloaded here:
http://www.parks.tas.gov.au/file.aspx?id=19258. The site is filled with historical
buildings of the former town of Darlington. Today, there is a large camping site there
plus accommodation is offered in some of the buildings.

The camping area was crowded with tame birds, wallabies and wombats, we spent a fair
amount of our birdwatching time right there. We tried to have lunch but our table was
quickly surrounded by Cape Barren Geese, Tasmanian Native-hens and Black
Currawongs. Even the shy Grey Currawong checked out our provisions. On anything
protruding from the ground, i.e. on stones, bushes, clothes drying lines, tent poles, etc.,
robins were perching (Dusky Robin, Scarlet Robin and Flame Robin). While we observed
a Tasmanian pademelon feeding her joey, Olive Whistler hopped out from under the
bush.

A flock of Green Rosellas was feeding among the tents. From the dense bracken ferns,
Tasmanian Scrubwrens and Common Blackbirds appeared. In the stand of tall
macrocarpa trees, Pallid Cuckoo and Satin Flycatcher were calling.

Paddocks around the old Darlington settlement are frequented by Tasmanian wildlife

Cattle Egrets were reported several times from the area near the campsite. If you are staying overnight, use a spotlight to locate Tasmanian Morepork, Tawny Frogmouth and perhaps the Tasmanian subspecies of Masked Owl; all of them are quite common on Maria Island. Be also on a lookout for the Tasmanian devils; they like to visit Darlington to check out the tourists' food and to rest under the buildings.

Counsel Creek Walk

A 3km section of this track between the Counsel Creek mouth and an intersection with the track leading to the Mount Maria summit is the most popular birdwatching site on the island. Forty-spotted Pardalote can be easily found in the manna gums. A map of the area is downloadable here: http://www.parks.tas.gov.au/file.aspx?id=19263

We first stopped at the mouth of Counsel Creek to observe a large colony of Tree Martins, established in dead trees to the east. A group of Chestnut Teals were dozing off in the creek mouth and a pair of Hooded Plovers stood on the beach.

Four Beautiful Firetails perched together with Scarlet Robins on dead branches over a field of bracken ferns. A dry swamp on the eastern side of the track was loud with piercing calls of Black Currawongs, plentiful in this spot. Dusky Woodswallows, Grey Fantails and Black-faced Cuckoo-shrikes were hunting insects over this area.

Next, we walked through the open forest dominated by blue gums and manna gums, with an understory of bracken fern. This is the 'Pardalote country'. Forty-spotted Pardalotes were relatively easy to locate high in the canopy of manna gums. Please keep in mind that Striated Pardalote and Spotted Pardalote are common on Maria Island so careful differentiation is needed.

The pardalote forest along the Counsel Creek Walk

In this area we also came across Eastern Rosella, Little Wattlebird, Yellow Wattlebird, Shining Bronze-Cuckoo, Fan-tailed Cuckoo and Tasmanian Thornbill. It is good to get experience with the Tasmanian Thornbill identification here as Brown Thornbill is practically absent or very rare, so no misidentification can occur.

Further down the track the vegetation changes to tall stringybark / white peppermint forest with the understory of blackthorn, silver wattle, blackwood and dogwood. Birds common here are mostly honeyeaters such as Black-headed Honeyeater, Strong-billed Honeyeater, Yellow-throated Honeyeater, New Holland Honeyeater, Crescent Honeyeater, Eastern Spinebill, Little Wattlebird and Yellow Wattlebird. Other birds in this area included Satin Flycatcher, Spotted Pardalote, Scarlet Robin, Green Rosella, Grey Fantail, Tasmanian Thornbill and Bassian Thrush.

Painted Cliffs Track

The weathered, pitted sandstone outcrop at the end of the Hopground Beach is called Painted Cliffs. Painted Cliffs Tk runs along the Hopground Beach and Painted Cliffs on the east shore of the island. The Painted Cliffs area map can be downloaded here: http://www.parks.tas.gov.au/file.aspx?id=19259.

Hooded Plovers nest on Hopground Beach. Other waders on the beach include Australian Pied Oystercatcher, Sooty Oystercatcher, Red-capped Plover, Ruddy Turnstone and Double-banded Plover.

Painted Cliffs Tk is another good area for Forty-spotted Pardalotes. It is also good place for Beautiful Firetail, Brush Bronzewing, Olive Whistler, White-fronted Chat and Tasmanian Scrubwren. Yellow Wattlebirds occur here in large numbers.

Reservoir Circuit

The 2km Reservoir Circuit is an excellent walk for birders, the area map can be downloaded here: http://www.parks.tas.gov.au/file.aspx?id=19260. The track runs from the Ranger's Station to the Reservoir. The way back is on the other side of the Bernacchis Creek, by the old cement works.

The track initially runs through the grassland, then through the bushland and woodland along the creek. The area near the Reservoir end is good for Forty-spotted Pardalote. You'll have a fair chance of finding Swift Parrot on this track. Look for them in the Tasmanian blue gums.

Other birds along the track include Olive Whistler, Satin Flycatcher, Tasmanian Thornbill, Pink Robin, Black-headed Honeyeater and Strong-billed Honeyeater. Nocturnal birds include Masked Owl and Tasmanian Morepork.

Australasian Grebes breed on the Reservoir. Look also for Chestnut Teal, Pacific Black Duck and White-faced Heron.

Fossil Cliffs Circuit

This 4km circular track takes you northeast of Darlington along the edge of Fossil Cliffs in the direction of twin peaks of Bishop and Clerk. The map of Fossil Cliffs Circuit can be downloaded here: http://www.parks.tas.gov.au/file.aspx?id=19258. First, you'll walk through the grassland along the cliff, then through the open forest along the Skipping Ridge. From the cliff you will have a view of Birds Rock, a favoured roosting place of seabirds such as Black-faced Cormorants, Australasian Gannets, terns and gulls. Peregrine Falcon is regularly found there, flying over the cliffs. Other raptors you may encounter in the area include White-bellied Sea-Eagle, Wedge-tailed Eagle and Brown Goshawk. On the beach you may find Hooded Plover, Australian Pied Oystercatcher and Caspian Tern.

The bushland of Skipping Ridge is a stronghold of Crescent Honeyeater. Other birds in this area include Satin Flycatcher, Striated Pardalote, Tasmanian Thornbill, Pallid Cuckoo, Black Currawong, Yellow Wattlebird, Yellow-throated Honeyeater and Black-headed Honeyeater.

Frenchs Farm

This camping site is located close to the Isthmus. It takes a long, 3hr walk from Darlington to get there, either via the coastal route of via the inland track through the bush. Frenchs Farm map can be downloaded here: http://www.parks.tas.gov.au/file.aspx?id=19262. There is another camping site nearby, at Encampment Cove 45min further south.

The area is good for Forty-spotted Pardalotes wherever manna gums are growing. Beautiful Firetails are common, particularly in the heath near the Isthmus. Other common birds in the area include Flame Robin, Scarlet Robin, Pallid Cuckoo, Musk Lorikeet, Yellow-tailed Black-Cockatoo and a wide selection of honeyeaters.

Flame Robins are very common on Maria Island

Several rare vagrants have been recorded in this area such as White-winged Triller and Common Sandpiper. The latter spent several months along the creek near Frenchs Farm.

Lake Dulverton Conservation Area

Lake Dulverton Conservation Area is located near the heritage old town of Oatlands, off Midland Hwy (1), about 85km north of Hobart and 115km south of Launceston. The town has the highest concentration of sandstone buildings from the Georgian era (over 80 in High St) in Australia.

If you stop in Oatlands on your way between Hobart and Launceston, have a picnic at Lake Dulverton. Turn off Midland Hwy (1) into a bypass of High St (C312) and continue to a windmill where you turn off to the Esplanade. This area is a free RV camping site with shelters, a shady picnic area, toilets and electric barbecues. A walking trail is provided along the lake. The best birdwatching is along the Esplanade. This site is very conveniently placed to see most of the waterbirds in Tasmania along a major travelling route.

This area used to be a lake prone to serious fluctuations of water levels until the lake dried out in 1993. The residents build a bund around the 2.2ha of the lake area and a 17km pipeline to supplement water to it from the Blackman River. Since 2009 when the lake filled up after heavy rains, that part of the lake and its surrounding wetlands have become permanent.

Over 90 bird species have been recorded at this small site. **Key species** is Great Crested Grebe. Dulveton Lake was the only place in Tasmania where this species was breeding until the lake dried out. It then disappeared from the area and selected new breeding sites in other parts of Tasmania. It came back when Dulveton Lake was restored and is now regularly spotted on the lake.

Lake Dulverton Conservation Area is home to an amazing variety of waterbirds. 13 duck species have been recorded. There are literally hundreds of common ducks (mostly Chestnut Teal, Grey Teal and Pacific Black Duck) together with Black Swans and Eurasian Coots there. Rarer species found among them include Hardhead, Australian Shelduck, Wandering Whistling-Duck, Australian Wood Duck, Pink-eared Duck, Musk Duck, Blue-billed Duck and Australasian Shoveler. All three grebe species (Australasian Grebe, Great Crested Grebe and Hoary-headed Grebe) are present. If you sit still, you may notice Australian Spotted Crake or Lewin's Rail feeding at the edge of the lake's rushes.

A sizable population of Northern Mallard lives here. We observed several birds looking pure-breed and a large number of hybrids with Pacific Black Duck.

Male Australasian Shoveler

The most common wader around the lake is Black-fronted Dotterel but when the wetland is drying out, Sharp-tailed Sandpiper, Common Greenshank and Latham's Snipe may appear. In 2015, a pair of Pied Stilts successfully bred here.

Welcome Swallows nest in little alcoves in the sandstone rock of the island. Listen for Little Grassbird's wailing call in the rushes and observe White-fronted Chats and Australasian Pipits around the lake.

You will most probably see the resident pair of White-bellied Sea-Eagles soaring over the water or a pair of Wedge-tailed Eagles patrolling the town. Other birds of prey in the wetlands include Whistling Kite, Swamp Harrier and Australian Hobby.

Ellesmere Dam

This large farm dam is located southeast of Lake Dulverton. It is also known as Mud Walls Road Dam. It was constructed on Ringwood Creek and is surrounded by endless pastures.

To get there, turn south off Midland Hwy (1) into Mud Walls Rd (B31) near Jericho. The dam will be on your right after a few kilometres, GPS coordinates are 42.25.11S and 147.18.33E.

Ellesmere Dam came to the attention of the birdwatching world in April 2014 when 60 Blue-billed Ducks were found on the lake. Since then, they are reported from this site regularly.

Waterbirds congregate on the lake in large numbers in autumn and winter, particularly Black Swan, Eurasian Coot, Chestnut Teal, Australian Shelduck, Hoary-headed Grebe and Great Cormorant. It is also a good place to find Musk Duck and Australasian Shoveler. Even Pink-eared Ducks were recorded here a couple of times.

Hoary-headed Grebes

On the surrounding paddocks, White-fronted Chat, Eurasian Skylark, Australasian Pipit and Flame Robin can be found. Swamp Harriers are often seen patrolling the dam. We observed five Wedge-tailed Eagles feeding on a carcass of a cow in the pasture.

Midlands Area

This site covers a vast area of grazing paddocks and fertile fields growing carrots, potatoes and other vegetables, located along Midland Hwy (1) and including small rural townships of Oatlands, Kempton, Cressy and Poatina. This seemingly boring and sterile agricultural land that may be passed without batting an eyelid, can yield a number of surprising bird species.

Key species are Banded Lapwing and Stubble Quail.

Banded Lapwings breed on the paddocks. After the breeding season they may form large post-breeding flocks. Seeing a crowd of these rare birds, marching behind a ploughing tractor, is a sight not easily forgotten.

Kempton

Kempton is a small town off Midland Hwy (1) located south of Oatlands. Flocks of Banded Lapwings are regularly reported from the paddocks opposite the town, some of them even from the Town Oval, usually in March-April.

While there, it is worth to visit the local sewage ponds located in the corner of Lonsdale Ln and Burnett Rd off Main St (C194). On the ponds, Hardhead, Hoary-headed Grebe, Australian Shelduck and Australasian Shoveler have been found.

Cressy

To get there, turn west into Powranna Rd (B53) from Midland Hwy (1), then turn north into Cressy Rd (B51).

A large flock of 70 Banded Lapwings was reported in February 2017 from a freshly harvested pea paddock near Cressy.

Stubble Quails breed in the area; reports exists of birds with small chicks. Other interesting records from the area include White-necked Heron, Little Corella and Sulphur-crested Cockatoo (flocks of a 100 birds).

Poatina

The township of Poatina is picturesquely situated on the plateau in the heart of the Great Western Tiers. It is a popular tourist destination. To get there, from Midland Hwy (1) take Powranna Rd (B53), then turn south into Cressy Rd (B51) to Poatina. The site is located about 60km from Launceston and 160km from Hobart.

Several interesting birding records exist from around the village. Small numbers of Banded Lapwings are regularly reported from the paddocks. Stubble Quails have been found nesting in a field of carrot seed crop. Latham's Snipe was observed feeding in a drainage canal near the village. In June 2013, White-necked Heron was reported from a wet lucerne paddock. Tasmanian Moreporks are often calling in the village.

Other birds in the area include White-belled Sea-Eagle, Swamp Harrier, Painted Button-quail (a dead body was found in a street in the village), Sacred Robin, Crescent Honeyeater, Eurasian Skylark and Australasian Pipit.

Rostrevor Lagoon

This large Lagoon is located on private land on the eastern side of Tasman Hwy (A3) about 1km north of Triabunna. The landowner has erected a small sign and installed stiles over the fence to identify the access point for foot access to the lagoon for anglers and birdwatchers. The owner requires a phone call before entering the land. Contact numbers are (03) 6257 3233, 0407 871967 and 0407 573233. As there may be no mobile coverage at the site, ring them in advance. On site, you will find a small parking area by the highway.

Over 60 bird species have been recorded here, with the birds often seen in large numbers. **Key species** are Blue-billed Duck, Hardhead, Musk Duck, Australasian Shoveler and Black-fronted Dotterel. Birds of interest also include Hoary-headed Grebe, Tasmanian Native-Hen, Little Grassbird, Latham's Snipe, Curlew Sandpiper, Little Grassbird and Tree Martin. Occasionally, you may find here White-necked Heron, Australian Pied Oystercatcher, Cape Barren Goose and White-throated Needletail.

This site is very good for rare duck species. Blue-billed Ducks have been recorded here in high numbers (flocks up to 80 birds). Musk Duck and Australasian Shoveler frequent this site regularly.

The Black Swan family after a successful defence against a White-Bellied Sea-Eagle

White-bellied Sea-Eagles often hang around this place. We observed a juvenile sea-eagle eyeing a group of five fluffy cygnets. The parents immediately closed ranks and made a very compact ball, with the adult birds close together and all chicks clumped tight under their wings. The sea-eagle could not break through that defence and after a few passes went away hungry.

Other birds recorded at this site include Caspian Tern, Red-capped Plover, Australian Shelduck, Common Greenfinch, Wedge-tailed Eagle, Swamp Harrier and Australian Hobby. A mainland vagrant, White-necked Heron, was recorded in Tasmania only a handful of times. A couple of these were from this lagoon.

Wielangta Forest

The forest is located on the south-east coast of Tasmania just opposite Maria Island, south off Tasman Hwy (A3) near Orford. It boasts a 100-year old blue gum eucalypt woodland with patches of rainforest along the creeks and gullies. It is a key habitat for many Tasmanian rare and threatened species such as Wedge-tailed Eagle (Tasmanian race) and Swift Parrot. The forest forms part of the south-east Tasmanian Key Biodiversity Area because of its significance to the conservation of a range of Tasmanian woodland birds.

Sandspit Forest Reserve in the centre of the Wielangta Forest offers a picnic area and short forest walks along the creek.

Birding is good along Wielangta Rd, an easy 35km 2-wheel drive. This road joins Rheban Rd (C320) in the north with Kellevie Rd (C336) in the south. This is an interesting scenic route, an alternative to Tasman Hwy as the connection between Orford and Bream Creek and Copping. You will find here several spectacular lookouts onto the coastline, Maria Island and the ocean. Wielangta Rd also provides access to the Thumbs Picnic Area and the lookout near Orford.

Over 60 species are on the Wielangta Forest's birdlist. **Key species** are Swift Parrot, Painted Button-quail, Bassian Thrush, Scrubtit, Australian Owlet-nightjar and Pink Robin. Other notable species include Olive Whistler, Tasmanian Scrubwren, Dusky Woodswallow, Yellow Wattlebird, Crescent Honeyeater, Black-headed Honeyeater and Strong-billed Honeyeater.

The most coveted species, Painted Button-quail, is regularly found along Wielangta Rd. A good selection of birds can be encountered on the walk from the Sandspit River Picnic Area carpark. Common birds there include Pink Robin, Bassian Thrush, Tasmanian Thornbill, Yellow-throated Honeyeater, Green Rosella, Olive Whistler, Scrubtit and

Striated Fieldwren. In the picnic area, Fan-tailed Cuckoo and Shining Bronze-Cuckoo are often calling.

A section of Rheban Rd just before its junction with Wielangta Rd is also worth checking, particularly in early autumn when birds are leaving Tasmania for the mainland. We noted sizeable flocks of Dusky Woodswallows, Silvereyes, Grey Fantails and Black-faced Cuckoo-shrikes at this location. Other birds here included Brush Bronzewing, Yellow-throated Honeyeater, Yellow-tailed Black-Cockatoo, Green Rosella, Black Currawong and Yellow-rumped Thornbill.

If you start exploring Wielangta Rd from its southern end, approaching from Sorell, check the paddocks – often, particularly in autumn, large flocks of Forest Ravens, Black Currawongs and Kelp Gulls can be seen there.

Freycinet National Park

The Park is located on Freycinet Peninsula that extends south into the Tasman Sea in the middle of the Tasmanian east coast. Freycinet is effectively two eroded blocks of granite - the Hazards and the Mt Graham/Mt Freycinet sections of the peninsula, joined by a sand isthmus. This is a truly magical park, the place of rare beauty with pure white beaches and pink granite mountains reflected in azure waters of the bay. This a one of the most popular Tasmanian tourist destinations.

Freycinet National Park – view from Cape Tourville

The Park stretches over 50km of the east coast, from Bicheno in the north to Schouten Island in the south, and covers almost 17,000ha. The vegetation consists of dry sclerophyll forest with a good fraction of old trees, heathland, coastal scrub, shallow wetlands and a small area of wet eucalypt forest. There are also patches of Oyster Bay pine forest.

Travel time is 2.5-3 hours from either Hobart or Launceston. Turn off the Tasman Highway (A3) onto the Coles Bay Road (C302) 12km south of Bicheno. The turnoff to the Friendly Beaches section of the park via gravel road comes about 9km after leaving the highway. The main park entrance and visitor reception are just past the Coles Bay township about 30km from the highway on a good sealed road. The dramatic peaks of the Hazards welcome you as you enter the park. The northern section of the Park can be reached from Bicheno via Harveys Farm Rd. A basic locality map is included in the Freycinet National Park brochure downloadable here:
http://www.parks.tas.gov.au/file.aspx?id=19033.

A good network of walking tracks has been developed, the Park is a bushwalker's paradise. Most of the tracks on the Peninsula originate from the Wineglass Bay carpark. The favourite birdwatching tracks is Wineglass Bay and Hazards Beach Circuit, see the downloadable map here: http://www.wineglassbay.com/wp-content/uploads/2014/09/freycinet_np_guide.pdf.

A vehicular sealed route in the Park is along Cape Tourville Rd, going to the lighthouse, Sleepy Bay and Bluestone Bay. There are also several 4WD roads and management tracks. Facilities in the Park include Visitor Centre, carparks and vehicular access camping areas at Richardson Beach, Honeymoon Bay, Isaacs Point and Whitewater Wall. A day use area with picnic tables, barbecues and a large shelter is located at Ranger Creek. Designated walk-in camping areas are provided for walkers and boaters along the walking tracks at Wineglass Bay, Hazards Beach and Cooks Beach.

Freycinet is a great place to go birdwatching. Over 140 species have been recorded in and around the Freycinet Peninsula, Schouten Island, Friendly Beaches and Moulting Lagoon. **Key species** are Hooded Plover, Spotted Quail-thrush and Swift Parrot. Other birds of interest include White-bellied Sea-Eagle, Wedge-tailed Eagle, Tasmanian Morepork, Green Rosella, Bassian Thrush, Brown Thornbill, Scarlet Robin, Satin Flycatcher and seabirds. Among rarer species that can be found here are Scrubtit, Tasmanian Thornbill, Painted Button-quail and Fiordland Penguin. The iconic Australian wildlife such as Tasmanian pademelon, Bennetts wallaby and echidna is plentiful, quite tame and easy to observe.

Swift Parrots come back each summer to breed in the old Tasmanian blue gum forest but due to the competition for hollows and predation from sugar gliders they are quite unsuccessful. The gliders were introduced to Tasmania from the mainland.

Hooded Plovers breed on the beaches around the Park, in particular on Friendly Beaches. Several pairs of White-bellied Sea-Eagles and a few pairs of Wedge-tailed Eagles breed in the Park. One of well-known White-bellied Sea-Eagle nests is located near Point Geographe opposite Schouten Island. Seabirds nest on the Nuggets and other coastal rock stacks.

The species rare in the Park, such as Scrubtit and Tasmanian Thornbill, can be found in the rainforest gullies of a saddle between Mt Mount Graham and Mt Freycinet. The area is not particularly accessible.

Freycinet Golf Club

The golf club is located 6.5km northwest of Visitor Centre, at Swanwick Rd off Coles Bay Rd, outside the National Park. You'll find here a good camping area adjacent to 8th tee. The site is fantastic for nocturnal birds. At night, you can see or hear Tasmanian Morepork, Masked Owl, Australian Owlet-nightjar and Tawny Frogmouth. There are also good numbers of Green Rosellas, Tasmania Scrubwrens, Brown Thornbills and Tasmanian Native-hens.

Visitor Centre

Laughing Kookaburra

Check the bushes and trees around the carpark and take a short walk to the beach and creek mouth below the Centre. The place is usually teeming with honeyeaters such as Yellow-throated Honeyeater, Black-headed Honeyeater, Strong-billed Honeyeater, Eastern Spinebill and Yellow Wattlebird. Plenty of small bush birds can be expected including Tasmanian Scrubwren, Silvereye and Superb Fairy-wren. You may also come across Laughing Kookaburra, Shining Bronze-Cuckoo, Fan-tailed Cuckoo, Satin Flycatcher, Green Rosella and Scarlet Robin. At the creek, we found Chestnut Teal with ducklings. There were Sooty Oystercatchers, Great Cormorants and Pacific Gulls on the beach. White-bellied Sea-Eagle was flying over the bay.

Friendly Beaches

This is the northern section of the Park, with long, beautiful beaches. A camping site and other facilities are located at Isaacs Point. This is the best place in the Park to find Hooded Plovers, they breed on the beach. Here, you'll also have the best chance of Spotted Quail-thrush sighting. Start looking along the walking track behind the airfield, walk along the ridge and scan the slopes, in particular the slopes overlooking the beach at the end of the trail in the eucalyptus/sheaoak woodland. Other birds here include Black-headed Honeyeater, Yellow-throated Honeyeater, Crescent Honeyeater, Eastern Spinebill, Black Currawong and Pallid Cuckoo.

In the coastal heath you may come across Tasmanian Scrubwren, Beautiful Firetail and New Holland Honeyeater.

On the beach, expect to find Sooty Oystercatcher, Caspian Tern and Pacific Gull and, occasionally, Double-banded Plover in winter. Fairy Terns have been sporadically recorded here.

Cape Tourville

This is the most visited part of the Park, expect crowds of people milling about. A good sealed road leads to the lookout with the outstanding views of the coastline up to Friendly Beaches. From the carpark, you will have a 20min easy walk to the lighthouse, passing a lookout towards the Nuggets on the way. As per information board on site, several bird species breed on the islands including Little Penguin (150 pairs), White-faced Storm-Petrel (250 pairs), Caspian Tern (30 pairs) and Short-tailed Shearwater (60 pairs). Nests of Fairy Prion, Common Diving-Petrel, Black-faced Cormorant and Pacific Gull are found in smaller numbers.

The walk is good to watch the seabirds flying by the shore. We observed a large flock of Short-tailed Shearwaters navigating close to the coast and a group of Little Penguins frolicking in the water near the Nuggets. Our sightings here also included Shy Albatross, Black-browed Albatross and Australasian Gannet. A large flock of Black-faced

Cormorants and Pacific Gulls was roosting on the Nuggets. White-bellied Sea-Eagle was patrolling the skies.

Other seabirds recorded around this area include Pomarine Jaeger, Arctic Jaeger, Cape Petrel, Northern Giant-Petrel, Indian Yellow-nosed Albatross and Buller's Albatross.

On the road to Cape Tourville, check the slopes for Spotted Quail-thrush; it was reported here several times. Other birds along the road include Green Rosella, Grey Butcherbird, Grey Currawong, Brown Thornbill and Common Bronzewing. In the carpark, there were Beautiful Firetails and a single Brush Bronzewing walking on the path. In the heath on our way to the lighthouse we found plenty of Tasmanian Scrubwrens, Silvereyes and New Holland Honeyeaters.

Ay night, you can hear Tasmanian Morepork and Australian Owlet-nightjar.

Bluestone Bay Track

This is a short 4WD track running down to Bluestone Bay. This a good place to look for Spotted Quail-thrush. Other birds that may be encountered at this site include Scarlet Robbin, Dusky Robin, Satin Flycatcher, Golden Whistler, Green Rosella, Black Currawong and Black-headed Honeyeater.

Wineglass Bay and Hazards Beach Circuit

This half a day walk takes you through a variety of habitats including dry sclerophyll woodland and vast areas of heath.

Hooded Plover can be found both in the Wineglass Bay and Hazards Beach. Robins including Dusky Robin, Flame Robin and Scarlet Robin are easy to spot in the bushes at the track verge. Yellow-tailed Black-Cockatoos are easy to observe when feeding and flying in raucous groups. Green Rosella is also common in the area. Swift Parrot is occasionally observed in summer.

Catch a glimpse of Bassian Thrush or Brush Bronzewing on the forest floor. Chances of a Spotted Quail-thrush sighting are however slim.

Other birds in this area include Satin Flycatcher, Tasmanian Scrubwren, Horsfield's Bronze-Cuckoo, Pallid Cuckoo, Brown Thornbill, Yellow-rumped Thornbill, Dusky Woodswallow and Grey Fantail. Honeyeaters include Yellow-throated Honeyeater, Crescent Honeyeater, New Holland Honeyeater, Eastern Spinebill, Yellow Wattlebird and Little Wattlebird.

Moulting Lagoon

This vast, 4,750ha shallow estuary is situated midway on the Tasmanian east coastline, 160km north of Hobart. The site is located at the mouth of Apsley and Swan Rivers, northwest of Freycinet NP, a few kilometres south of Bicheno and 10km north of Swansea. It is a wetland of international importance (Ramsar site). Moulting Lagoon is a place of extraordinary beauty, with the Hazards of Freycinet providing a scenic backdrop to this charming place.

The lagoon contains both the areas of deep and shallow water, surrounded by periodically exposed saltmarshes and mudflats. Further away from the water is a dense scrub and farmland. The most conspicuous plant is beaded glasswort (samphire) that covers large areas of saltmarshes. At some time in a year the tips of this groundcover plant turn deep red to form a richly-coloured carpet against the background of the Hazards.

The richly-coloured swamp around Moulting Lagoon

The Lagoon is generally an excellent birdwatching destination. However, due to its large size and vast numbers of waterfowl in the water, some rarer species can be difficult to spot. This area is, sadly, also a game reserve and when the hunting season starts the birds wisely move out.

The Lagoon holds the largest concentration of Black Swan in Tasmania. On average, 8,000-10,000 swans live here. In drought periods, up to 20,000 birds were recorded. Even the lagoon's name is derived from feather shedding by the swans. In the moulting seasons piles of feathers can be seen on the beaches. The site also boasts the largest numbers of Common Greenshanks in Tasmania in summer.

There are several points of access to the Lagoon, mostly via rural roads in between private land. These include:

- *Nine Mile Beach at the Bagot Point Reserve*. Head north from Tasman Hwy (A3) from Swansea and take the first turnoff to the right called Dolphin Sands Rd. It runs to Nine Mile Beach and Dolphin Sands. Go to the end of this road where you'll find a carpark. Walk to the beach.
- *Sherbourne Rd*. Head north from Tasman Hwy (A3) from Swansea and pass the turnoff to Nine Mile Beach. At the bottom of a steep hill, 1km before the township of Apslawn, look for Sherbourne Rd on the right. Take it and drive to the Lagoon.
- *Route from Coles Bay Rd (C302)*. Continuing north on A3 past Apslawn, turn right into Coles Bay Rd. This road passes close to the edge of the Lagoon several times within the first 10km. You can stop on the roadside and scan the Lagoon with a scope. 18km from the highway turnoff look for Flacks Rd. This is the most favoured approach route to the Lagoon. This good unsealed road will lead you through the bushland to a carpark at the end of the road. Stiles are provided over the fence to walk to the lagoon. Another access point from Coles Bay Rd is River and Rocks Rd, 2km from Flacks Rd, running along Swanwick Bay.

There are no facilities around the Lagoon, the closest facilities and accommodation are located at Coles Bay and Swanwick.

Over 100 bird species are on the site's birdlist. **Key species** are Black Swan, Common Greenshank and Hooded Plover. Other birds of interest include Sharp-tailed Sandpiper, Eastern Curlew, Australian Pied Oystercatcher, White-fronted Chat, Dusky Woodswallow, Pallid Cuckoo, Beautiful Firetail and Striated Fieldwren. Among the rarer species are Great Crested Grebe, Blue-billed Duck, Lesser Sand Plover, Marsh Sandpiper and Black-shouldered Kite.

Nine Mile Beach

Yellow-tailed Black-Cockatoo feeding on pine cones

Dolphin Sands Rd leading to Nine Mile Beach is surrounded with dense coastal scrub dominated by banksias, grass on the dunes and patches of pine trees. As we drove along this road, flocks of Yellow-tailed Black-Cockatoos were feeding on the pine cones. In the flowering banksias we got New Holland Honeyeater, Crescent Honeyeater, Little Wattlebird and Musk Lorikeet. Mixed flocks of Silvereyes, Brown Thornbills, Tasmanian Scrubwrens, Spotted Pardalotes and Grey Shrike-thrushes were moving through the dense bushes. On the power line we observed large numbers of Dusky Woodswallows. Pallid Cuckoo was calling from a treetop position. In the low coastal scrub and grass on the dunes we scored Beautiful Firetail and Striated Fieldwren. A flock of Brown Quails crossed the road. Eastern Rosellas were common along the road, feeding on the ground.

At Point Bagot we observed a large number of shorebirds on the sandbar at the outlet of the lagoon into Great Oyster Bay. A huge flock of Crested Terns and Silver Gulls included a few Caspian Terns, Fairy Terns, Kelp Gulls, Pacific Gulls, Sooty Oystercatchers and Australian Pied Oystercatchers. We also sighted two Hooded Plovers, the highlight of the day.

On the opposite bank of the outlet, Black-faced and Great Cormorants were roosting on the moored boats. On the mudflats near the oyster farms we spotted a small group of Eastern Curlews, Red-necked Stints and Bar-tailed Godwits.

The Hazards of Freycinet National Park as seen from the Nine Mile Beach

Flacks Road

The dense bush and heath along Flacks Rd is very good for birdwatching. Common birds here include Green Rosella, New Holland Honeyeater, Crescent Honeyeater, Little Wattlebird, Yellow Wattlebird, Golden Whistler, Pallid Cuckoo and Fan-tailed Cuckoo. The heath around the Tasmanian devil enclosure may yield Beautiful Firetail and Superb Fairy-wren. The carpark at the end of the road may produce Yellow-rumped Thornbill, Scarlet Robin and Flame Robin.

When crossing the expanse of samphire saltmarshes, we observed large numbers of White-fronted Chats and Australasian Pipits. Heads of Red-capped Plovers and Pacific Golden Plovers were sticking out of the groundcover. A couple of Black-fronted Dotterels and Eastern Curlews were standing at the edge of the swamp. Far away in the water we saw plenty of Black Swans, Australian Shelducks and Chestnut Teals. Swamp Harrier and Brown Falcon were flying over the saltmarshes.

In winter, this is the place to look for Double-banded Plovers visiting from New Zealand.

River and Rocks Road

River and Rocks Rd runs along Swanwick Bay, at multiple points giving access to the Lagoon. This location is known for waders - they favour this site as a feeding and roosting area. We observed a large group of Australian Pied Oystercatchers (80) and Common Greenshanks (30) roosting on the beach. There were also small numbers of Sooty Oystercatchers, Red-capped Plovers, Bar-tailed Godwits and Sharp-tailed Sandpipers. On the water were plenty of Black Swans, Chestnut Teals, Black-faced Cormorants, Hoary-headed Grebes and a single Musk Duck.

A small camping area is located in the bush by this road. In the heath near the campsite we located Beautiful Firetail, Scarlet Robin and Crescent Honeyeater. Green Rosellas were feeding on the ground in good numbers. In the evening, Tasmanian Morepork was calling from the bush. Tasmanian Native-Hens were foraging in the camp.

Other birds recorded at this site include Little Egret, Eastern Great Egret, Caspian Tern, Olive Whistler, Australasian Pipit, Black-headed Honeyeater, Dusky Robin and White-bellied Sea-Eagle.

Lake Leake

Lake Leake is a large man-made storage reservoir near Lake Leake Rd (B34) which connects Midland Hwy (1) at Campbell Town with Tasman Hwy (A3) near the turnoff to the Freycinet National Park. Turn into Lake Rd to get to the western part of the lake, or from the Lake Leake village you'll have a couple of choices to get the water.

Over 60 bird species have been reported from the lake. **Key species** are Swift Parrot, Spotted Quail-thrush and Satin Flycatcher. Other birds of interest include Dusky Robin, Dusky Woodswallow, Brown Thornbill, Grey Currawong and Green Rosella.

Swift Parrots are found in summer in trees through the village. Spotted Quail-thrushes have been reported from the bushland near the Lake Leake Inn carpark in Lake Rd.

On the lake, you should find a good selection of waterbirds such as Hardhead, Chestnut Teal, Black Swan, Caspian Tern and large rafts of Eurasian Coots. White-belled Sea-Eagles regularly patrol the lake.

In the forest, look for Yellow-throated Honeyeater, Yellow Wattlebird, Eastern Spinebill, Flame Robin, Scarlet Robin and Fan-tailed Cuckoo.

Bicheno

Bicheno is a small, charming township on the Tasmanian east coast, located about 180km northeast of Hobart and 160km southeast of Launceston. It is a popular summer tourist spot that makes a good base for exploring birding destinations in the area such as the Douglas-Apsley National Park.

In the township itself there are diverse habitats that support a large variety of bird species. The gardens and parks are full of native plants providing food and shelter for honeyeaters and parrots including Swift Parrot.

The good birding spots include Bicheno Blowhole, Governor Island, Diamond Island with the corresponding stretch of the coastline and a walk to the top of the rocky outcrop. Over 100 species are on the town's birdlist. **Key species** are Little Penguin and Swift Parrot. Bicheno is home to the finest Little Penguin viewing area on the Tasmanian east coast. In summer, flocks of Swift Parrots regularly move through the gardens and bushland of the township. Other notable species include Crested Tern, Yellow Wattlebird, Musk Lorikeet, Yellow-throated Honeyeater, Tasmanian Scrubwren, Green Rosella and Brown Thornbill. Bicheno is known for vagrants that add to the total Tasmania birdlist such as Red-backed Kingfisher and Fiordland Penguin.

Diamond Island Nature Reserve

The site is located 1km north of the town centre. The coastal part of the reserve can be explored along a walking track in the coastal scrub. At low tide the island is linked to the mainland by a sandy bank and accessible on foot, just watch your tides.

This section of the coast is the prime viewing area for Little Penguins. They nest in hollows under the rocks, in the dunes, in the scrub, and under the floors of the neighbouring houses and garages. The best way to observe the penguins retuning home at night is to join a guided tour. For detail see the website: https://www.bichenopenguintours.com.au/ or call (03) 6375 1333.

Red Path Beach, a part of Diamond Island Reserve, can be reached from Gordon St. This is the place where Hooded Plovers are recorded from time to time. Other interesting species here include Australian Pied Oystercatcher, Sooty Oystercatcher, Red-capped Plover, Crested Tern and Pacific Gull.

On the other end of the Diamond Island Reserve, east of the Sealife Centre, at the end of Jetty Rd, Bicheno Beach is located. This is one of the places where Little Penguins like to get out in groups in the evening but without the infrared torches and professional guides they may be difficult to spot. Seabirds seen from Bicheno Beach include Shy Albatross,

Short-tailed Shearwater, Pomarine Jaeger, Black-faced Cormorant, Australasian Gannet and White-bellied Sea-Eagle.

Governor Island

This small, rocky, 2ha island is separated from the mainland by a 50m-wide stretch of water known as Waubs Gulch. Governor Island, a few other small rocks and the waters in a 400m radius semicircle form together the marine reserve which is arguably the best temperate diving location in Australia. The divers report that the underwater scenery and sealife are simply exceptional.

A small boat harbour on the Esplanade opposite to the island is a good place to watch seabirds breeding on the island. The largest Tasmanian breeding colony of Crested Terns is on Governor Island. Juvenile birds often congregate on the western side of the island which is facing the wharf. Many other seabirds can be seen roosting on the island including Black-faced Cormorant, Pacific Gull, Kelp Gull, Sooty Oystercatcher and Australasian Gannet.

Black-faced Cormorants can often be seen around the harbour

Bicheno Blowhole

Bicheno Blowhole is located south of Bicheno. To get there, take Tasman Hwy (A3), turn east into Douglas St at the Blowhole road sign then turn south at the T-junction with the Esplanade.

The bush strip along the Esplanade is the best place to look for Swift Parrots in summer. Other bush birds here include Musk Lorikeet, Eastern Spinebill, New Holland Honeyeater, Crescent Honeyeater, Little Wattlebird, Brown Thornbill and Grey Fantail. An area of heath about 200m south of the blowhole is good for Beautiful Firetails, often seen popping out of the bushes to drink from water puddles on the track.

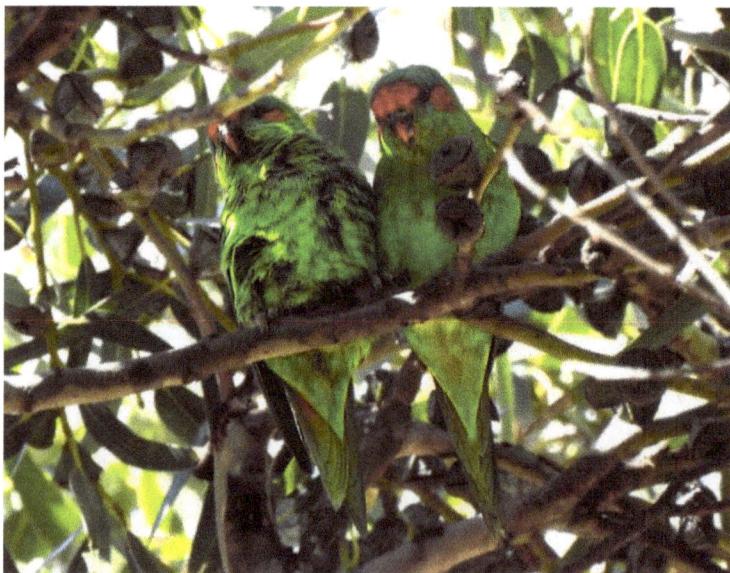

Musk Lorikeets in a tree on the Esplanade

On the rocks near the Blowhole there should be plenty of roosting seabirds such as Black-faced Cormorant, Great Cormorant, Crested Tern, Pacific Gull and Kelp Gull. Other seabirds recorded in the area include Buller's Albatross, Arctic Jaeger, Northern Giant-Petrel and Little Penguin. A small breeding colony of Crested Gulls is located on one of the rocks. When we were there most of the crevices in the rocks were taken over by breeding Common Starlings, busy bringing in nesting materials.

Granite Outcrop

This is a large rock that dominates the landscape of south Bicheno. White-bellied Sea-Eagles like to roost there. A short walk through the bushland leads to the top of the rock. A view from top is spectacular. Birds in the bush include Common Bronzewing, Eastern Spinebill, Yellow Wattlebird, Yellow-throated Honeyeater, Black-headed Honeyeater, Crescent Honeyeater, Green Rosella, Black Currawong and Tasmanian Scrubwren.

Douglas-Apsley National Park

Douglas-Apsley NP is located approximately 185km northeast of Hobart and 160km southeast of Launceston, just a few kilometres north of a coastal township of Bicheno. It is situated between Douglas and Apsley Rivers which rise in the marshland to the west and then cut through the deep gorges full of large boulders, to create cascades, waterfalls and waterholes in the eastern section. The Park protects the largest area of unlogged dry eucalypt forest in Tasmania. You will find here white peppermint, Tasmanian blue gum and stringybark. Rarer plants include Tasmanian ironbark, South Esk pine and Oyster Bay pine. There is also an area of heathland which delivers stunning wildflower displays in the spring.

The main vehicular access is to the south of the Park where Apsley Waterhole is located. To get there, from Bicheno drive on Tasman Hwy (A3) for 4km then turn west onto Rosedale Rd. Follow this road 7km to the carpark (including 5km on a decent dirt road). From the carpark, there is a short but steep walk to the waterhole where a bush campsite is located. Several other walking tracks also start from this carpark.

Access to the northern section of the Park (Thompsons Marshes) is via 'E' Rd. From Bicheno, drive 24km north on Tasman Hwy (A3) then turn west onto 'E' Rd after seeing a National Park directional road sign. This road is unsealed and its last section is very steep and treacherous, 4WD only.

The Park is a bushwalkers' paradise with a network of shorter and longer tracks through the rugged terrain. Facilities (very basic) are located only in the southern section of the Park. General site information with a basic locality map can be found in the Park's Fact Sheet downloadable here: http://www.parks.tas.gov.au/file.aspx?id=19015.

Around 65 bird species have been recorded in the Park. Most of Tasmanian endemics can be found here, even small flocks of Forty-spotted Pardalotes are sighted occasionally. **Key species** include Wedge-tailed Eagle (a pair is breeding here), Beautiful Firetail, Scarlet Robin, Brush Bronzewing and Bassian Thrush. Occasionally seen rarer species include Spotted Quail-thrush, White-throated Needletail, Pink Robin, Olive Whistler, Australian Owlet-nightjar, Whistling Kite and Tasmanian Morepork.

On route to the Park along Rosedale Rd look for Eastern Rosella, Tasmanian Native-Hen, Australasian Pipit, Eurasian Skylark, Forest Raven, Brown Falcon and Swamp Harrier.

The area around the carpark is a good birding spot. At the time of our visit, Yellow Wattlebirds were the most vocal, calling from the trees around the carpark. A couple of Brush Bronzewings and a Bassian Thrush were on the ground. We also found Grey Fantail, Golden Whistler, Green Rosella, Superb Fairy-wren, Scarlet Robin, Yellow-throated Honeyeater and Grey Butcherbird. Look also for Tawny Frogmouth and Satin Flycatcher; these were reported several times from this area.

Grey Fantail

The 500m steep descent to Apsley Waterhole also proved to be productive. We scored several honeyeaters such as Black-headed Honeyeater, Strong-billed Honeyeater, Crescent Honeyeater and Eastern Spinebill. Small bush birds included Tasmanian Scrubwren, Tasmanian Thornbill and Striated Pardalote. A pair of Wedge-tailed Eagles were flying over the hills.

You have a good chance to spot Beautiful Firetail in the bushes around the waterhole. Occasionally, waterbirds appear at the waterhole; Australasian Shoveler and Musk Duck were recorded. Other birds here include Grey Shrike-thrush, Golden Whistler, Laughing Kookaburra, Grey Currawong and Scarlet Robin.

Another waterhole is located a few hundred metres further on; this is also worth checking.

Northeastern Tasmania

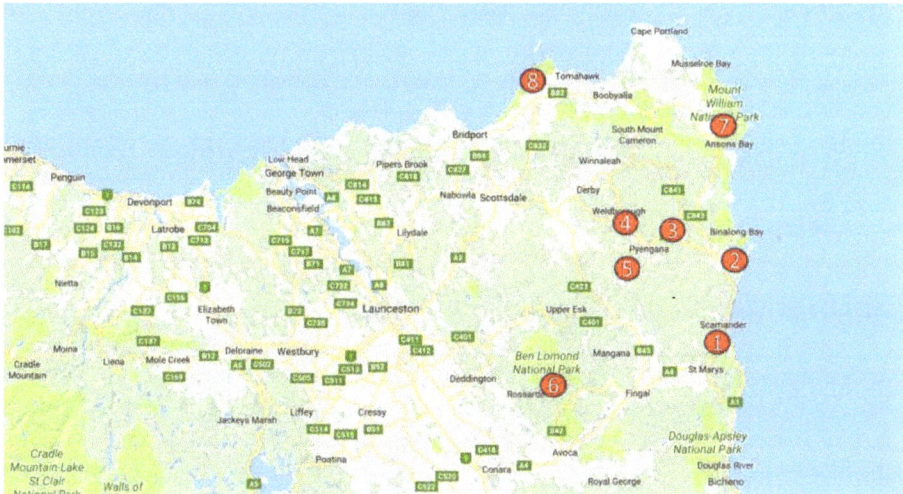

Scamander Area

Scamander is a little coastal town located on Tasman Hwy (A3) at the mouth of Scamander River. It features wide sandy beaches and several nature reserves. The site is located 15km south of St Helens and 180km (2.5hr drive) southeast of Launceston.

Popular birding sites in the area include Winifred Curtis Scamander Reserve near the Henderson Lagoon, Scamander Forest Reserve and the mouth of Scamander River. **Key species** are Hooded Plover, Little Tern and Fairy Tern. Other species of interest include waders, Tasmanian Scrubwren, Tasmanian Morepork, Masked Owl and White-bellied Sea-Eagle. Occasionally, rarities such as White-necked Heron, Black-tailed Godwit and Sanderling are recorded.

Scamander River Mouth

Access to the river mouth is from Lagoon Esplanade. You will find here a fenced-off beach area set aside as a breeding site for Little Terns, Fairy Terns, Hooded Plovers and Australian Pied Oystercatchers. We only saw the latter and these were nesting outside the fence.

Other shorebirds in the river mouth included Red-capped Plover, Red-necked Stint, Pacific Gull (60+) and Caspian Tern. Two Fork-tailed Swifts were flying over the lagoon, mixed in a flock of Welcome Swallows and Tree Martins. Australian Hobby was sitting on top of a small tree near the beach.

Scamander Sanctuary Tourist Park

This is a nice place for both holidaying and birdwatching. The tourist park is surrounded by bushland and wetland and has private access to the beach through a belt of dense heath. To get there, turn off Tasman Hwy (A3) into Winifred Dr in Scamander.

You'll find plenty Tasmanian Native-hens in the grounds. You may also see Dusky Woodswallow, Scarlet Robin and Yellow-throated Honeyeater. During the night, Australian Owlet-nightjar is calling. Tawny Frogmouth hunts for moths around the lamp posts.

In the heath, we got Brush Bronzewing, Little Wattlebird and New Holland Honeyeater. Occasionally, Buff-banded Rail may come up into the open from the wetlands. The dunes yielded White-fronted Chat, Australasian Pipit and Striated Fieldwren. On the beach, we found Fairy Tern, Hooded Plover, Sooty Oystercatcher and Australian Pied Oystercatcher. Occasionally, Sanderlings are reported from this beach.

Scamander Forest Reserve

The site, stretched on the banks of the Scamander River, offers good camping and picnic areas and a boat ramp for fishing and canoeing. To get there, turn west in Scamander off Tasman Hwy (A3) into Coach Rd, then into Skyline Rd. Travel along this road in the forest.

The forest along Skyline Rd and Dogs Tk is good for Masked Owl, Tasmanian Morepork, Satin Flycatcher, Flame Robin, Pallid Cuckoo, Wedge-tailed Eagle and honeyeaters.

Winifred Curtis Scamander Reserve

This is a lovely little (80ha) reserve, adjacent to the Henderson Lagoon, located off Tasman Hwy (A3) just south of Scamander. The entrance to the Reserve is situated directly opposite Upper Scamander Rd (C421) about 2km south of Scamander.

The reserve offers a carpark and 8km of walking tracks, see the map below, photographed from the information board at the entry to the Reserve.

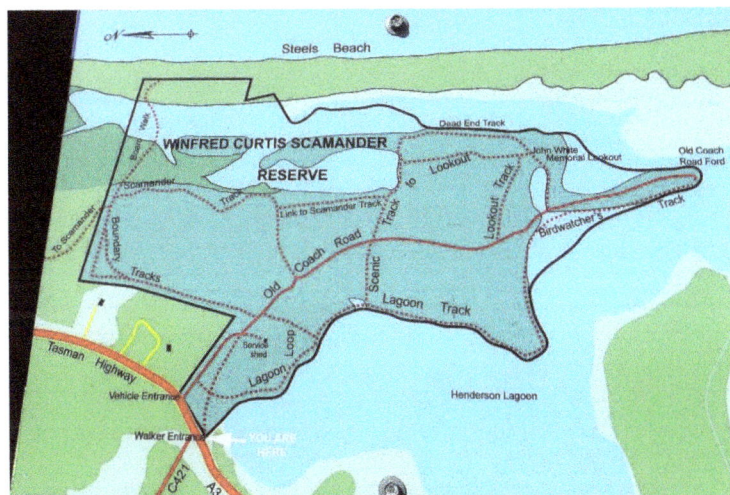

Information board with a map of Winifred Curtis Scamander Reserve

The site is covered by dry sclerophyll bushland, heathland, marshland, wetlands and dunes. A severe fire destroyed in 2006 most of the tree canopy so at present it is mostly heathland with new trees sprouting up. The heath is very dense and consists of bracken fern, hakea, common heath and many species of bush wattle.

Heathland habitat in the Winifred Curtis Scamander Reserve

Over 60 bird species have been recorded in the Reserve. **Key species** are Brush Bronzewing, Tasmanian Scrubwren and White-bellied Sea-Eagle. Other notable species include Horsfield's Bronze-Cuckoo, White-fronted Chat, Fairy Tern and Swamp Harrier. On the list of rarer species are Musk Duck, Little Tern, Eastern Great Egret, Swift Parrot and Olive Whistler. A single White-necked Heron spent a few months in 2014 around the Henderson Lagoon.

Tasmanian Scrubwren is the most common bird in the heath; we saw hundreds of them everywhere on every track. In the northern part of the Reserve were several Striated Fieldwrens; one was singing from the top of a small bush. Brown Quails run across the path a few times. Eastern Spinebills were very active and vocal. The heath also yielded White-fronted Chat, Brown Thornbill, Superb Fairy-wren and Silvereye. At the entrance to the Reserve, Grey Butcherbird was singing beautifully and Dusky Woodswallows perched in a tree on the other side of the road. A Swamp Harrier and a juvenile White-bellied Sea-Eagle were patrolling the lagoon.

On the water of Henderson Lagoon were Chestnut Teals, Grey Teals, Hoary-headed Grebes, Australian Pelicans and a pair of Black Swans with cygnets. Black-fronted Dotterels are regularly observed at the edges of the lagoon. Double-banded Plovers from New Zealand regularly winter in the area.

On the ocean-side beach, we got Sooty and Australian Pied Oystercatcher, Red-capped Plover and Pacific Gull. The rare Lesser Sand Plover has also been recorded in this location.

Swift Parrot used to visit this site regularly but since the fire they appear only occasionally because the blue gums have perished and there is no more blossom.

St Helens Area

The township of St Helens is located on Georges Bay on the east coast of Tasmania. Access is easy both from Hobart and Launceston via Tasman Hwy (A3), the Island's main thoroughfare. Georges Bay carves in deeply into the land and both arms of this long and narrow coastal inlet offer excellent wader-watching opportunities. Waders can be observed both at low tide when feeding on the mudflats in the mouth of Colchis Creek as well as at high tide when they roost on sandspits near the Pelican Point, Granny's Gut Creek, Mcdonalds Point or St Helens Point.

Several reserves are located close to town including St Helens Point Conservation Reserve, Medeas Cove Conservation Area and Bay of Fires Conservation Area.

Bay of Fires Conservation Area

Bay of Fires is a place of rare splendour, voted by the Lonely Planet to be in the top 10 of the most beautiful places in the world. It is located 12km north of St Helens, stretching from Binalong Bay in the south to Eddystone Point in the north. There are three sections in this stretch of coast. The 13km southern section between Binalong Bay and The Gardens has been protected as Bay of Fires Conservation Area. The middle section is called Policemans Point and is situated along Ansons Bay. The northern section, Eddystone Point, is part of the Mt William National Park.

The Bay of Fires Conservation Area has rocky headlands, long sandy beaches, several lagoons and countless small rocks stacks and islets. Vegetation types include dry sclerophyll forest, sheaoak forest, wet heathland, coastal scrub and saltmarshes.

To get there, take Binalong Bay Rd (C850) from St Helens to the seaside village of Binalong Bay, the gateway to the Bay of Fires. An easy walk leads to the Humbug Point. From Binalong Bay take Gardens Rd (C848) as far as The Gardens (13km). Several short detours lead to the coves, lagoons and beaches. Several camping areas are provided, varying from basic tent sites to sites designed for RVs and caravans. The park brochure with a locality map can be downloaded here:
http://www.parks.tas.gov.au/file.aspx?id=6390.

Over 80 species are on the site's birdlist. **Key species** are Ground Parrot, Hooded Plover, Southern Emu-wren and Ruddy Turnstone. Among other species of interest are Sanderling, Tawny-crowned Honeyeater, Striated Fieldwren, White-bellied Sea-Eagle and Grey Goshawk. Rarities include Swift Parrot, Azure Kingfisher, Fairy Tern, Little Tern and Eastern Curlew.

White-bellied Sea-Eagle clutching prey in its right foot

Sloop Lagoon to Big Lagoon

The area features a beautiful, healthy heath, stretching from the Sloop Lagoon in the south to Big Lagoon in the north. This place is the best for the heathland species in the whole Bay area. A network of unnamed tracks is useful for birding but watch your direction, you may easily get lost. The low heath along Seaton Tramway Tk is the place to look for Ground Parrots. These birds, rare on the East Coast of Tasmania, were recorded here several times. Southern Emu-wren, Tawny-crowned Honeyeater and Striated Fieldwren are common and quite easy to find. A good population of Beautiful Firetails lives in the heath south of Big Lagoon. We found several birds perched on a fence nearby. Swamp Harriers often hunt over the heathland. Other notable birds in this area include White-fronted Chat, Tasmanian Scrubwren, Golden Whistler, Bassian Thrush, Australasian Pipit (plenty along Gardens Rd) and Tree Martin.

In the lagoons, you can count on a selection of waterbirds and waders such as Australian Shelduck, Chestnut Teal, Eastern Great Egret and Australian Pied Oystercatcher.

On the beachside, look for Hooded Plover, Ruddy Turnstone, Sanderling, Red-capped Plover, Sooty Oystercatcher and Australian Pied Oystercatcher. Pairs of Hooded Plovers are scattered along the beaches so look for them at each stop. Flocks of Ruddy Turnstones are most often seen north of Ansons Bay near the Mt William National Park.

The Gardens

At the end of Gardens Rd, you'll find a myriad of confusing tracks through the dunes and scrub, leading to the beach shacks. Plenty of Australasian Pipits can be found along these tracks. The site is good for seabirds such as Shy Albatross, Black-browed Albatross, Australasian Gannet, Black-faced Cormorant, Pacific Gull, Crested Tern and Little Penguin. A walk along the beach can yield Ruddy Turnstone, Sooty Oystercatcher and Red-capped Plover and occasionally Fairy Tern. Scarlet Robins are quite common among the beach shacks. Black Falcons are regularly seen hunting over the dunes.

Bush birds here include Yellow-rumped Thornbill, Brown Thornbill, Crescent Honeyeater, Eastern Spinebill, Little Wattlebird, Golden Whistler and Tree Martin.

Check the roadside paddocks – small flocks of Cattle Egrets sometimes appear here.

Georges Bay

To get there, turn east off Tasman Hwy (A3) to Binalong Bay Rd (C850). Several access points to the water are available along this road.

Waders are common in the Georges Bay area including summer migrants including Bar-tailed Godwit, Red-necked Stint, Eastern Curlew, Common Greenshank, Sharp-tailed Sandpiper, Ruddy Turnstone and Sanderling. Rarer species such as Whimbrel, Red Knot and Grey-tailed Tattler are found here occasionally. In winter, Double-banded Plover, a New Zealand migrant, can be found in good numbers on the mudflats in Colchis Creek which is the best place in the area for the waders. Native waders including Australian Pied Oystercatcher, Sooty Oystercatcher, Red-capped Plover and even Hooded Plover can be seen around the Bay the whole year round.

Look in the paddocks around the township for Banded Lapwings - they may be spotted there in small numbers.

St Helens Sewage Ponds

Sewage ponds are adjacent to the Colchis Creek mouth. They provide a good environment for the waterfowl. Hundreds of Australian Shelducks and Black Swans live there. The latter are sometimes so numerous that they seem to fill the ponds to the brim. Smaller numbers of Australasian Shovelers, Chestnut Teals, Hardheads and Australasian Grebes can also be found. Rarities such as Australian Wood Duck, a recent colonizer of Tasmania, and Musk Duck, breed on the ponds. Little Egret and Black-fronted Dotterel are regularly observed feeding on the ponds. Small flocks of Cattle Egrets, otherwise uncommon in the St Helens area, were found several times roosting around the ponds.

In the saltmarshes around the ponds, good numbers of Tawny-crowned Honeyeaters can easily be spotted. Look also for Striated Fieldwren, White-fronted Chat and Australasian Pipit. White-bellied Sea-Eagle and occasionally Peregrine Falcon have been reported to patrol Georges Bay and the sewage ponds.

Medeas Cove Conservation Area

The site, comprising a large cove and a bushland area at its west end, is located on the western side of Tasman Hwy (A3). Birding is possible along Medeas Cove Esplanade off A3. The road changes its name to Eagle St in the bushland section. Bird composition in the cove is similar to that of the Georges Bay but they occur here in smaller numbers. This is a good place for Eastern Great Egret which has been reported regularly. Occasionally, Musk Duck can be found here. Tasmanian Native-hens are very common, feeding on the shores. Small groups of Australian Pelicans can often be seen on the water; this bird, plentiful on the mainland, is rather uncommon in Tasmania.

When driving along the coast, look for Striated Pardalotes. Several colonies are established in the embankment. You can observe the birds flitting between their holes and the gum trees and in the quiet air you may even hear the youngsters chattering underground.

Bush in the Conservation Area may produce Yellow Wattlebird, Yellow-throated Honeyeater, Eastern Spinebill and Common Bronzewing. All four species of cuckoo can be found here in summer. Also, Swift Parrot and Grey Goshawk occasionally visit in summer.

St Helens Point Conservation Reserve

This coastal 1,066ha Reserve stretches from Dianas Basin in the south to St Helens Point in the north. The main features of this site are extensive and impressive Peron Dunes and wonderful, endless pristine beaches. As dunes are a very sensitive habitat, prone to damage, vehicular use has been reduced to a small area put aside for the 4WD and beach buggy enthusiasts. Other habitats protected in the Reserve include coastal heathland, coastal scrub, woodland and wetland. The offshore islets in the area, including St Helens Island and Paddys Island, are also part of the Reserve. They offer fantastic breeding grounds for many seabirds such as Little Penguin, White-faced Storm-Petrel, Short-tailed Shearwater, Black-faced Cormorant, Sooty Oystercatcher, gulls and terns.

Peron coastal dunes

To get to the northern, main section of the Reserve, turn east off Tasman Hwy (A3) into St Helens Point Rd (C851) signposted to Parkside. Drive 11km along the bay to St Helens Point. The southern section of the Reserve, the Dianas Basin, can be accessed from Tasman Hwy (A3) about 6km south of St Helens. The turnoffs to Dianas Basin are well-signposted.

A network of tracks runs through the Reserve, allowing access to different sections of the beach. Other facilities include basic camping and picnic areas in Dianas Basin, St Helens Point and Stieglitz Beach.

Over 100 bird species have been recorded in this Reserve. **Key species** are Hooded Plover, Musk Duck and Ruddy Turnstone. Birds of interest also include Sooty Oystercatcher, Sanderling, Striated Fieldwren, White-fronted Chat, Tasmanian Native-hen and seabirds. Among the rarities here are Great Frigatebird, Lesser Frigatebird, Fairy Tern, Little Tern, Grey-tailed Tattler and Black-shouldered Kite.

In June 2016, a small group of four Great Frigatebirds and two Lesser Frigatebirds appeared in the St Helens area. For a couple of weeks, the birds were flying over the Beerbarrel Beach and Burns Bay harassing Australasian Gannets and Crested Terns to steal their food.

We started birdwatching from the northern section, adjacent to Georges Bay. We soon found out that popping into some nearby locations accessible from St Helens Point Rd was worth it.

Windmill Lagoon

Access to the area is from St Helens Point Rd (C851), turning into Dawson St which later changes name to Stieglitz Tk. Sewage treatment ponds are located on the west side of Stieglitz Tk while Windmill Lagoon with a swamp are situated on the east side.

The lagoon is a good placed for Musk Duck which breeds in the swamp. Australasian Bittern was recorded a few times here.

The lagoon is surrounded by coastal heath and scrub teeming with the honeyeaters (Tawny-crowned Honeyeater, Yellow-throated Honeyeater, New Holland Honeyeater, Crescent Honeyeater, Eastern Spinebill, Little Wattlebird and Yellow Wattlebird), White-fronted Chats, Beautiful Firetails, Brush Bronzewings and Brown Thornbills. In the vegetation around the lagoon verges Little Grassbirds can be heard, wailing incessantly.

Flocks of White-throated Needletails up to a hundred strong have been reported flying over the lagoon in autumn (March-April). Welcome Swallows, Tree Martins and Dusky Woodswallows can often be seen mixed in the needletail flocks.

Stieglitz Sewage Ponds

The sewage treatment ponds are located on the west side of the Stieglitz Tk. There is no direct access but you can scan the ponds with your binoculars when visiting Windmill Lagoon.

A good selection of waterbirds can be found on the ponds. Regularly found are Musk Duck, Chestnut Teal, Hardhead, Australasian Shoveler, Australian Shelduck, Hoary-headed Grebe, Eurasian Coot and Rd-capped Plover. Pink-eared Duck was recorded a few times.

Two male Chestnut Teals

Other birds here include White-fronted Chat, Australasian Pipit, Scarlet Robin, White-bellied Sea-Eagle and Australian Hobby.

Maurouard Beach

This beautiful beach is located midway through the Reserve. It can be reached via Stieglitz Tk past Windmill Lagoon (see above). The beach is one of the best areas for Hooded Plovers; they congregate here in flocks up to 10 birds. Other waders at this site include Red-capped Plover, Australian Pied Oystercatcher and Double-banded Plovers (in winter).

In the dune vegetation along the beach there are plenty of White-fronted Chats. In autumn they form 50-100 strong flocks. You can also find here Striated Fieldwren and Tawny-crowned Honeyeater.

Moriarty Lagoon

Turn east from St Helens Point Rd (C851) into Moriarty Rd just before Pelican Point. The lagoon is situated along Moriarty Rd. This is another good spot for Musk Duck in the area. Look also for Green Rosella, Tasmanian Native-hen, Australasian Pipit and Swamp Harrier.

Pelican Point

This is one of the good high-tide roosting sites in the area. Find a track leading to the Point from St Helens Point Rd (C851) past Simeon Pl.

During our visit, we observed Red-necked Stints, Eastern Curlews, Bar-tailed Godwits, Australian Pied Oystercatchers and White-faced Herons feeding on the mudflats. A White-bellied Sea-Eagle was perching in the tree.

Blanche Beach

This small sandy beach is situated at the narrow ocean outlet of Georges Bay. We found it occupied by Hooded Plovers, Sanderlings and both oystercatchers. There were also plenty of Crested Terns and all three species of gulls. Forest Ravens were fossicking on the beach. Occasionally, Fairy Terns are reported from this location.

In the scrub nearby, we got Tasmanian Scrubwren, Brown Thornbill and Crescent Honeyeater.

Burns Bay

This is the bay with a boat ramp, just before St Helens Point. In the dense scrub look for Bassian Thrush (differentiate with the female Common Blackbird, the species common in Tasmania). Rocks by the bay may be occupied by Black-faced Cormorants, Sooty Oystercatchers, Pacific Gulls and Chestnut Teals.

The site is good for seabirds; Brown Skua and Pomarine Jaeger have been reported from this location. There is also a record of Black-shouldered Kite flying over this area.

Beerbarrel Beach

Access is via St Helens Point Rd (C851). A carpark is provided near the end of the road. Signposted tracks lead to the Beerbarrel Beach from there, one (longer) along the coast and the other (shorter) through the scrub.

Near the carpark at St Helens Point Rd there were Scarlet Robins, Beautiful Firetails and plenty of Australasian Pipits.

This is a good seabird-watching site. Thousands of Short-tailed Shearwaters can often be observed flying along the coastline. Many seabirds breed and roost on the coastal rocks nearby. When a shoal of fish moves near the cost, bird feeding frenzy has been observed many times, involving hundreds of Great Cormorants, Little Black Cormorants, Australasian Gannets, gulls and terns.

On exposed rocks look for waders including Ruddy Turnstone, Pacific Golden Plover and Sanderling. Reported occasionally are Grey Plover and Grey-tailed Tattler. There is a good chance to spot Hooded Plovers on the beach; one pair is there most of the time.

Heath along the beach may yield Tawny-crowned Honeyeater, Yellow-throated Honeyeater, Horsfield's Bronze-Cuckoo, Brown Thornbill, Striated Fieldwren, White-fronted Chat and occasionally Olive Whistler. If you are the area in the evening, you may experience a dark cloud of Common Starlings descending *en masse* into the scrub around the St Helens Point for the night roost.

Dianas Basin

This site is located in the southern section of the Reserve just off Tasman Hwy (A3). This is a large lagoon surrounded by heath and woodland. A large carpark and a shady camping area are provided on the northern side of the lagoon. Stieglitz Tk runs along the southern shore (it doesn't connect with Stieglitz Tk at St Helens Point).

Dianas Basin is a good place to stop for Musk Duck; it is nearly always there. Other regular findings include Eastern Great Egret, Hoary-headed Grebe, Swamp Harrier and White-bellied Sea-Eagle. Plenty of Yellow-throated Honeyeaters can usually be observed around the carpark. Yellow-tailed Black-Cockatoos often fly overhead or feed in the casuarina trees.

On the beach-side, a fenced-off area is provided for the nesting Hooded Plovers. In the heath by the beach, look for Striated Fieldwren, White-fronted Chat, Horsfield's Bronze-Cuckoo and Dusky Woodswallow.

Loila Tier Reserve

Birdwatchers visit this reserve to find Spotted Quail-thrush which occurs here in good numbers.

Loila Tier is a small reserve in the middle of a large pristine area of dry sclerophyll forest. The defining features of that area are prominent, narrow ridges running north to south with deep creek gullies and steep slopes. A proposal was put forward to create a large Constable Creek-Loila Tier Reserve that would cover the area of 13,000ha, stretching from Scamander to St. Helens. At the moment, Loila Tier Reserve is still small and sits on the ridge, with several communication towers on top of the hill. The dominant vegetation type is ironbark forest with open canopy and sparse understory of small shrubs. There also small patches of black peppermint and stringybark forest.

To get there, from Tasman Hwy (A3) turn west into Flagstaff Rd a few kilometres south of St Helens. Drive as far along this road as you can. When the road becomes too steep, walk up to the communication towers and go briding along the ridge. The area near the towers offers stunning panoramic views over the coast and the countryside.

Spotted Quail-thrush is easy to find while driving or walking along the mountain ridge. The favoured habitat for this species is the stringybark forest above 300m with the understory of boronia and grass trees (*Xanthorrhoea* spp.) growing on stony slopes. They are often seen foraging along the track and, when frightened, would fly onto the rocky slopes to disappear into the stony ground. The best place for them is a few hundred metres before the towers.

The area around the towers is also good for other birds including Brush Bronzewing, Eastern Spinebill, Crested Honeyeater, Black-headed Honeyeater and Strong-billed Honeyeater. Robins are quite common (Dusky Robin, Flame Robin and Scarlet Robin) and can be found the easiest when walking along the ridge.

In autumn, Grey Currawongs congregate in the Reserve in large numbers. Wedge-tailed Eagles breed in the Reserve, with two nests known.

When driving at night on Flagstaff Road, Masked Owl, Tawny Frogmouth and Tasmanian Morepork can be found, in particular near the turnoff from Tasman Hwy. Australian Owlet-nightjar's calls can be heard frequently along this road; the birds seem to be attracted to the car headlamps.

Halls Falls, Blue Tier

Halls Falls is situated near Pyengana in the Blue Tier section of North East Highlands. Turn off Tasman Hwy (A3) into Anchor Rd approximately 25km west of St Helens. Find a small carpark and a picnic area from where you may take a walk to the Falls (40min return). At first, you'll be walking through the dense scrub, then through the open forest and last through a beautiful rainforest in a gorge where the path winds along the river bank lined with giant tree ferns. You can also access the falls by taking a 90min walk from St Columba Falls nearby.

Halls Falls area is adjacent to the Blue Tier Reserve that was saved from logging. That site is practically non-accessible.

There is a good selection of rainforest bird species here. **Key species** are Tasmanian Thornbill, Scrubtit, Pink Robin and Satin Flycatcher. Other birds of interest include Bassian Thrush, Golden Whistler, Olive Whistler, Tasmanian Scrubwren, Flame Robin, Scarlet Robin, Dusky Robin, Eastern Spinebill and Green Rosella.

Weldborough Pass Scenic Reserve

The site is located east of a tiny township of Weldborough, off Tasman Hwy (A3), well signposted. It is a short, 20min circular walk through the spectacular tree fern display. The ferns are growing under a canopy of old beech myrtles, blackwood and sassafras. The site positively looks enchanted, medieval, with ancient-looking trees covered in thick mosses, dripping with moisture. The king of the forest is the "Grandfather Myrtle", a magnificent beech myrtle with a 10m circumference.

During our visit, birds common on the walk included Scrubtit, Tasmanian Thornbill, Pink Robin, Crescent Honeyeater and Bassian Thrush. A pair of Wedge-tailed Eagles was soaring over the forest.

An enchanted rainforest walk in the Weldborough Pass Scenic Reserve

St Columba Falls State Reserve

This 295ha Reserve is located 25km west of St. Helens. It features stunning falls that plunge nearly 90m from the Mt Victoria foothills to the valley of South George River. The falls are surrounded by the rainforest of the neighbouring Blue Tier with towering sassafras and beech myrtles, a middle layer of blackwood, and the understory of tree ferns. This was the favourite habitat of the extinct Tasmania Tiger. The locals believe they can still see it around. Some 4,000 sightings were reported in the last 50 years but no animal was produced, alive or dead.

To get there, turn into St Columba Falls Rd (C248) from Tasman Hwy (A3) about 500m east of Willows Roadhouse. Drive 24km to the Falls. You can also reach St Columba Falls via a 90min walk from Halls Falls. Facilities in the reserve include a carpark and 800m walk to the falls where you'll find a viewing platform.

Birds common in the area and easy to find include Scrubtit, Pink Robin, Tasmanian Thornbill, Tasmanian Scrubwren and Bassian Thrush. Flame Robins are nesting in the bushes near the falls.

Look also for Olive Whistler, Grey Butcherbird, Black Currawong, Dusky Robin, Silvereye, Green Rosella and Yellow-tailed Black-Cockatoo.

Ben Lomond National Park

The main feature of the Park is the magnificent massif of Ben Lomond, towering above the farmland and forest and visible over much of the northern Tasmania. An alpine plateau, 13km long and 8km wide, is located on the top. The unobtrusive summit, called Legges Tor, rises to the height of 1,572m over the sea level and is the second highest peak in Tasmania (after Mt Ossa, 1,617m). The Park is home to the Tasmania's only commercial ski field.

Most of the plateau is stony, with low alpine vegetation clinging the dear life among the stones. The rest of the mountain is covered in vegetation ranging from alpine heathland to dense wet forest. The Park is in a stark contrast to the dry sclerophyll environment of coastal Parks in Tasmania.

Ben Lomond National Park is located 50km (1hr drive) southeast of Launceston and 3rh drive north of Hobart. From Launceston, take St Leonards Rd (C401) to White Hills. From White Hills continue on Blessington Rd (C401) until turning right into Ben Lomond Rd (C432) 3.5km before Upper Blessington. This unsealed road will take you to the Alpine

Village. From Hobart, take Midland Hwy (1). Turn into Leighlands Rd (B41) to Evandale. From Evandale, take the partially sealed Logan Rd (C413). At the T-junction turn left into Deddinton Rd (C420), then right into Blessington Rd (C401) not far away from your turnoff into Ben Lomond Rd (C432). The locality map can be downloaded here: http://www.parks.tas.gov.au/file.aspx?id=19013.

The 18km Ben Lomond Rd is unsealed and features some entertaining hairpin bends. In particular, the Jakob's Ladder section is very steep and narrow and has several very tight zig-zags in a close sequence. After you've conquered your fear and got through, you'll find modest facilities in the Alpine Village including a carpark and a public day shelter (with heating). There are several short walks from the Alpine Village to explore the birdlife. The only camping area with six unpowered sites and drinking water is located 1km into the National Park. Bush camping is also permitted.

About 50 bird species have been recorded in the Park. **Key species** are Spotted Quail-thrush, Scrubtit and Tasmanian Thornbill. Birds of interest also include Crescent Honeyeater, Scarlet Robin, Flame Robin and Australasian Pipit. Ten out of twelve endemic species inhabit the Park.

Tasmania Morepork is common in the foothills. Look there also for Scrubtit, Tasmanian Thornbill, Tasmanian Scrubwren, Green Rosella, Crescent Honeyeater, Yellow-throated Honeyeater, Grey Currawong and Satin Flycatcher.

On your way to the Alpine Village look for Spotted Quail-thrush but do not take your eyes off the road.

Birds common in the Alpine Village include Australasian Pipit, Forest Raven, Black Currawong, Welcome Swallow, Scarlet Robin, Flame Robin and Crescent Honeyeater. Wedge-tailed Eagles soar majestically over the ridge.

Mount William National Park

This idyllic 14,000ha Park, located in the northeastern corner of Tasmania, is quite remote. It was established in 1973 on failed tobacco farms to protect the last at that time population of Forester kangaroo. The Park has large areas of grassland, supporting thousands of wallabies, kangaroos, wombats and other herbivores. Additionally, the Park boast extensive, magnificent coastal heathland, dry sclerophyll woodlands, granite outcrops and beautiful beaches that stretch to rocky headlands. There are two large lagoons in the Park, Musselroe Lagoon in the north and Ansons Bay Lagoon in the south. Several small coastal islets also belong to the Park; these are favourite breeding grounds for many seabirds.

A locality map can be downloaded here:
http://www.parks.tas.gov.au/file.aspx?id=19047. Two main routes lead to the Park:

- Travel to Gladstone via Scottsdale (on Tasman Hwy A3 and Waterhouse Rd B82). From Gladstone it is 17km on gravel roads (North Ansons Rd, C843, and Musselroe Rd, C845) to the entrance at the northern end of the park.
- The southern end of the park, near Eddystone Point, can be reached by gravel roads from St Helens via Ansons Bay (North Ansons Rd, C843, and Eddystone Point Rd, C846) or from Gladstone on the North Ansons Rd (C843).

There are four basic camping areas at the northern sections with picnic tables and fireplaces. Electric barbecues are available only in Camping No.4 at Stumpys Bay. Two camping areas are available in the southern section, at Deep Creek and Eddystone Point. No drinking water is available in the Park, you must bring your own.

In the northern section, a circuit track called Forester Kangaroo Dr is a major Park attraction, particularly when you come at dusk and drive slowly between the foraging kangaroo mobs, wombats and other marsupials.

Over 100 species are on the Park's birdlist. **Key species** are Hooded Plover, Tawny-crowned Honeyeater and Fairy Tern. Other birds of interest include Brown Quail, Tasmanian Native-hen, Yellow-tailed Black-Cockatoo (large flocks) and Crescent Honeyeater. Among the rarities are Ground Parrot, Swift Parrot, Little Tern, Banded Lapwing, Banded Stilt and Grey Plover.

The Park is well-known for the seabirds and both native and migratory waders. On the beaches, you can observe gulls (Pacific Gull, Silver Gull, Kelp Gull), terns (Caspian Tern, Crested Tern, Fairy Tern), cormorants (Black-faced Cormorant, Little Black Cormorant, Little Pied Cormorant), oystercatchers (Australian Pied Oystercatcher, Sooty Oystercatcher) and plovers (Red-capped Plover, Hooded Plover).

In autumn, the Park experiences a surge in the bird numbers as it serves as a staging point in the seasonal migration to the mainland. The most abundant are Silvereyes, Dusky Woodswallows, Black-faced Cuckoo-shrikes and Grey Fantails.

Corner of North Ansons Rd and Musselroe Rd

This is a worthy stopover on your way to the National Park. Check the paddocks: Banded Lapwings were recorded here several times. One pair was even breeding in the area. On the dam nearby, Australian Wood Ducks were found.

Other birds of interest include Cape Barren Goose, Australian Shelduck, Australasian Pipit, Wedge-tailed Eagle and Brown Falcon.

Musselroe Bay Conservation Area

The site is located just north of Mount William National Park and is not a part of it. Musselroe Bay Conservation Area includes a large lagoon and the surrounding heath and grassland. To get there, drive on Musselroe Rd (C845) until the end of the road where a campsite is located.

The lagoon is good for waders. Flocks feeding on the incoming tide usually include Common Greenshanks, Ruddy Turnstones, Red-necked Stints, Curlew Sandpipers, Sharp-tailed Sandpipers and Australian Pied Oystercatchers. Fairy Terns often fish in the lagoon. Other birds common in the area include Black Swan, Great Cormorant, Australian Pelican, Masked Lapwing and the common waterfowl.

Masked Lapwings congregate in Musselroe Bay Conservation Area in large numbers

Little Musselroe Bay

Drive 27km along Cape Portland Rd (C844) north of Gladstone, and then 200m into a sheltered bayside camping area. Best to come here between Christmas and Easter, when vehicular access to the campground is possible for small off-road vehicles; otherwise there is access on foot from the road.

Little Musselroe Bay and Estuary are important breeding areas for many shorebirds. It is also an important feeding and roosting stop for the migratory waders. Threatened species known to reside in this area include Grey Goshawk, Wedge-tailed Eagle, White-bellied Sea-Eagle, Eastern Curlew and Fairy Tern.

The Bay area boasts a very high diversity of resident species and is a stronghold for Double-banded Plover, Sooty Oystercatcher and Little Tern. Hooded Plover, Red-capped Plover and Australian Pied Oystercatcher can also be easily found here. This is a breeding area for Fairy Terns.

Migratory waders such as Bar-tailed Godwit and Red-necked Stint can be observed in good numbers in the summer season.

Northern Section of the Park

The most productive birding habitats in the northern section of the Park are the coastal scrub and buttongrass swamp. Tawny-crowned Honeyeaters are plentiful there. The heath is also full of Yellow-throated Honeyeaters, New Holland Honeyeaters, Crescent Honeyeaters, Eastern Spinebills and Little Wattlebirds. Striated Fieldwren, Tasmanian Scrubwren, Brown Thornbill and White-fronted Chat are also common in the area.

There is a chance of flushing a Brown Quail. Swift Parrots are often seen flying in between stands of gum trees in the buttongrass swamp. Ground Parrots were recorded several times in patches of knee-high heath. Large flocks of Yellow-tailed Black-Cockatoos fly over the heathland to feed on banksia cones.

In the coastal woodland, Dusky Woodswallow and Green Rosella are abundant. Golden Whistler, Black Currawong and Grey Currawong are common. You may hear Tasmanian Morepork at night.

Raptors are not common but Wedge-tailed Eagle, Brown Falcon and Swamp Harrier may be found.

Common birds near the campsites include Australasian Pipit, Common Bronzewing, Black Currawong, Scarlet Robin and Flame Robin.

Eddystone Point

From North Ansons Rd (C843) turn north into Eddystone Point Rd (C846) and drive to the lighthouse. The best way of birding is to walk to the beach through the coastal scrub, then walk on the beach in the direction of the lighthouse. The waders usually congregate on the beach south of the lighthouse. In summer, you may expect large flocks of Sanderlings and Red-necked Stints. There will also be a few Ruddy Turnstones around.

Year-round on the beach you may encounter Hooded Plover (breeding there), Red-capped Plover, Australian Pied Oystercatcher, Sooty Oystercatcher, Fairy Tern, Pacific Gull and Kelp Gull. In the dunes, look for Australasian Pipit, White-fronted Chat and Brown Falcon. Coastal scrub behind the dunes may produce Horsfield's Bronze-Cuckoo, Fan-tailed Cuckoo, Brown Thornbill, Little Wattlebird and New Holland Honeyeater.

In the patches of woodland, you may come across Crescent Honeyeater, Pallid Cuckoo, Dusky Woodswallow, Brown Thornbill and Laughing Kookaburra.

Small flocks of White-throated Needletails have often been observed flying over the lighthouse, usually accompanied by Tree Martins and Welcome Swallows.

Approximately 8km north of Eddystone Point a group of small islands, called Georges Rocks, is located. They are important breeding grounds for Little Penguin, Short-tailed Shearwater, White-faced Storm-Petrel, Common Diving-Petrel, Black-faced Cormorant, gulls and terns. Hooded Plovers breed on the islands' beaches.

Ansons Bay

To get there, from Ansons Bay Rd (C843) turn left into Grooves Rd and left again to Acacia Dr which runs along the Bay. The site came to the attention of the birdwatching world when 30 Banded Stilts decided to spend a few weeks here in February 2016.

Musk Ducks are often found in the lagoon. In the surrounding heath and scrub there are plenty of honeyeaters including Yellow-throated Honeyeater, Strong-billed Honeyeater, New Holland Honeyeater, Yellow Wattlebird and Eastern Spinebill. Other birds in the area include Pallid Cuckoo, Brown Thornbill, Dusky Woodswallow and Grey Butcherbird.

Policemans Point

The site is located in the mouth of Ansons Bay. To get there, from Ansons Bay Rd (C843) urn left into Policemans Point Rd and drive to the camping site at the end of the road. The area contains mudflats, beaches, sandspits and coastal heathland.

It is a good place for waders including Hooded Plover, Red-capped Plover, Australian Pied Oystercatcher, Ruddy Turnstone and Red-necked Stint. You will see White-bellied Sea-Eagle soaring in the sky.

Waterhouse Conservation Area

The 7,000ha Waterhouse Conservation Area is located west of Bridport, spreading to Tomahawk Beach along the northeastern coast of Tasmania. This a top birding area, famous for the highest species counts that can be obtained in Tasmania in a day. The area contains many wetlands including three major permanent deep water lagoons: Blackmans Lagoon, Big Waterhouse Lake and Little Waterhouse Lake. The latter is listed under the Ramsar Convention as the internationally significant wetland. Waterhouse Conservation Area includes one of the largest areas of heathland in northeast Tasmania.

Access is easy from Launceston – take East Tamar Hwy (A8) north, then turn right into Bridport Rd (B82). From Bridport, continue west on Waterhouse Rd (B82) for approximately 25km. Take a turnoff left for Blackmans Lagoon Rd to get to Blackmans Lagoon. If you carry on along Waterhouse Rd for a few more kilometres, you'll get to a turnoff to Homestead Rd that leads to all other sites of the Waterhouse Conservation Area.

Several designated bush camping areas are provided. Bring drinking water and other supplies with you; there are no facilities except for pit toilets there. The site map indicating the approved bush camp locations can be downloaded here: http://www.parks.tas.gov.au/file.aspx?id=6670.

Over 140 bird species have been recorded within the Waterhouse Conservation Area, including six of Tasmania's 12 endemic birds. **Key species** are Hooded Plover, Australasian Bittern, Banded Lapwing, Cape Barren Goose and Musk Duck. Other birds of interest include Brown Falcon, White-fronted Chat, Latham's Snipe, Australasian Shoveler, Eastern Great Egret and Tawny-crowned Honeyeater. Among the rarities recorded here are Yellow-billed Spoonbill, Pied Stilt, Cattle Egret, Common Sandpiper, Fairy Tern, Peregrine Falcon and Grey Goshawk.

Blackmans Lagoon

Access from Waterhouse Rd (B82) is via Blackmans Lagoon Rd, a 2km-long dirt road leading to the edge of the lagoon. You will find here a carpark and a camping site.

When we drove there, paddocks on the way to the lagoon yielded plenty of White-fronted Chats, Yellow-rumped Thornbills and Australasian Pipits. The fence lines were adorned with numerous Scarlet Robins, Flame Robins and Dusky Robins. In a belt of dense vegetation along the road we got Striated Fieldwren and Beautiful Firetail. Three Brown Falcons were hunting over the fields.

A pair of Australian Hobbies were nesting in a pine tree near the carpark. A small group of Yellow-tailed Black-Cockatoos were lunching on the cone pines. We heard Olive Whistler calling from the dense bushes near the carpark. A couple of Common Bronzewings were foraging on the road to the farmhouse near the campsite. Heathland around the lagoon was teeming with and Superb Fairy-wrens and Tasmanian Scrubwrens. A family of Tasmanian Native-hens was foraging at the edge of the heath.

Australasian Bittern flew over the reeds at the northern part of the lagoon. Hundreds of Black Swans and Eurasian Coots were present on the water. A raft of about 60 Hoary-headed Grebes displayed their expert fishing skills. Other common species in this area include Musk Duck (breeding there, always present), Australasian Shoveler, Chestnut Teal and Australian Shelduck.

A raft of Eurasian Coots on Blackmans Lagoon

Wader records for this site include Red-capped Plover, Black-fronted Dotterel, Australian Pied Oystercatcher and Latham's Snipe. Among the rarities are Pacific Golden Plover and Common Sandpiper. In 2012, Yellow-billed Spoonbill was recorded.

Raptors of Blackmans Lagoon include White-bellied Sea-Eagle, Wedge-tailed Eagle, Swamp Harrier and Peregrine Falcon.

Homestead Road

Turn left into Homestead Rd from Waterhouse Rd (B82) soon after you see the turnoff to Old Waterhouse Rd on the right. The paddocks along Homestead Rd are the best place for Banded Lapwing in Tasmania. Banded Lapwings breed here and are present year-round; flocks up to 47 birds were recorded.

Banded Lapwing

Cape Barren Goose is also abundant, with flocks of up to a hundred-strong observed feeding in the paddocks in autumn. Other species to watch for along the road include Flame Robin, Yellow-tailed Black-Cockatoo, cuckoos in summer (Pallid Cuckoo and Fan-tailed Cuckoo), Australasian Pipit, White-fronted Chat, Brown Falcon and Grey Goshawk.

Flooding occurs from time to time and then you can observe hundreds of ducks, Masked Lapwings and huge flocks of Kelp Gulls on the wet paddocks.

Big Waterhouse Lake

To get there, from Waterhouse Rd (B82) turn north into Homestead Rd. Be on a lookout for an obscure wooden sign directing to Big Waterhouse Lake. Turn left into a narrow, overgrown track called Big Waterhouse Lake Rd. Drive to the parking and camping area in the bush near the water. The lake is partially surrounded by scrub and partially by coastal heath and sand dunes.

Big Waterhouse Lake

In the dense banksia and wattle bushland, we found Brush Bronzewing, Yellow-throated Honeyeater, New Holland Honeyeater, Golden Whistler and Grey Shrike-thrush. We could hear plenty of Little Grassbirds from the wetland vegetation at the water edge. On the neighbouring paddock were Cape Barren Geese, Australian Shelducks, White-fronted Chats, Australasian Pipits and Eurasian Skylarks.

Waterbirds were dozing off in a large group at the northern side of the lagoon, mostly European Coots, Australian Shelducks and Black Swans. Among them were a few Australasian Shovelers and Musk Ducks. Eastern Great Egrets were hunting in the rushes while Swamp Harrier and White-bellied Sea-Eagle were on the patrol over the lagoon.

Yellow-tailed Black-Cockatoos can be seen in flocks of hundreds here. Other parrots recorded in this area include Green Rosella, Blue-winged Parrot and Swift Parrot. Australasian Bittern and Fairy Tern are regularly sighted here. Other birds of interest include Grey Goshawk, often seen feeding on the roadkill, Australian Wood Duck and Hoary-headed Grebe.

Little Waterhouse Lake

This is a Ramsar site. To get there, from Homestead Rd take next left into South Croppies Rd after passing the Big Waterhouse Lake turnoff. This junction is well-signposted but the road is rather terrible (deep sand). After about 1km turn left into Little Waterhouse Lake Rd. From this turnoff up to the lake you'll go through a large area of coastal heath teeming with honeyeaters, mainly Tawny-crowned Honeyeaters. Other birds here include New Holland Honeyeater, Little Wattlebird, Dusky Woodswallow, Brown Thornbill, Horsfield's Bronze-cuckoo and Fan-tailed Cuckoo.

Little Waterhouse Lake is known for its population of Latham's Snipes; look for them around the northern perimeter of the lake. Other birds on the lake include Australasian Grebe, Hoary-headed Grebe, Tasmanian Native-hen (plenty), White-fronted Chat and Green Rosella.

White-bellied Sea-Eagles are easy to see in the area. Wedge-tailed Eagle has a nest in the Tower Hill area.

Herbies Landing

Access is from Homestead Rd when the road turns sharply right. The turnoff to Herbies Landing is signposted. This is a reliable place for Hooded Plover. Look also for Pacific Golden Plover, in summer they are often observed foraging on the rocky beach.

Other birds of interest in this area include Sooty Oystercatcher, Australian Pied Oystercatcher, Caspian Tern, Pacific Gull and Black-faced Cormorant.

Ransons Beach

This is a sandy beach with coastal heathland and a few pockets of melaleuca and gums. The site is located at the end of Homestead Rd, access is by 4WD only.

The beach an excellent place for Hooded Plover; these breed here from October to January. Flocks of Black-faced Cormorants can be observed on the beach. The beach is also a good spot for gulls (Pacific Gull, Silver Gull, Kelp Gull) and terns (Caspian Tern, Crested Tern and even Fairy Tern).

Launceston and Surrounds

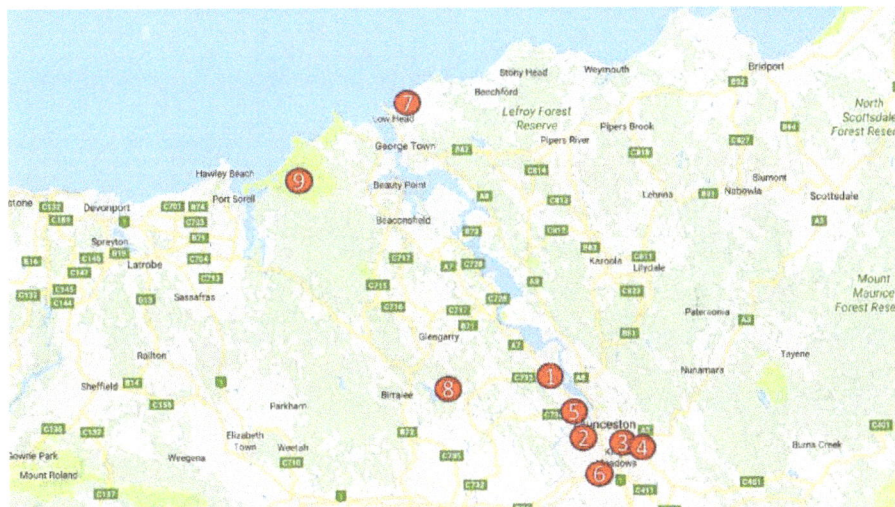

Tamar Island Wetlands

This is a very popular wetland reserve, only 10min drive north of the Launceston CBD, located on the west bank of Tamar River. The Reserve protect 60ha of lagoons, mudflats and islands and includes one of the largest remaining areas of common reeds. This is the best habitat for Australasian Bitten. There are also small patches of paperbark swamp around the bird hide as well as grassland on Tamar Island. This a unique place where, instead of hanging around the edges, you can walk in comfort to the heart of a large wetland.

To get there, take West Tamar Hwy (A7) towards Riverside. The wetlands are signposted from the suburbs of Riverside and Legana. There is a large carpark with an 80m-long boardwalk leading to an excellent Visitor Centre. Even from the toilet, birdwatching is still possible, observing the birds fleeting between the reeds from the windows. From the Visitor Centre the boardwalk extends for further 1.5km to Tamar Island. On the island, you'll find a gravel track and a picnic area with barbecues. Other facilities on site include a bird hide and viewing platforms. Look for the old shipwrecks before reaching the Island, plenty of waterbirds choose to roost there.

Tamar Island Wetlands with a boardwalk and Visitor Centre

Over 110 bird species have been recorded in Tamar Island Wetlands, including 55 waterbirds. **Key species** are Australasian Bittern, Lewin's Rail, Spotless Crake, Australian Spotted Crake, Australasian Shoveler and Dusky Moorhen. Other notable species include Eastern Great Egret, Little Grassbird, Black-fronted Dotterel, Hoary-headed Grebe, Nankeen Night-Heron and White-bellied Sea-Eagle. Among the rarities are Pied Stilt, Pink-eared Duck, Freckled Duck, Musk Duck, Great Crested Grebe and Whistling Kite.

We paid short visits to this site twice in different years and it rained persistently on both occasions. Nevertheless, we were still able to record over 40 species each time, mostly waterbirds. Walking in the rain, we could hear a booming call of Australasian Bittern from the reeds. We ticked off Eastern Great Egret, Cape Barren Goose and Hoary-headed Grebe. Spotless Crakes were foraging cautiously in the open near the Visitor Centre. Lewin's Rail popped up onto the levee near the bird hide. Little Grassbirds and Australian Reed-Warblers were calling constantly from the dense vegetation. Each time, there were hundreds of ducks, mostly Chestnut Teals and Grey Teals, also plenty of Black Swans as well as literally thousands of Silver Gulls. Look for the Australasian Shovelers and Australian Shelducks in the duck crowds (we found them on the ponds near the carpark).

On the island, Tasmanian Native-hens, Purple Swamphens and Black Swans were foraging on the pasture. We also found White-fronted Chat, Australasian Pipit, Galah and Tasmanian Scrubwren. Introduced finches (Common Greenfinch, European Goldfinch) and Eurasian Skylark are common at this site.

When the swamp is drying out in summer, look for waders on the mudflats including Common Greenshank, Red-necked Stint, Curlew Sandpiper and Red-capped Plover. In winter, Double-banded Plovers occasionally visit the site.

The area is good for the rarities such as Little Egret, Cattle Egret, Royal Spoonbill and Nankeen Night-Heron. A pair of Nankeen Night-Herons often roost near the Visitor Centre. Try to flush Latham's Snipe from the vegetation.

Raptors hunting in Tamar Wetlands include White-bellied Sea-Eagle, Swamp Harrier (common), Whistling Kite and Brown Falcon.

Tamar Island Wetlands are located in the middle of a large regional town

Cataract Gorge

This is the Launceston's own piece of wilderness, 1.5km from the CBD. It is a picturesque river gorge located at the lower section of South Esk River, close to the Trevallyn Reserve. Cataract Gorge is the region's prime attraction and one of the most visited places in Tasmania. The grounds are spacious, set in a heritage parkland full of old trees. In the last 50 years, native bushland has also been incorporated in the landscaping design. The site is a gem for the birdwatchers, with 8 of 12 endemic species present. The grounds are open round the clock so a spotlighting visit at night is an appealing possibility.

The most direct way to get to the site is by walking from the CBD to Kings Bridge. Walk across the bridge and take Cataract Walkway along the gorge. Besides walking, there are several ways to access the site by car. The easiest way of approach on the eastern side of the river is via Basin Rd in West Launceston. On site, you'll find a large carpark, a café, a swimming pool and access to the chairlift transferring you over the gorge. It is arguably the longest chairlift in the world. The western side of the river is accessed via Gorge Rd in Trevallyn. You'll find a small carpark at the end of the road, a café and gardens around the Band Rotunda.

Other fantastic site facilities include visitor displays, picnic areas, lookouts and several kilometres of walking tracks. The Launceston Heritage Walks brochure, containing a good map of the Cataract Gorge and walks in the area can be downloaded here: http://www.destinationlaunceston.com.au/resources/uploads/routes_trails/1heritagewalksprintablebro.pdf.

Over 80 bird species have been recorded at Cataract Gorge. **Key species** are Indian Peafowl, Nankeen Night-Heron and Grey Goshawk. Other birds of interest include Dusky Woodswallow, Scarlet Robin, Common Bronzewing, Dusky Moorhen, Beautiful Firetail, Tawny Frogmouth and four cuckoo species. Rarities include Painted Button-quail and Swift Parrot.

The population of 30-50 Indian Peafowls in the Park has been on site for over 100 years (according to the local Rangers), obviously breeding there and self-sustaining. They can be found in the Rotunda parklands and in the picnic areas around the gorge.

At the Kings Bridge end of the gorge, look for Tasmanian Morepork, Brown Goshawk, Golden Whistler and Nankeen Night-Heron. Cataract Walkway (also called Main Walk) runs from Kings Bridge to First Basin on the western side of South Esk River. At several view points you can observe the waterbirds such as Hoary-headed Grebe, Australian Shelduck, Chestnut Teal, Hardhead and Black Swan. In the bush and forest across the river look for Dusky Woodswallow, Grey Shrike-thrush, Musk Lorikeet, Fan-tailed Cuckoo, Satin Flycatcher and Black-faced Cuckoo-shrike. Eagle Eyrie Lookout is the regular hangout of a pair of Peregrine Falcons, they nest in the area and can often be seen flying over the gorge. With luck, you may also observe aerial courtship displays of Grey Goshawks.

The walkway branches out in several directions at the Band Rotunda. Wild peacocks will be the most eye-catching birds in here. In spring and summer, the lawns will be speckled with colourful Flame and Scarlet Robins. In the bushes, look for Bassian Thrush, Brown Thornbill, Yellow-throated Honeyeater, Crescent Honeyeater, Green Rosella and Musk Lorikeet. Occasionally, a few Rainbow Lorikeets can be found.

In the chairlift area on the eastern side of the river, Grey Goshawks are often seen. Other birds here include Shining Bronze-cuckoo, Eastern Spinebill, Forest Raven and Brown Goshawk. Check the trees around the carpark; a family of Tawny Frogmouths often roosts there.

In the bush along Zig Zag Tk look for Brush Bronzewing, Black-headed Honeyeater, Brown Thornbill, Beautiful Firetail, Dusky Robin and Yellow-tailed Black-Cockatoo.

Queechy Lake

Queechy Lake is a small water body located southeast of Launceston CBD in the suburb of Newstead. It is surrounded by dense reeds. Access is from Queechy Rd off Penquite Rd in Norwood to Queechy Park. This small park gives the only access to Queechy Lake, other sides of the lake have been fenced off and taken over by residential housing or overgrown by bush.

This is one of the favourite birding spots in Launceston. Over 90 species are on the site's birdlist. **Key species** are Australasian Bittern, Royal Spoonbill, Australasian Shoveler and Great Cormorant. Other species of interest include Cattle Egret, Tasmanian Native-hen, Australasian Grebe, Hoary-headed Grebe and Musk Lorikeet. Among rarer species are Freckled Duck, Pink-eared Duck, Blue-billed Duck, Musk Duck, and Rainbow Lorikeet. Intermediate Egret was also recorded here.

The lake is well-known for large flocks of Cattle Egrets (100+ birds), roosting here in winter, and for resident Royal Spoonbills, Nankeen Night-Herons and Eastern Great Herons. Nankeen Night-Herons can often be seen roosting on a submerged willow tree.

Willow bushes on the small island have been taken over by a breeding colony of Great Cormorants. Among them nest Little Pied Cormorants and Little Black Cormorants. There are also a few nests of Royal Spoonbills. The latter first appeared here at the turn of the century and since have grown to about 15 birds, breeding regularly on site.

Great Cormorants breed on Queechy Lake

Duck species found on the lake include, apart those mentioned above, Chestnut Teal (highest numbers), Australian Wood Duck, Australian Shelduck, Pacific Black Duck, Australasian Shoveler, Grey Teal, Hardhead and Northern Mallard. In 2007, a small flock of Freckled Ducks stayed here for several months.

Coots and gallinules are always here (Dusky Moorhen which is rare in Tasmania, Purple Swamphen, Tasmanian Native-hen and Eurasian Coot). Little Grassbirds and Australian Reed-Warblers are common in the reeds and bulrushes surrounding the lake. Caspian Terns and Pacific Gulls frequent the area.

In the bushes you will find honeyeaters (Yellow-throated Honeyeater, Crescent Honeyeater, New Holland Honeyeater, Eastern Spinebill, Little Wattlebird and Yellow Wattlebird), cuckoos in summer (Shining Bronze-Cuckoo, Pallid Cuckoo, Fan-tailed Cuckoo), Brown Thornbill – very common, parrots (Green Rosella, Eastern Rosella, Musk Lorikeet, Yellow-tailed Black-Cockatoo). Swift Parrots and Rainbow Lorikeets have been reported a few times from this area.

A good range of raptor species at low numbers can be found around the lake including White-bellied Sea-Eagle, Grey Goshawk, Brown Goshawk and Swamp Harrier, as well as Wedge-tailed Eagle, Australian Hobby and Brown Falcon.

Old Mac's Farm and Fishery

Two large lakes with islands are the main feature of this site. Access is restricted as it is a RV park. Please ask permission to enter the site to view birds.

Old Mac's is located close to Queechy Lake and birds are moving between the two sites. Follow the road signs on Penquite Rd in Norwood directing to the "Old Mac's Farm". Turn into Queechy Rd and drive to the end. Turn right into Sundown Rd at the T-junction. Follow the road sharply down, passing the Stonesthrow restaurant. Drive and walk around the lakes.

There are about 50 species on the site's birdlist. Bird composition is similar to that of Queechy Lake.

During our visit, a small group of Freckled Ducks were foraging on the first lake along a good selection of other waterbirds such as Australian Shelduck, Australasian Shoveler, Musk Duck, Hardhead (dominant species on the lake), Hoary-headed Grebe and Australasian Grebe.

Tasmanian Native-hens, often with chicks, were running among the parked caravans. A pair of Common Bronzewings found shelter under a caravan, Black-fronted Dotterels were feeding at the lake edge.

Bush birds on the site included Yellow-throated Honeyeater, Little Wattlebird, Yellow Wattlebird, Dusky Woodswallow, Grey Shrike-thrush and Grey Butcherbird. Stands of willows near the lake were a good roosting place for the introduced Common Starlings, European Goldfinches and Common Greenfinches.

Grey Butcherbird sitting on a farm fence at the Old Mac's Farm

Trevallyn Reserve

The 44ha Trevallyn Nature Recreation Area is located on the South Esk River, Tasmania's longest river, adjacent to Cataract Gorge, only 4km from the centre of Launceston. The South Esk River gorge, with 60m-high cliffs and buttresses, is the dominant feature of its landscape. The reserve has originally been established as a recreational area but its important nature conservation role was quickly recognised. It protects dry open grassy forest and woodland communities, including 28 species of threatened plants. The aquatic and riparian habitats of the South Esk River gorge are particularly biodiversity-rich.

From Launceston, drive East Tamar Hwy (A7) and take a signposted turnoff to Lake Trevallyn. Follow the signs until you get to Reatta Rd which provides access to Lake Trevally Rd leading to the lake, and to Duck Reach Rd leading to the main gate and day use areas of Village Green and Hoo Hoo Hut. You may also get here by taking a 45min walk from the picturesque Cataract Gorge. The site is open from early morning till sunset. A network of 35km of walking tracks and mountain bike trails in a natural bush setting facilitates good birdwatching.

Over 60 bird species have been recorded in the Reserve. **Key species** are Peregrine Falcon, Painted Button-quail and nocturnal birds such as Tasmanian Morepork, Australian Owlet-nightjar, Masked Owl and Tawny Frogmouth. Other notable species include Grey Goshawk, Tasmanian Scrubwren, Brown Thornbill, Dusky Woodswallow, Yellow-throated Honeyeater, Dusky Robin, Scarlet Robin and Black Currawong.

A pair of Peregrine Falcons has a nest high on the cliffs. The nesting birds can be observed from the lookouts, take care not to disturb them.

Painted Button-quails breed in the Trevallyn Reserve and with luck can be found along Duck Reach Rd. Cuckoos are very common in summer (Shining Bronze-Cuckoo, Horsfield's Bronze-Cuckoo, Pallid Cuckoo and Fan-tailed Cuckoo). Honeyeaters are plentiful (especially Yellow-throated Honeyeater, Eastern Spinebill and Yellow Wattlebird). Small flocks of Dusky Woodswallows and Yellow-tailed Black-Cockatoos are regular visitors to this area. A small population of wild Indian Peafowl is resident in the Reserve and the neighbouring Cataract Gorge.

The carpark with a picnic area by the dam is a good birding spot. You may find here Brush Bronzewing, Common Bronzewing, Scarlet Robin (plenty), Yellow-rumped Thornbill, Grey Butcherbird, Green Rosella and four species of cuckoos. Another good birdwatching spot is Dead Mans Knob Tk. Look there for Beautiful Firetail, Yellow-tailed Black-Cockatoo, Golden Whistler, Grey Goshawk and Wedge-tailed Eagle.

Other birds in the Reserve include Dusky Robin, Tasmanian Scrubwren, Yellow-rumped Thornbill, Brown Thornbill, Grey Fantail and Striated Pardalote.

Kate Reed State Recreation Reserve

This 120ha reserve is situated on the southern outskirts of the Launceston's suburb of Prospect. The site is flanked on two sides by the Bass and Midlands highways. You'll find here remnants of native vegetation, mostly woodland dominated by black peppermint and swamp gum, with patches of native grassland and sedgeland.

There are three main entrances to the reserve: through the Silverdome complex, from the Bass Hwy and from the Kings Meadows connector on the Midlands Hwy. Access routes:

- *Silverdome complex entrance*: from the Launceston CBD follow Westbury Rd towards Prospect. Take the left turn into Oakden Rd and drive to a boom gate at the Silverdome complex. Because the gate is only open during office hours, if you are early leave the car by the right side of the road and walk to the Reserve. When the gate is open, drive right through to the Reserve. Otherwise, take the overpass and follow the road to the left around the complex to the top of the overflow carpark.
- *Bass Hwy entrance*: there is an entry from the Bass Hwy (1), driving southwest past Midlands Hwy (1) interchange.
- *Kings Meadows connector entrance*: the reserve can also be accessed from the Kings Meadows connector on the Midlands Hwy (1). This is on the western side of the highway, with limited parking available near the entrance.

A network of 15km of tracks has been established in the Reserve, used mostly by the mountain bikers, so be careful and best keep to the shared tracks.

Over 60 species are on the Reserve's birdlist. **Key species** are Grey Goshawk, Beautiful Firetail, Dusky Robin and Scarlet Robin.

Beautiful Firetail is common in the native grassland habitat. We observed two birds displaying on the power line with a male presenting a grass blade to the female. Scarlet Robins, Dusky Woodswallows and Grey Fantails were nearly on every track. Grey Goshawk was being chased by Forest Ravens.

Near the carpark we found Common Bronzewing, Striated Pardalote, Grey Currawong and a large flock of Sulphur-crested Cockatoos. The selection of bush birds here also includes Black-headed Honeyeater, Yellow-throated Honeyeater, Crescent Honeyeater, Eastern Spinebill, Brown Thornbill, Green Rosella, Superb Fairy-wren, Golden Whistler and Satin Flycatcher. Large flocks of Yellow-tailed Black-Cockatoos regularly frequent the Reserve.

Low Head Coastal Reserve

The Reserve is located in northeast Tasmania, a few kilometres north of George Town and about 50km north of Launceston. This site is home to the largest Tasmanian mainland Little Penguin rookery. The penguin burrows are hidden in dense box thorn bushes that cover the Head's stony shores. There are several historic buildings in the Reserve such as Pilot Station and Lighthouse underneath which the penguins also like to nest.

To get there from Launceston, take East Tamar Hwy (A8) north and drive to George Town. Continue north along A8 past the town (the road at some stage changes name to Low Head Rd). We must admit that driving along A8 was a traumatic experience due to the wildlife road carnage, including echidnas, pademelons, possums and other native fauna. This road is called by some "the roadkill capital of the world". The amount of fresh roadkill we saw was disgusting and horrifying even for Tasmania where roadkill is truly a hecatomb, worse than in the mainland Australia where it is really bad.

The penguins emerge from the ocean in the evening onto the beach facing the Bass Strait. To watch them, it is best to take East Beach Rd off Low Head Rd and go to a viewing platform on the beach. The bird numbers vary depending on the time of the year, the numbers are the greatest in the breeding season Nov-Feb, with 100-200 penguins coming up from the sea each night. However, the best way to see penguins is with the Low Head Penguin Tours, mob. 0418 361860. They are located on 486 Low Head Rd near the penguin colony, check the website:
http://penguintourstasmania.com.au/.

Other seabirds and shorebirds around Low Head include Shy Albatross, Australasian Gannet, Short-tailed Shearwater, Australian Pied Oystercatcher, Sooty Oystercatcher and Pacific Gull (often in large flocks).

The Lagoon Beach, located at the turnoff to East Beach Rd from Low Head Rd, is also worth checking. A large flock of Rock Doves (we counted 200 birds) lives there and Peregrine Falcon uses this colony as its private pantry, we observed one constantly harassing the pigeons.

George Town Wildlife Sanctuary

George Town sprawls handsomely on the eastern banks of the Tamar River estuary. Access is via East Tamar Hwy (A8). You'll find George Town Wildlife Sanctuary near the Tamar River. To get there, turn into Arthur St from East Tamar Hwy and observe the birds from Esplanade North. Most waders can usually be found on the mudflats in front of Lovers Islet. You can expect to find Eastern Curlew, Bar-tailed Godwit, Ruddy Turnstone, Common Greenshank, Australian Pied Oystercatcher, Sooty Oystercatcher and Whimbrel.

Common Greenshank

In the mouth of Tamar River, you'll see plenty of Black Swans mixed with a few Australian Pelicans, Chestnut Teals, Little Pied Cormorants and Great Cormorants. On the beaches and town lawns there are hundreds of Silver Gulls, Pacific Gulls and Crested Terns with an occasional Caspian Tern in the mix.

Coastal heath supports good numbers of White-fronted Chats and Little Wattlebirds.

Four Springs Lakes

Four Springs is a popular trout fishing location north of Selbourne, about half an hour drive west of Launceston. The dam was constructed in 1990' at the confluence of four creeks. It is a purpose-built fishery with a lot of shallows covered in underwater meadows, providing rich feeding grounds for fish and waterfowl. There are also large areas of deep water, good for diving ducks. The lake is surrounded by open forest and grassland.

The easiest way to get there is to take to Bass Hwy (1) west of Launceston and then turn into Meander Valley Rd (B54). In the vicinity of Hagley, turn north into Selbourne Rd (C735). Next, turn right into Four Springs Rd that will take you to the lake (north of the village of Selbourne). You will find here a boat ramp with a jetty. A track runs along the south and west edge of the lake.

Key species are diving ducks, especially Musk Duck which breeds here, and Hardhead. The rarities recorded here include Freckled Duck, Blue-billed Duck, Cape Barren Goose, Royal Spoonbill and Spotless Crake.

In the Selbourne village, flocks of Banded Lapwings (up to 60 birds) have been recoded several times near a local church.

The lake generally runs in a north-south direction and is quite narrow. The shoreline around it is fringed by the forest and marshes. The area is good for the rare ducks such as Musk Duck, Blue-billed Duck, Hardhead and Australian Shelduck. Large flocks (300+) of Hoary-headed Grebes have been observed. There are years when the lake is literally covered with Eurasian Coots which may form rafts of up to 2,000 birds.

The lake margin's vegetation is teeming with Little Grassbirds that are calling incessantly. Honeyeaters (Yellow-throated Honeyeater, Crescent Honeyeater, Little Wattlebird and Yellow Wattlebird) are quite common. You can find a few tame Black Currawongs at the picnic site by the lake. Tawny Frogmouth's nesting and roosting site is located near the boat ramp. A flock of Long-billed Corellas has for years been hanging around the lake.

At the interphase of forest and pasture, look for Scarlet Robin, Flame Robin, Olive Whistler and Beautiful Firetail. Raptors here include White-bellied Sea-Eagle, Brown Falcon and Grey Goshawk.

Other species found at Four Springs Lakes include Brown Thornbill, Pallid Cuckoo, Yellow Wattlebird, Crescent Honeyeater, Yellow-throated Honeyeater and Eastern Spinebill.

Narawntapu National Park and surrounds

Narawntapu National Park, formerly known as Asbestos Range National Park, covers 4,300ha and is situated in central-north coast of Tasmania, extending from Port Sorell estuary in the west to Greens Beach near the mouth of River Tamar in the east. The Park stretches from the low coastal ranges to Bass Strait beaches, and includes inlets, small islands, headlands, wetlands, dunes and lagoons, all with an amazing variety of plants and animals. Dubbed the "Serengeti of Tasmania", Narawntapu is one of the best places in Tasmania to view the wildlife. The park boasts a rich array of easily observed animals that come out in the evening to graze on the grasslands. With not much trouble you will see Forester kangaroo, Bennet's wallaby and wombats. You may even catch a glimpse of a Tasmanian devil.

Coastal heathland is the dominant vegetation type in the Park. Dry sclerophyll woodland grows on the hills. Around the North East Arm, you'll find the areas of extensive saltmarshes and tidal mudflats. Bakers Beach dunes are covered with coastal heath and thicket of coastal wattle, herbland in the swales and patches of swamp forest in between the dunes.

Coastal heath of Narawntapu National Park

The main entrance to the Park is located in the western section of the Park (Bakers Beach and Springlawn), 40km east of Devonport. It can be accessed via Frankford Rd (B71), turning north into Bakers Beach Rd (C740) which will take you to the Park entrance and Springlawn. Access to West Head is from Greens Beach via West Tamar Hwy (A7). Turn left into Gardners Rd in Greens Beach and drive 4km to the lookout (signposted). To get to Badger Beach in the central section of the Park, from Launceston take West Tamar Hwy (A7) in the northerly direction. At Beaconsfield, take Greens Beach Rd (C720) and then turn left and follow an unsealed Badger Head Rd (C721).

There are four basic camping areas with toilets, fireplaces and picnic tables in the western section of the Park. Electric barbecues are only in the Springlawn Campground which also has a Visitor Centre, usually manned only in summer. There is also a network of dirt roads and tracks and a boardwalk leading to a bird hide near the lagoon. A basic locality map can be downloaded here: http://www.parks.tas.gov.au/file.aspx?id=19050.

Over 120 species are on the site's birdlist. Ten out of twelve endemic birds are recorded in the Park. The only absentees are Forty-spotted Pardalote and Scrubtit. **Key species** are Painted Button-quail, Musk Duck, Blue-billed Duck, Hooded Plover, Tawny-crowned Honeyeater and Brown Quail. Other birds of interest include Australasian Shoveler, Striated Fieldwren, Olive Whistler, Tasmanian Morepork, Dusky Woodswallow, Eastern Great Egret and White-bellied Sea-Eagle. Rarities include Ground Parrot, Fairy Tern, Dusky Moorhen, Great Crested Grebe, Banded Stilt, Whimbrel and Freckled Duck.

The most important birding area is located in the western section around Springlawn, North East Arm and Bakers Beach.

Banded Lapwings are regularly reported west of Port Sorell and from the paddocks near Bakers Beach along the access road to the Park.

Springlawn Campground and Lagoon

Painted Button-quails are regularly found on Springlawn Tk leading to the bird hide in the northern part of the lagoon. Look for their platelets along the track before the boardwalk over the swamp. Springlawn Tk may also produce Tasmanian Thornbill, Golden Whistler, Grey Fantail, Tasmanian Scrubwren and White-fronted Chat.

Silvereye working on a bush in the Springlawn Campground

On the lawns in front of the Visitor Centre, expect to find Australasian Pipit, Eurasian Skylark, Forest Raven, Yellow-rumped Thornbill, Flame Robin, Cape Barren Goose and large flocks of Tasmanian Native-hens. Blue-winged Parrots are often observed on the lawn. In the campground, Silvereye, Grey Fantail, Green Rosella, Fan-tailed Cuckoo, Dusky Robin, Crescent Honeyeater, Yellow-throated Honeyeater and Little Wattlebird are common. Tasmanian Morepork can be heard at night.

We observed a large flock of 100+ Yellow-tailed Black-Cockatoo flying from the direction of Port Sorell towards Bakers Beach.

The lagoon in the Park supports an abundance of waterfowl. There should be plenty of Black Swans, Australian Shelducks, Chestnut Teals and cormorants (Black-faced Cormorant, Little Pied Cormorant, Great Cormorant and Little Black Cormorant). Musk Duck and Australasian Shoveler breed here and flocks of 6-10 birds are not uncommon. There is also a resident population of Australian Wood Ducks on the lagoon; flocks up to 100 ducks have been recorded. If you are lucky, you may come across Cape Barren Goose, Levin's Rail, Spotless Crake, Freckled Duck, Blue-billed Duck or even Australasian Bittern. All three grebe species have been reported from the lagoon, with Hoary-headed Grebe being sighted most consistently. Waders in the lagoon include Black-fronted Dotterel, Red-capped Plover and occasionally Double-banded Plover in winter and Common Greenshank.

Small flocks of Brown Quails are regularly found in the wet grass near the lagoon and Visitor Centre. In late summer, flocks of White-throated Needletails can be seen flying over Springlawn. In February 2017, 400 birds were counted in a single flock.

A walk through the woodland and scrub behind the dunes may produce sightings of many honeyeater species (Yellow-throated Honeyeater, New Holland Honeyeater, Crescent Honeyeater, Black-headed Honeyeater, Strong-billed Honeyeater, Eastern Spinebill, Little Wattlebird and Yellow Wattlebird), cuckoos in summer (Shining Bronze-Cuckoo, Pallid Cuckoo, Fan-tailed Cuckoo), thornbills (Yellow-rumped Thornbill, Brown Thornbill, Tasmanian Scrubwren), robins (Dusky Robin, Scarlett Robin, Flame Robin), pigeons (Brush Bronzewing, Common Bronzewing), Green Rosella, Golden Whistler, Olive Whistler, Satin Flycatcher and Bassian Thrush.

In the dune vegetation look for Striated Fieldwren, White-fronted Chat and Australasian Pipit. On the beaches accessible from the Springlawn Campground, Hooded Plovers are regularly found. Look also for Australian Pied Oystercatcher, Sooty Oystercatcher, Crested Tern, Silver Gull and Pacific Gull.

Raptors patrolling the lagoon and the surrounding bush include White-bellied Sea-Eagle, Brown Goshawk, Swamp Harrier, Wedge-tailed Eagle and Brown Falcon, with rare records of Peregrine Falcon and Nankeen Kestrel.

Brown Falcon

Bakers Point

It is good to take a walk along the estuary mudflats between the North East Arm and Bakers Point. It is a fantastic place for the shorebirds. Sooty Oystercatchers breed there. Australian Pied Oystercatchers congregate in large numbers; we counted 200 birds. Double-banded Plovers have been recorded in winter in flocks up to 200 birds. Other waders found on the beach include Eastern Curlew, Black-fronted Dotterel, Red-necked Stint, and occasionally an odd Pectoral Sandpiper, Curlew Sandpiper or Pacific Golden Plover.

On the beaches near Bakers Beach, Red-capped Plover and Hooded Plover are breeding. Occasionally, Fairy Terns are found here.

Heathland from Springlawn to Bakers Beach is a good habitat for the elusive Ground Parrot; it is occasionally reported from this area. Finding it is however not guaranteed, in contrary to Tawny-crowned Honeyeater, Crescent Honeyeater and New Holland Honeyeater which are always there. Look also for White-fronted Chat, Striated Fieldwren and Beautiful Firetail in the heathland and marsh vegetation.

Western Section

Masked Owls can be found in the Park, with some good spots near Greens Beach.

Beaches from Greens Beach village to Kelso are known for wintering flocks of Double-banded Plovers.

Northwestern Tasmania

Moorland Beach, Devonport

This beautiful beach is located north of the Devonport Airport. The site includes a variety of habitats such as sandy beaches, rocky points, lagoons, heathland, coastal scrub and grazing paddocks. Pardoe Northdown Conservation Reserve is located at this beach.

To get there, from Mill Rd (C701) in Devonport turn north into Moorland Beach Rd and drive to the beach.

Over 70 species are on the site's birdlist. **Key species** are Ruddy Turnstone, Banded Lapwing and Hooded Plover. Other birds of interest include Musk Duck, Australian Shelduck, Striated Fieldwren, Cattle Egret and Peregrine Falcon. Rarities include Fairy Tern, Pacific Golden Plover and Tasmanian Morepork.

Check the paddocks along Moorland Beach Rd. Banded Lapwings are observed regularly, even breeding here. After the breeding season, small flocks of Banded Lapwings can sometimes be seen on the beach among the other waders. In winter, flocks of Cattle Egrets are reported from the paddocks. Australasian Pipit, Eurasian Skylark, Masked Lapwing, Forest Raven and plenty of Common Starlings are also found there.

Ruddy Turnstones are regularly found on the beach which is home to about 80 bird species often seen roosting at high tide on the strandline. Some Ruddy Turnstones even winter here. A pair of Hooded Plovers regularly attempt to breed at the western end of the beach. Other birds here include Sooty Oystercatcher, Australasian Pied Oystercatcher, Red-capped Plover, Double-banded Plover (in winter), Pacific Gull and Caspian Tern. On rocky points, Black-faced Cormorants and Little Pied Cormorants are often roosting.

The chain of lagoons behind the dunes may produce a wide range of waterbirds such as Musk Duck, Chestnut Teal, Australasian Shoveler, Eastern Great Egret, Hoary-headed Grebe, Australasian Grebe and Black Swan. In the vegetation around the lagoons look for Striated Fieldwren, White-fronted Chat, New Holland Honeyeater and Brown Thornbill.

A pair of White-bellied Sea-Eagles is often seen patrolling this section of the coast. We observed a Peregrine Falcon, consuming a large Masked Lapwing on the ground, being attacked by a group of distraught lapwings and other birds. This created quite a ruckus. This however did not distract the raptor which calmly carried on with feather plucking from its meal.

Lillico Beach Conservation Area

The narrow coastal strip of the Lillico Beach is home to a large colony of Little Penguins. From the viewing platform you can observe these cute creatures returning to their burrows in the evening. Local volunteers and/or Park Rangers are on site in the penguin breeding season (September to May). The site is located 20km west of Devonport, just off Bass Hwy (A2). It is well signposted and a large carpark is provided near the viewing platform.

Little Penguin in its nesting box

During our visit, Swamp Harrier was flying over the coastal strip. On the rocky beach we found Black-faced Cormorant, Sooty Oystercatcher, Australian Pied Oystercatcher and a juvenile Pacific Gull. In the dense shrubbery near the carpark, we found New Holland Honeyeater, Silvereye, Grey Fantail, Superb Fairy-wren and Common Starling.

Other birds recorded here include Kelp Gull, Red-capped Plover, Australian Hobby and Grey Goshawk.

Mountain Valley Wilderness Centre, Loongana

This 61ha "Land for Wildlife" private nature reserve is hidden in the valley of Loongana, 65km southwest of Devonport. This is the eco-style retreat with cosy log cabins built at the foothill of Black Bluff Mountain in a fantastic bushland setting. On offer is plenty of wildlife, both birds and other animals. This reserve is a release site for the rehabilitated wildlife, coming off human care for injured or orphaned animals. You may see here a spotted-tailed quoll or Tasmanian devil out of your cabin window. Wildlife also includes platypus, Tasmanian pademelon, wombats, etc.

Access is restricted to the guests of the Centre and to volunteers. The site is located at 1519 Loongana Rd, Loongana. For bookings and further information see their website at http://mountainvalley.com.au/ or call (03) 6429 1394. To get there, from Bass Hwy (A2) turn south into Castra Rd (B15) near Ulverstone. At Nietta, turn into Loongana Rd (C128). You will have approximately 16km of winding dirt road to the Wilderness Centre.

Over 80 species are on the site's birdlist. **Key species** are Scrubtit, Satin Flycatcher, Strong-billed Honeyeater and Grey Goshawk. Other birds of interest include Pink Robin, Olive Whistler, Bassian Thrush, Black Currawong, Australian Owlet-nightjar, Masked Owl and Wedge-tailed Eagle.

The site offers exciting possibilities for spotlighting. Apart from Australian Owlet-nightjar and Masked Owl mentioned above, you may get Tasmanian Morepork and Tawny Frogmouth. As most of the marsupials are nocturnal, they can be discovered in the spotlights, too.

All but one Tasmanian endemics can be found here with the relative ease. The odd one out is Forty-spotted Pardalote. Grey Goshawk is resident in the area, often seen close to the release aviary, attempting to steal some food out of the captive birds' plate.

Other birds recorded here include Brush Bronzewing, Common Bronzewing, Beautiful Firetail, Satin Flycatcher, Striated Fieldwren, Grey Currawong, Crescent Honeyeater and Grey Butcherbird.

Mole Creek Karst National Park

Mole Creek is a small National Park located on the slopes of Great Western Tiers in northwest Tasmania, about 60km south of Devonport. It protects internationally significant karst geological system. The word 'karst' is a Slovenic term for a landscape shaped by erosion of limestone by acidic water. Caves and sinkholes are the main feature of this system.

More than 300 caves, underground creeks and sinkholes have been found in the Mole Creek Karst Park. Majority of them are not open to public but two, King Salomon Cave and Marakoopa Cave, are the major Tasmanian tourist attractions. Marakoopa Cave boasts the largest glow-worm display in Australia.

The Park comprises twelve separate blocks of land, surrounded mostly by farmland but also by some forest and bushland. Almost all of the Park is covered with open forest dominated with stringybark, swamp gum, manna gum, black peppermint and silver acacia. There are also small areas of rainforest in damp gullies, where beech myrtle, sassafras and tree ferns reign.

From Launceston or Devonport get to Deloraine via Bass Hwy (1). From Deloraine it is a 45min drive to the Park. First, take Mole Creek Rd (B12) and about 4km past the Mole Creek township turn let to the Marakoopa Cave. For the King Salomon Cave, continue on Mole Creek Rd for another 11km. Day use facilities at both sites include electric barbecues, shelters, picnic areas and walking tracks. No camping is allowed. A basic map of the area can be downloaded here: http://www.parks.tas.gov.au/file.aspx?id=19046.

Over 60 species are on the site's birdlist. **Key species** are Scrubtit, Pink Robin and Grey Goshawk. Other birds of interest include Cape Barren Goose, Dusky Moorhen, Green Rosella, Tasmanian Morepork, Masked Owl and Tasmanian Scrubwren.

Pink Robins are common and tame around the Marakoopa Cave. A pair of White-bellied Sea-Eagles can often be seen in this area. Other birds here include Shining Bronze-cuckoo, Scarlet Robin, Dusky Robin, Tasmanian Thornbill, Yellow-throated Honeyeater, Tree Martin, Yellow-tailed Black-Cockatoo and Green Rosella. A small wetland in the Marakoopa Cave block may produce Australian Shelduck, Hardhead, Hoary-headed Grebe, Dusky Moorhen, Black Swan and Purple Swamphen.

Burnie

Burnie is a large coastal town located in northwestern Tasmania. In the 1980' it was an important industrial hub, full of smoke stacks and pollution. Most of the heavy industry since died so the town needed to reinvent itself. Now it is known for restoring and protecting natural habitats. The only industries left are agriculture with a couple of boutique cheese-making factories, forestry and a large harbour. The town can now offer several wonderful wildlife-watching opportunities, especially the Little Penguin Observation Centre and a viewing platform for the platypus in the Fern Glade Reserve. Swift Parrots are regularly observed in town, particularly when they are returning to Tasmania from the mainland in September.

Fern Glade Reserve

The peaceful Emu River valley is Burnie's most valuable natural asset. The Reserve is located along Emu River in South Burnie just 4km from the city centre. The main attraction of the reserve is the platypus; with luck you'll see it from the viewing platform.

Access is from Bass Hwy (A3). If driving in westerly direction, pass the Emu River bridge and turn left into Massy-Greene Dr (C112) at the lights. Soon turn sharp left into Fern Glade Rd leading to fern Glade Reserve. There is another entry to the reserve from Old Surrey Rd (C112), turning into Wattle Av and then right to Fern Glade Dr. Site facilities include a carpark, viewing platform, picnic area, fireplaces (bring your own firewood) and long walking tracks along the Emu River.

About 80 species are on the Reserve's birdlist. **Key species** are White-bellied Sea-Eagle, Dusky Robin, Beautiful Firetail, Bassian Thrush and Scrubtit (rare). Other birds of interest include Masked Owl, Australian Owlet-nightjar, Pink Robin, Olive Whistler, Satin Flycatcher, Dusky Woodswallow and Strong-billed Honeyeater. Rarities here include Tawny-crowned Honeyeater, Dusky Moorhen, Eastern Rosella and Grey Goshawk.

The Reserve is an easily accessible birding spot for Beautiful Firetail and Dusky Robin; they are common here. Look for Tawny Frogmouth roosting in a tree near the carpark. In this area there are also Pink Robins, Brush Bronzewings and Dusky Woodswallows.

Tasmanian Native-hens are plentiful, often running before you on a walking track. Honeyeaters are plentiful in the bush, including Crescent Honeyeater, Yellow-throated Honeyeater, Black-headed Honeyeater, Eastern Spinebill and Yellow Wattlebird. All four cuckoos occurring in Tasmania can be found here. We observed a Horsfield's Bronze-cuckoo chick being fed by Tasmanian Scrubwren near the viewing platform.

Common in the river are Hoary-headed Grebe, Chestnut Teal, Australian Wood Duck and Great Cormorant.

A pair of White-bellied Sea-Eagles can often be observed flying over the Reserve. Look also for Collared Sparrowhawk, Brown Falcon and Wedge-tailed Eagle.

Romaine Reserve

This large recreational reserve is located in South Burnie along the Romaine Creek. The site is part of the walkways and boardwalks that circumnavigate Burnie. Vegetation includes both native and exotic trees and is dominated by mountain ash and manna gum with the understory of blackwood and tree ferns.

To get there, turn south off Bass Hwy (A3) into Reeves St which changes name to Collins St, then to Roslyn Av. Take a left on the roundabout into Blackwood Pde and finally turn left into Amanda Ct which will lead you to the Reserve's carpark. A fitness track runs around the dam.

The Reserve is very good for parrots as it offers plenty of hollows in the old trees. Yellow-tailed Black-Cockatoo, Galah and Green Rosella are common. Swift Parrots are regularly seen and even breed here. We observed a pair of Rainbow Lorikeets investigating the hollows, so probably breeding in the Reserve, too.

On the ground look for Scarlet Robin, Forest Raven and Grey Butcherbird. Bush birds here include Shining Bronze-Cuckoo, Golden Whistler, Satin Flycatcher and a great selection of honeyeaters. Black-Headed Honeyeater, Yellow-throated Honeyeater and Little Wattlebird are regularly recorded.

On the water expect to see Hardhead, Chestnut Teal, Australian Wood Duck, Hoary-headed Grebe, Australasian Grebe and Northern Mallard (pure-breed). Black Swans nest on the dam.

We observed a large flock (50+) of White-throated Needletails flying high with Welcome Swallows over the Reserve.

Little Penguin Observation Centre

The Centre is located at Parsonage Point next to West Beach. To get there, from Bass Hwy (A3) turn north at the lights into an unnamed street next to the West Park Oval, leading into a large carpark. A picnic area is provided near the Surf Club and another in Burnie Park on the land side of Bass Hwy.

The Centre is in the right-hand corner of the carpark, near the beach. From the carpark you can get to the viewing platform on the beach. The area of bush and beach where penguins are nesting is fenced off. To see the penguins, visit the Centre about an hour after sunset, use the viewing platform and walk along the fence. Remain very quiet and do not use a torch or flash. The area is not very dark due to the street lamps around.

Little Penguin colony in Burnie

To see the shorebirds, visit the West Beach located to the east of the Little Penguin Observation Centre. Look for Australian Pied Oystercatcher, Sooty Oystercatcher, Red-capped Plover, Pacific Gull, Crested Tern and White-bellied Sea-Eagle. In winter, Double-banded Plover appears here. Seabirds that can be observed from the shore include Australasian Gannet, Short-tailed Shearwater and Shy Albatross. We found Black-faced Cormorants nesting on the pier in the harbour. A group of Pacific Gulls were standing on top of a woodchip pile ready for shipping.

Burnie Regional Hospital Grounds

Access is from Bass Hwy (A3), turning south into Brickport Rd. Swift Parrots visit the hospital grounds every year in spring and summer, you can find them in the stands of flowering Tasmanian blue gums. You can also find here Green Rosella, Galah, Yellow Wattlebird and Australian Hobby.

Wynyard

Wynyard is a relaxed coastal town, famous for its flat-topped Table Cape and fields of stunning tulips flowering in spring. It is located on the northwest coast Tasmania, 70km west of Burnie. A good range of birding opportunities can be found here, particularly along the shoreline and Inglis River. A good initiative in this city is a free (donation-based) Wynyard Little Penguin tour, greatly appreciated by the birdwatchers and tourists alike. Contact Keith at 0417 153244 or by email at wyneardpenguins@hotmail.com; bookings are essential.

Inglis River Walking Track

This well-signposted 6km one-way walk follows closely the forested banks of Inglis River in Wynyard. The track runs between the Table Cape Bridge and a pedestrian crossing below the Bass Hwy Bridge. It is best to start from the Table Cape Bridge parking area off Saunders St (C234) where Table Cape Bridge Reserve is located.

Follow the track through a forest dominated by the Tasmanian blue gums until you reach the Big Creek Bridge. Past that bridge you enter the 16ha York Street Reserve. The reserve features an old eucalypt forest with plenty of hollows with the understory of tea trees, paperbarks, Boronia, bushpeas, etc. The Reserve can be accessed directly from York St where a carpark is provided. A circular walking track runs through the site.

Past the York Street Reserve, the last leg of Inglis River Walking Tk runs through extensive pastures with only a narrow belt of trees lining the river bed. You can come back to your car walking along River Rd on the other side of the river.

Over 80 bird species have been recorded along this track. **Key species** is Azure Kingfisher – this is the best place to see this bird in Tasmania. Other notable species include Grey Goshawk, Satin Flycatcher, Swift Parrot, Eastern Great Egret, Dusky Robin and a variety of honeyeaters. Among the rarities are Forest Kingfisher and Sacred Kingfisher.

Look for Azure Kingfisher along the entire distance but the best place to find it is at the Table Cape Bridge Reserve where the birds are often seen catching crabs at low tide. Other good spots are near the footbridge across the Big Creek and about 700m downstream the Bass Hwy Bridge. The rare vagrants, Forest Kingfisher and Sacred Kingfisher, have also been found here in similar environments.

Easter Great Egret is often spotted at the river banks around the Table Cape Bridge.

The most common birds along the Inglis River Walking Tk are, as nearly everywhere else in Tasmania, Common Blackbirds. You may also come across Tasmanian Native-hen, Grey Butcherbird, Green Rosella, Scarlet Robin, Shining Bronze-Cuckoo, Pallid Cuckoo, Tree Martin, Collared Sparrowhawk and Australian Hobby.

Platypus is known to inhabit the river so keep an eye on the water for its V-shaped trail.

The best place for bush birds is the York Street Reserve. We encountered several birds on the nests or feeding their young. Among them were Golden Whistler, Satin Flycatcher and Grey Shrike-thrush. Parrots such as Sulphur-crested Cockatoos and Galahs were investigating the hollows or already breeding in them. Spotted Pardalotes were nesting in the banks of Big Creek near the footbridge.

Brush Bronzewing was walking in front of us on the track. Brown Thornbills were extremely common everywhere in the Reserve. Other birds in the York Street Reserve included Crescent Honeyeater, Yellow-throated Honeyeater, Black-headed Honeyeater, Dusky Woodswallow, Tasmanian Scrubwren and Grey Fantail. Look also for Grey Goshawks; a pair has been nesting in this reserve for ages. Swift Parrots are regular visitors to the Reserve in summer.

Camp Creek Mouth

The mouth of Camp Creek is another good birding spot in Wynyard. It can be accessed from Old Bass Hwy (C240) in Wynyard. You'll find walking and cycling tracks on both sides of the creek.

About 50 species are on the site's birdlist. **Key species** are Latham's Snipe, Eastern Great Egret, Nankeen Night-Heron and Australian Pelican. Other birds of interest include Tasmanian Native-hen, Hoary-headed Grebe, Chestnut Teal, Black-headed Honeyeater and Musk Lorikeet. Occasionally, Royal Spoonbill is recorded.

An old hospital site near a creek is a good place for birds. Latham's Snipes are regularly found there and Nankeen Night-Herons often roost in trees by the water. Eastern Great Egret and sometimes Royal Spoonbill can be found under the road bridge.

Bush birds around this site include Yellow-throated Honeyeater, New Holland Honeyeater, Little Wattlebird, Golden Whistler, Scarlet Robin and Yellow-tailed Black-Cockatoo.

Wynyard Shoreline

The coast along Old Bass Hwy (B240) east of Camp Creek to Bruce's Café is worth checking. This area is very good for Double-banded Plover, arriving here regularly in winter, with a few birds occasionally staying over for the summer.

Common birds on the beach include Red-capped Plover, Sooty Oystercatcher, Australian Pied Oystercatcher, Pacific Gull and Crested Tern. There are sporadic records of Fairy Tern, Whimbrel and Red Knot. On the rocks along the coast you'll find plenty of Black Cormorants, they nest on the old port wall.

Other birds in the area include Tasmanian Native-hen, Red-necked Stint and White-bellied Sea-Eagle.

Flowerdale

The small locality of Flowerdale is situated a few kilometres west of Wynyard. Flowerdale River is meandering through the pastures. For birdwatchers, the most interesting site is a large dam near the Flowerdale River.

Wedge-tailed Eagle, a dark morph Tasmanian subspecies

To get there from Wynyard, drive west on Bass Hwy (A3) and turn left into Flowerdale Rd (C229). On Google Maps this road is called Preolenna Rd. The dam is on the right about 1km from the turnoff from Bass Hwy. This easy to find dam is an excellent birding site. You'll find here a wide range of waterbirds and the resident Wedge-tailed Eagles. When we arrived, three of them were perched on a lone pine tree on a nearby hill. They later started to fly which startled all waterfowl into the air. These were mostly Australian Shelducks, Musk Lapwings, Pacific Black Ducks and Chestnut Teals. Only a few Freckled Ducks stayed calmly on the water.

Black Swans and small flocks of Cape Barren Geese were grazing on the pasture. We also recorded Tasmanian Native-hen, Eurasian Skylark, White-faced Heron, Forest Raven, Black Currawong and Brown Falcon. There were plenty of introduced finches around.

We flushed a couple of Blue-winged Parrots from the road verge. A single Dusky Moorhen (a rarity in western Tasmania) was on a small pond near the main road.

In winter, a large flock of Cattle Egrets (up to 250 birds) takes residence in this area for a few months. Other rare birds recorded here include Royal Spoonbill and Blue-billed Duck.

Rocky Cape National Park

This small, 3,060ha Park is located on the northwest coast of Tasmania half way between Wynyard and Stanley. You'll find here fantastic views across the Bass Strait, spectacular wildflower displays in spring and sheltered picturesque beaches. Vegetation here is hardy, windswept and salt-resistant, mostly coastal heath. The long spikes of grass trees protrude out of the sea of heath everywhere.

The Park is located 2hr drive west of Launceston along Bass Hwy (A2). It can be accessed in two ways:
- The main entrance in the west can be reached by turning into Rocky Cape Rd (C227), 2.5km west of the Rocky Cape township. After 3km, turn right to the Burgess Cove boat ramp or take second right to the Rocky Cape Lighthouse and a walking track to the North Cave.
- Eastern section is accessible via Port Rd (C232) 12km west of Wynyard. After 1.5km veer left to Sisters Beach Rd (C233). On your way you will pass the eastern entrance to Postmans Tk on your right and to Lake Llewellyn on your left. Sisters Beach Rd ends in the Sisters Beach village. At the end of the road you'll find walking tracks leading into the National Park.

The tracks in the Rocky Cape National Park intertwine so you may choose a short walk or a 25km trek throughout the whole Park. Facilities in the Park include a picnic area with fireplaces at Mary Ann Cove. There is also a picnic area at Sisters Beach with electric barbecues and drinking water. Camping is not allowed in the Park but a variety of accommodation is available in Sisters Beach, Rocky Cape and Wynyard. The Rocky Cape brochure with a basic locality map can be downloaded here: http://www.parks.tas.gov.au/file.aspx?id=19051.

Over 90 species are on the Park's birdlist. **Key species** are Ground Parrot, Painted Button-quail, Brown Quail and Hooded Plover. Other birds of interest include Scrubtit, Tasmanian Scrubwren, Tasmanian Thornbill, Southern Emu-wren, Beautiful Firetail, Black-headed Honeyeater, Bassian Thrush and Peregrine Falcon. Among the rarities are Spotted Quail-thrush and Swift Parrot.

Ground Parrots are resident in the Park but these elusive birds seldom flush from the heath. They reside in the central section of the Park where the walking tracks are scarce so access is difficult.

Postmans Track

The eastern entrance to Postmans Tk is from Sisters Beach Rd (C233) on your way to the Park and the western entrance is in Sisters Beach. In the heath along the track look for Southern Emu-wren, Beautiful Firetail and Superb Fairy-wren. You may also come across Crescent Honeyeater, Yellow-throated Honeyeater, New Holland Honeyeater and Little Wattlebird. At the western entrance to the track (near the township) look for Brown Quails that come out from the heath to forage on the lawns. At the carpark near the eastern entrance, Spotted Quail-thrush was recorded several times.

Other birds along Postmans Tk include Satin Flycatcher, Bassian Thrush, Scarlet Robin, Dusky Robin, Blue-winged Parrot, Golden Whistler and Tasmanian Thornbill.

Lake Llewellyn

As you enter the Park, turn left from Sisters Beach Rd (C233) into the short Tink Taylor Av. Looking from this street onto the lake, we got a single Blue-billed Duck and a couple of Australian Shelducks and Pacific Black Ducks. White-faced Heron had a huge nest with two chicks in a tree by one of the houses. On the forest track at the end of the street were Pink Robin, Scrubtit, Dusky Robin, Green Rosella, Yellow-throated Honeyeater, Golden Whistler and eight Yellow-tailed Black-Cockatoos.

White-faced Heron at Lake Llewellyn, taking a break from its parental duties

Rocky Cape Road

About 1.5km into this road check a large farm dam on your left. It was drying up during our visit. On the water were a couple of Chestnut Teals, Great Cormorant and White-faced Heron. In the dead vegetation on the mudflats were Black-fronted Dotterels, White-fronted Chats and Australasian Pipits. Latham Snipe flushed from the edge of the dam. Peregrine Falcon was flying over the area.

Sisters Beach

This quaint, pretty village is surrounded by the magnificent Rocky Cape National Park from three sides and the Bass Strait beaches from the north. It is located 15min drive west of Wynyard in the Tasmanian northwest coast. The unique feature of this place is the prevalence of old man banksia (*Banksia serrata*). In Tasmania, this species grows only in the open woodland and sedgeland around Sisters Hills. The village boasts the very old, giant trees. Sisters Beach is known for unusual, rare bird sightings.

Access is via Port Rd (C232) 12km west of Wynyard. After 1.5km veer left to Sisters Beach Rd (C233). Sisters Beach Rd ends in the Sisters Beach village (no through road, you go back the same way you came in). Facilities include a picnic area with electric barbecues and drinking water and a variety of accommodation in the village. There is a foot bridge over the creek and a short walking path to a cave.

Footbridge at Sisters Beach where Azure Kingfisher is often found

Over 70 species are on the Sisters Bach birdlist. **Key species** are Azure Kingfisher and Hooded Plover. Other birds of interest include White-throated Needletail, Scarlet Robin, Dusky Robin, Green Rosella, Tasmanian Scrubwren, Yellow-throated Honeyeater, Crescent Honeyeater, Australian Owlet-nightjar and Masked Owl. Among the rare birds are White-necked Heron, Stubble Quail, Nankeen Night-Heron, Rainbow Lorikeet and Swift Parrot.

Azure Kingfishers are regularly recorded hunting in the area near the foot bridge. This is where we saw two of them, too. On the beach were a couple of Hooded Plovers, Australian Pied Oystercatchers, Sooty Oystercatchers and Pacific Gulls. A pair of White-bellied sea-Eagles were flying over the waves. Common Greenfinches were foraging among the debris on the beach.

Female Superb Fairy-wren at a picnic site in Sisters Beach

Banksias were flowering profusely at a picnic site by the beach, attracting masses of honeyeaters including Yellow-throated Honeyeater, New Holland Honeyeater, Crescent Honeyeater, Black-headed Honeyeater, Eastern Spinebill and Little Wattlebird. In the bush along the creek we found Brush Bronzewing, Scarlet Robin, Dusky Robin, Black Currawong, Golden Whistler, Pallid Cuckoo and Superb Fairy-wren. Tasmanian Native-hens are often seen walking through the village.

In summer, flocks of White-throated Needletails make a regular appearance in the village, often flying with Tree Martins. In bad weather, seabirds may come close to the shore. Look for Shy Albatross, Short-tailed Shearwater and Brown Skua.

Crayfish Creek

The Crayfish Creek mouth is a fantastic birding spot, especially if you stay in Crayfish Creek Tourist Park. The cabins and caravan sites are scattered in dense bushland along the creek mouth. The area is teeming with birds and other wildlife. The site is located along Bass Hwy (A2) just east of Port Latta, 40 km west of Wynyard and 25km east of Stanley. The coordinates for the tourist park are 40.51.28 E and 145.23.55 S.

When we stayed there, Masked Owl and Tasmanian Morepork were calling through the night. A white spot clearly visible in one of the dead trees in the camp proved to be Grey Goshawk. The most common honeyeaters were Yellow-throated Honeyeaters; these were everywhere. Tame Pink Robins and Dusky Robins perched along the driveways to caravan sites. Green Rosellas were plentiful. Yellow-tailed Black-Cockatoos landed with the big noise to roost on the opposite side of the creek.

The abundance of small bush birds included Brown Thornbill, Tasmanian Scrubwren, Silvereye and Grey Fantail. We also saw Brush Bronzewing, Golden Whistler, Eastern Spinebill, New Holland Honeyeater, Brown Goshawk, Laughing Kookaburra and Grey Currawong.

In the mouth of the creek on the beach on the other side of Bass Hwy were Australian Pied Oystercatcher, Pacific Gull, Crested Tern and a group of Little Penguins in the water. White-bellied Sea-Eagle was circling over the shore.

Yellow-throated Honeyeater

Stanley and The Nut

The beautiful historic township of Stanley is located on the far northwest coast of Tasmania, on the large cape called The Nut. The massif of The Nut is the most significant landmark in all of the northwest coast of Tasmania. This huge rock is the plug of an extinct volcano which stands 134m tall and has steep sides with a flat top. To reach the top you may either walk which takes around 15min or get there the easy way - by the chairlift.

The Nut State Reserve is established on the plateau, featuring a 2.3km walk circular walk by the edge, taking around 45min. The views form the top are simply breathtaking. Before, the Reserve was hopelessly overgrown by gorse but thanks to the huge efforts the gorse got under control. The habitats include large areas of tall grassland and patches of lush planted bushland in sheltered spots. The Nut Reserve protects the nationally endangered straw daisy and provides an important breeding site for 15,000 pairs of Short-tailed Shearwaters (mutton birds) as well as Peregrine Falcon and Nankeen Kestrel.

The characteristic silhouette of The Nut dominates the Stanley landscape

To get there from Launceston, take a scenic route west on Bass Highway (National 1 changing into A2) along the northern coast. About 18km west of Crayfish Creek you will get to a large intersection where you turn north onto Stanley Hwy (B21). To get to the chairlift when you reach the town, turn left into Marshall St from Church St, then right into Browns Rd which will take you to the carpark and café at the Chairlift station. The

chairlift operates 7 days per week from 9:30am to 5pm but it's closed from late June to late August. A site map can be downloaded here:
http://www.circularhead.tas.gov.au/webdata/resources/files/map4.pdf.

Over 80 bird species have been recorded in the Stanley area. **Key species** are Little Penguin, Short-tailed Shearwater, Peregrine Falcon and Nankeen Kestrel. Other birds of interest include Hooded Plover, Striated Fieldwren, Crescent Honeyeater, Dusky Woodswallow, Tasmanian Scrubwren, Grey Fantail and Silvereye. Occasionally, the rare Orange-bellied Parrots utilise The Nut as a launching or landing pad for their trip to or from the mainland.

Little Penguin Colony

The colony is situated on the western slopes of The Nut. Penguins come in the evening onto Godfreys Beach. From Church St turn into Harrison Tce and get to Kings Park. Go through the gate to the colony and wait until dark on a path at the bottom of the cliff to see the penguins coming ashore. Dress warm. No flashlights are allowed unless you have a red filter.

During the day, on Godfreys Beach you can find Australian Pied Oystercatcher, Sooty Oystercatcher, Pacific Gull, Black-faced Cormorant and Red-capped Plover.

The Nut State Reserve

Common Starling on top of the Chairlift Station's antenna on The Nut.

Birdwatching started for us at the chairlift station where we found plenty of introduced birds such as Common Starling, Common Blackbird, European Goldfinch and Common Greenfinch. Common Starling was singing his heart out from an antenna on the Chairlift Station. He was mimicking other bird calls in his song and we were able to recognise the voices of Sulphur-crested Cockatoo, European Goldfinch, Australian Pied Oystercatcher and Yellow-tailed Black-Cockatoo.

Grey Shrike-thrushes were calling loudly as we were riding to the top in the chairlift. In the grass and weeds on the plateau we observed Tasmanian Scrubwren, Superb Fairy-wren, New Holland Honeyeater, Grey Fantail and Australasian Pipit. Striated Fieldwren is common in the heath; we saw one calling from the gorse.

Good numbers of honeyeaters hanged out in the planted bushland including Crescent Honeyeater, New Holland Honeyeater, Yellow-throated Honeyeater and Eastern Spinebill. In the same habitat we also found Dusky Woodswallow and Pallid Cuckoo.

The Nut is a very important staging point for the migratory birds on their departure and return to Tasmania. In autumn in particular, large numbers of Grey Fantails, Silvereyes, Dusky Woodswallows, Welcome Swallows, Black Cuckoo-shrikes, etc. gather here before crossing the Straits.

Weeds are growing rapaciously in the well-fertilized soil of a shearwater colony on The Nut

Such a massive bird get-together is a magnet for raptors. We saw seven raptor species around The Nut and the township. A pair of White-bellied Sea-Eagles were soaring on the uplift air. Swamp Harrier had a nest in the tall weeds in the shearwater colony. Nankeen Kestrel, the rarest bird of prey in Tasmania, was hovering over the plateau. Peregrine Falcon, regularly nesting on the eastern cliffs of The Nut, was hunting over the harbour. Wedge-tailed Eagle, Brown Falcon and Australian Hobby were flying over the Highfield Historic Site and the sewage lagoons.

If you stay on the plateau until dark between September and March, you will witness the spectacle of Short-tailed Shearwaters returning noisily in massive numbers to their burrows. During the day, you may see other seabirds from the plateau such as Australasian Gannet, Shy Albatross, Black-browed Albatross and various cormorants, including Black-faced Cormorant.

Sewage Lagoons

Sewage Lagoons are located along Godfreys Beach on Green Hills Rd north of town. Birds to be found there include Hardhead, Australasian Shoveler, Chestnut Teal, Australian Shelduck, Australasian Grebe (occasionally) and Hoary-headed Grebe.

Along the access road look for Tasmanian Native-hen, Purple Swamphen, Eurasian Skylark and Australasian Pipit.

West Inlet

The site is accessed via West Inlet Tk (not signposted). Look for it on the left a few kilometres before reaching Stanley.

This is a good water spot. Hooded Plovers breed there. Australian Pied Oystercatchers form post-breeding flocks of up to 100 birds. Double-banded Plover is frequently found here in winter. Other birds include Red-capped Plover, Sooty Oystercatcher and Eastern Curlew (very rare).

Smithton

Smithton is a small coastal town located on Bass Hwy (A2) in the far-northwest corner of Tasmania in the mouth of Duck River. The distance to Burnie is 85km. The rich green farmland surrounding the town brings life and prosperity to it. The town is the last stop for the travellers to Arthur River and the Tarkine Wilderness.

Several good birding areas are scattered around the town including the sewage ponds and the mouth of Duck River. Over 70 bird species have been recorded. The **key species** is Latham's Snipe. Other birds of interest include White-fronted Chat, Eastern Great Egret, Black-fronted Dotterel, Australian Pelican, Yellow-throated Honeyeater and Brown Falcon. Several rare species have been reported from the area including Orange-bellied Parrot, Swift Parrot, Galah, Straw-necked Ibis, Azure Kingfisher, Royal Spoonbill, Blue-billed Duck and Pink-eared Duck.

Azure Kingfisher is occasionally found around Duck River. The best place is 1km upstream of Watsons Corner.

Duck River Boardwalk

This is a well-known Latham's Snipe's roosting site. Up to 100 birds have been counted during the season.

To get there, from Bass Hwy (A2) turn north onto Nelson St (C215) and drive to the junction with Key St where you'll find Rotaract Park with mudflats and boardwalk over the saltmarshes. These saltmarshes are the favourite roost of Latham's Snipes.

In the flowering gums in the Rotaract Park we found Little Wattlebird, Black-headed Honeyeater, New Holland Honeyeater and Yellow-throated Honeyeater as well as Green Rosella, Pallid Cuckoo and Brown Falcon.

Swift Parrots were reported from this site several times.

In the saltmarshes we found a couple of Latham's Snipes but the show was stolen by hundreds of White-fronted Chats in the samphire. They let us to get close enough to them for a photo. In April 2017, a few Orange-bellied Parrots were found here in the samphire. Pacific Golden Plover is occasionally reported.

A male White-fronted Chat in the Rotaract Park saltmarsh

On the Duck River mudflats, we found Chestnut Teals, White-faced Herons and Pacific Gulls. A couple of Eastern Great Egrets were standing on the other side of the river. This is a good place for migratory waders such as Red-necked Stint, Curlew Sandpiper and sometimes Sharp-tailed Sandpiper and Ruddy Turnstone.

Smithton Sewage Ponds

To get there, after crossing over the Duck River bridge on Smith St (C215) in the westerly direction turn immediately right into West Esplanade and then go onto a dirt track called Pelican Ln. At a T-junction turn right into Pelican Point Rd. Drive to the end of the road and scan the ponds from the outside.

To pond came to the birdwatchers' attention after several rarities were found there including Blue-billed Duck, Pink-eared Duck, Royal Spoonbill and Straw-necked Ibis.

When driving to the site among the paddocks we found plenty Eurasian Skylarks, Australasian Pipits, Tasmanian Native-hens, Purple Swamphens, Kelp Gulls, Flame Robins and hundreds of Goldfinches and Greenfinches.

European Goldfinches on an old farm fence

One of the sewage ponds was drying out and featured ten Black-fronted Dotterels, two Red-capped Plovers and two Curlew Sandpipers. In the weeds surrounding that pond we found White-fronted Chats.

On the ponds with water were hundreds of Australian Shelducks and small numbers of Grey Teals, Chestnut Teals, Australian Wood Ducks and Black Swans. Swamp Harrier was flying over the area.

Tarkine Forest Adventure

This 640has adventure park, also known as Dismal Swamp, is located at the northern edge of the Tarkine Wilderness. It is situated along Bass Hwy (A2) 20min west of Smithton. The swamp has formed in a giant sinkhole. Visitor Centre is located at the edge of the sinkhole. You can take 110m high slide to the sinkhole or, more sedately, take a steep 360m-long walk. A 1.2km boardwalk runs among the thousand year old giant trees and the tree ferns at the bottom of the hole.

The operation is closed in winter. For the opening times and further information visit the website at http://dismalswamptasmania.com.au/.

The site is known for its wide variety of rainforest bird species such as Bassian Thrush, Pink Robin, Scrubtit and Tasmanian Thornbill.

On arrival, you'll be greeted by the colourful robins such as Pink, Flame and Scarlet Robin which perch among the tree ferns scattered between the carpark and Visitor Centre. Masked Owl is often heard calling from the swamp at night. Other birds in the area include Dusky Robin, Golden Whistler, Green Rosella, Grey Fantail, Crescent Honeyeater, Tasmanian Morepork and Grey Goshawk.

Marrawah Area

Marrawah is a small rural town located in the northwest corner of Tasmania with access to very good surfing beaches.

Key species are Hooded Plover and Banded Lapwing. Other birds of interest include White-fronted Chat, Australasian Shoveler, Hoary-headed Grebe, Striated Fieldwren and Brown Falcon. White-necked Heron is the only rarity, found in April 2016 on a flooded paddock a few kilometres east of Marrawah.

The farmland around Marrawah is good for raptors. Brown Falcon, Wedge-tailed Eagle, White-bellied Sea-Eagle, Brown Goshawk and Grey Goshawk have been recorded.

Green Point Campground

The site is located on the coast a few kilometres west of town. From Bass Hwy (A2) take Comeback Rd (C213) to Marrawah, then turn west into Green Point Rd to get to the campground.

The beach near the campground is good for the waders, particularly for Hooded Plover and Ruddy Turnstone. Other shorebirds there include Red-capped Plover, Sooty Oystercatcher, Australian Pied Oystercatcher, Caspian Tern, Crested Tern and Pacific Gull. Seabirds visible from the shore include Short-tailed Shearwater, Shy Albatross and Black-faced Cormorant.

In the surrounding heath look for Striated Fieldwren, White-fronted Chat and Superb Fairy-wren. On the farmland along the road, Australasian Pipit, Eurasian Skylark, Forest Raven and Brown Falcon can be found.

Green Point Lagoon

This large lagoon is located about 1km past the Green Point Campground along Green Point Rd. Banded Lapwings are resident on the paddocks around the lagoon.

Waterbirds on the lagoon include Black Swan, Hardhead, Australian Shelduck, Australasian Shoveler, Chestnut Teal, Hoary-headed Grebe, Great Cormorant and Black-fronted Dotterel.

A pair of Australian Shelducks

West Point State Reserve

This is a small coastal reserve with beautiful beaches and coastal heath behind the dunes. It is located north of Arthur River and south of Marrawah. Turn off Arthur River Rd (C214) to West Point Rd, an awful dirt track that will get you to the Reserve. Site coordinates are 40.56.39 S and 144.37.04 E.

This site is suitable for the observation of seabirds and shorebirds. Hooded Plovers regularly breed there. Other waders in the area include Ruddy Turnstone, Red-capped Plover, Sooty Oystercatcher and Australian Pied Oystercatcher. Among the seabirds you'll usually find large numbers of Short-tailed Shearwaters coming back to their burrows along the shore. There should also be some Shy Albatrosses, Australasian Gannets, Pacific Gulls and Black-faced Cormorants.

Birds in the heath and surrounding paddocks include White-fronted Chat, Crescent Honeyeater, Swamp Harrier, Australasian Pipit, Forest Raven and Brown Falcon.

Arthur River Area

The tiny (population 25) coastal township of Arthur River is located in the northwestern corner of Tasmania at the mouth of Arthur River about 2hr drive (150km) from Burnie. It is surrounded by the lush rainforest and serves as a base for the exploration of Tarkine Wilderness, the Tasmania's largest expanse of temperate rainforest. On the southern side of the Arthur River mouth you'll find a plaque claiming that this is the 'edge of the world'. It truly feels like it.

To get there drive on Bass Hwy (A2) to Marrawah where you turn left into Arthur River Rd (C214).

The coastline is gorgeous and remote. Because it lies within the violent grasp of the Roaring Forties, the winds and the weather here can make quite an impression on an unsuspecting visitor.

The heavily tannin-stained waters of Arthur River run completely wild; this is the only river in Tasmania that is not dammed. The best way to explore the river is to take a cruise or you can hire a boat or a kayak.

A network of shorter and longer tracks run on both sides of the river. You'll find here picnic sites with barbecues. Accommodation ranges from good campsites to holiday houses. There are three campgrounds: Manuka, Peppermint and Prickly Wattle. Meals are available in the Tavern. The area is heaven for the 4-wheel drivers with a choice of tough 4WD tracks around.

Over 70 bird species have been found in the area. **Key species** are Azure Kingfisher, Hooded Plover, Southern Emu-wren and Tawny-crowned Honeyeater. Other birds of interest include Brown Quail, White-throated Needletail, Striated Fieldwren, Beautiful Firetail, White-bellied Sea-Eagle and Grey Goshawk.

Birdwatchers come here to look for the endangered Tasmanian form of Azure Kingfisher. The easiest way to get this bird is to take one of the river cruises (for details see http://www.arthurrivercruises.com.au/) and travel a few kilometres upstream. The birds can be found in the small inlets and channels along the northern banks of the river. Another good place is a series of small waterfalls and the tracks leading to them – most cruises stop there so you can venture out on a quick walk. Travelling on foot, you may get a glimpse of the birds from the bridge over the river.

The most visible bird on a river cruise is usually White-bellied Sea-Eagle. The birds breed along the river. Other birds noticeable on a cruise include Green Rosella, Black Currawong, White-faced Heron, Nanking Night-Heron (occasionally) and Grey Goshawk.

Black Currawong

A beach 500m north of Arthur River estuary is good for Hooded Plover, Red-capped Plover and Double-banded Plover (in winter).

Gardiner Point

Gardiner Point and the Edge of the World are located at the southern bank of Arthur River. To get there, from Temma Rd (C214) turn into Airey St and drive to the end of the road.

Scan the ocean for seabirds from the lookout. You may get Indian Yellow-nosed Albatross, Shy Albatross, Cape Petrel and Northern Giant-Petrel.

On the rocky headland, beaches and dunes, look for Hooded Plover, Red-capped Plover, Black-faced Cormorant, Pacific Gull, Australian Pied Oystercatcher, Sooty Oystercatcher and Masked Lapwing. Occasionally, Latham's Snipes are reported from the swamps behind the dunes.

Manuka Campground

The site is located before the Arthur River hamlet, just off Arthur River Rd (C214). There are several tracks around the campsite that may prove to be good for birdwatching. There should be plenty of honeyeaters such as Yellow-throated Honeyeater, Crescent Honeyeater, Little Wattlebird and Eastern Spinebill. Flocks of Yellow-tailed Black-Cockatoos often roost near the campground. Wedge-tailed Eagle and Swamp Harrier often fly over the camp. White-throated Needletails are regularly found flying over the river in summer. At night, you may hear Tasmanian Morepork.

Other birds in the area include Green Rosella, Fan-tailed Cuckoo, Yellow-rumped Thornbill, Tasmanian Scrubwren, Dusky Robbin, Black Currawong and Forest Raven.

Arthur River Road Heathland

A stretch of Arthur River Rd (C214) north of Arthur River runs through an extensive area of heathland on both sides of the road. This is an excellent place to look for heathland birds such as Tawny-crowned Honeyeater, Southern Emu-wren, Beautiful Firetail, White-fronted Chat, Brown Quail and Striated Fieldwren. You may also come across New Holland Honeyeater, Little Wattlebird, Tasmanian Scrubwren and Australasian Pipit.

Western Tasmania

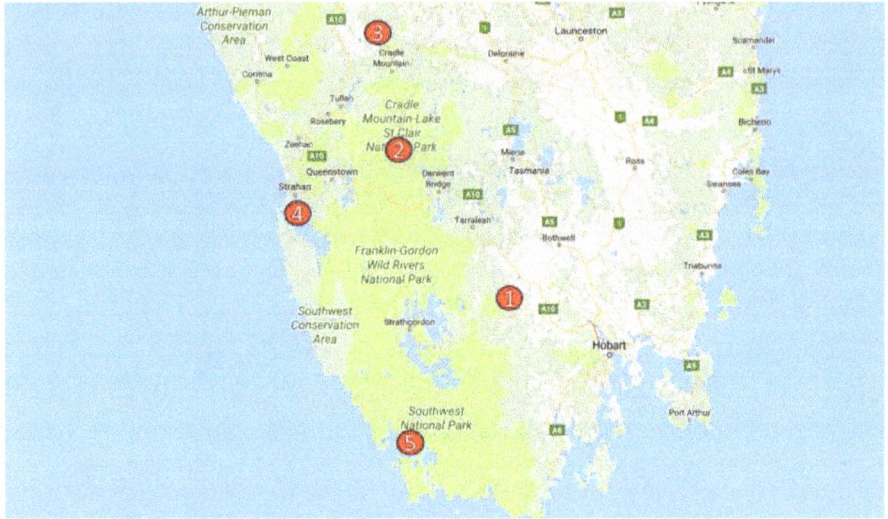

1   Mount Field National Park
2   Cradle Mountain - Lake St Clair National Park
3   Lake Lea
4   Strahan and Macquarie Harbour
5   Melaleuca

Mount Field National Park

This 17,000ha Park is one of the most loved places in Tasmania. It was declared a National Park in 1916 and together with the Freycinet shares the distinction of the first Tasmanian National Park. Sadly, the status of much of the original area was later revoked to allow logging, continuing till today.

The spread of habitats corresponds to the difference of altitudes from 160m above the sea level at the Park entrance to 1,434m at the top of Mt Field. Few other places in Australia can offer such a diversity of vegetation. The tall mountain ash forest with the understory of giant tree ferns grows at the base of the mountain. Cool temperate rainforest dominated by beech myrtle, sassafras, Huon pine and leatherwood occurs around Lake Dobson. In the alpine zone you'll find dwarf shrubland, bogs and tarns.

To get there from Hobart, take Brooker Hwy (1), extending into Lyell Hwy (A10) to New Norfolk, following River Derwent upstream. Past New Norfolk take Glenora Rd (B62), turning left into Gordon River Rd (B61) at a T-junction. At the National Park village turn right into Lake Dobson Rd (C609).

There are two visitor sectors, separated by a distance of 16km. The first sector is located around the Park entrance. You will find here a picnic area, shops, café, a caravan park and a track among the fern trees to Russell Falls. These trees lighten up like Christmas trees at night thanks to the glow worms that live in them. The second sector is at the Lake Dobson where skiing fields, long walking tracks and public shelters with tables and wood heaters are located. A useful map is included in the site brochure downloadable here: http://www.parks.tas.gov.au/file.aspx?id=34556.

Over 90 bird species have been recorded in the Park. **Key species** are Superb Lyrebird, Scrubtit, Pink Robin and Dusky Robin. Other birds of interest include Tasmanian Thornbill, Tasmanian Morepork, Olive Whistler, Wedge-tailed Eagle and Peregrine Falcon. 11 out of 12 Tasmanian endemics can be found here. The only one missing is Forty-spotted Pardalote.

Lyrebird Walk

At Lyrebird Walk you'll have a good chance of finding Superb Lyrebird or at least its tracks along the path. Look around when you see fresh scratchings in the litter.

Scrubtit, Tasmanian Thornbill and Crescent Honeyeater are common. Other birds on the track include Olive Whistler, Bassian Thrush, Black Currawong and Tasmanian Morepork.

Russell Falls Track

This is one of the best birdwatching walks in the Park. Pink Robin or Scrubtit may be hanging upside down on a woolly tree fern's trunk. The track goes past the falls to join Horseshoe Falls Tk, Lady Barron Falls Tk and Tall Trees Tk to form a 4hr circuit in the Park. The tracks run through stringybark, mountain ash, manna gum and Antarctic beech forests.

Near Russell Falls, Sulphur-crested Cockatoos are very common, you are also bound to see Bassian Thrush, Golden Whistler, Tasmanian Scrubwren and Yellow Wattlebird.

Continuing from Russell Falls along Horseshoe Falls Tk, you'll be walking through wet sclerophyll forest. Look for Olive Whistler, Beautiful Firetail, Swift Parrot, Yellow-throated Honeyeater and Grey Goshawk.

The area around the Lady Barron Falls should produce Brush Bronzewing, Dusky Robin, Tasmanian Scrubwren and Tasmanian Morepork.

On you way back to the Visitor Centre via Tall Trees Tk, look for and listen again to Superb Lyrebirds. There are usually plenty of Black Currawongs around here. There should be also Pink Robin, Scrubtit, Tasmanian Thornbill, Bassian Thrush and Yellow Wattlebird.

The area near the Visitor Centre and the Campground is typically dotted with robins including Flame Robin, Scarlet Robin and Dusky Robin. Black Currawongs beg around the picnic tables while Tasmanian Native-hens strut about at the lawn edges with their chicks. Other birds here include Green Rosella, Common Bronzewing and Forest Raven.

Lake Dobson

Heathland about 1km before Lake Dobson is good for Striated Fieldwren. You will also have a chance of spotting Southern Emu-wren and Olive Whistler here. Another good place for Southern Emu-wren is in the heath near Robert Tarn between Newdegate Pass and Robert Tarn.

On the water, look for the waterfowl such as Australian Shelduck, Hardhead, Australian Wood Duck, Black Swan, Hoary-headed Grebe and Eurasian Coot.

Female Hardhead on Lake Dobson

Bush birds around the lake include Scrubtit, Crescent Honeyeater, Strong-billed Honeyeater, Eastern Spinebill and Pink Robin.

Alpine vegetation may yield Australasian Pipit, Flame Robin, Forest Raven and Black Currawong. At high altitudes, look into the sky in search of Peregrine Falcon and Wedge-tailed Eagle.

Cradle Mountain - Lake St Clair National Park

Cradle Mountain is a must for every visitor to Tasmania who can allocate at least two days with an overnight stay to get there and back. The hauntingly beautiful, majestic scenery and an abundant wildlife make this trip worthwhile for every nature lover. The Park covers 161,00ha of ancient rainforest and alpine heath. Glacial lakes and icy streams cascading down the mountains add to the wild beauty of this unforgettable place.

While the remnants of the glacial era are few and far between on the mainland, Tasmania bears plenty of signs of the past global freeze events. The whole Cradle Valley was shaped in a number of glacial periods that started about 2 million years ago. Dove Lake and Cradle Lake were created by a massive glacier that moved across the north of the island, leaving behind a trail of ridges and mounds and piles of huge boulders. Cradle Mountain is of volcanic origin but it was shaped and scarred into today's look by the glaciers. The hard, volcanic dolerite of Cradle Mountain resisted erosion and remained in place while other rock components crumbled and fell with the time passage.

The Park comprises two sections: the northern Cradle Mountain section and the southern St Claire section. A basic locality map of the Park can be downloaded here: http://www.parks.tas.gov.au/file.aspx?id=19014.

Cradle Mountain Section

The jagged contour of Cradle Mountain, standing 1,545m above the sea level, is an unmistakable landmark of the area. This part of the Park is the most visited wilderness region of Tasmania. The famous 80km Overland Tk starts at the Cradle Mountain and runs to the Lake St Clair. The weather here is absolutely unpredictable so bring clothes for every season, focusing on warm windbreakers and raincoats.

Cradle Mountain can be reached in a number of ways. The main routes are:
- from Launceston or Devonport, get to Sheffield. It is still 1.5 hr drive from there. Take Claude Rd (C136) in Sheffield, then turn south into Cradle Mountain Rd (C132). It will get you to the entrance of the Park.
- From Hobart, drive to Queenstown and take Murchison Hwy (A10), then turn east into Belvoir Rd (C132). Next, turn south into Cradle Mountain Rd to get to the Park entrance.

The facilities are good, spreading across a range of localities in the Park. A Visitor Centre with a large carpark, shelters and a café, is located on the Park boundary. Free shuttle bus services to Dove Lake operate from spring to autumn. Cradle Mountain Campground and a range of other accommodation, a shop and meals are located at the entry to the Park. Deep inside in the Park, you may stay at Waldheim Cabins. A number of short walking tracks start at the Cradle Mountain Lodge or you can drive or walk to Dove Lake. The map of the northern section of the National Park can be found in the brochure downloadable here: http://www.parks.tas.gov.au/file.aspx?id=34557.

Over 80 bird species have been found in the Cradle Mountain section of the National Park. **Key species** are Scrubtit, Olive Whistler, Pink Robin and Crescent Honeyeater. Other birds of interest include Black Currawong, Tasmanian Morepork, Wedge-tailed Eagle, Striated Fieldwren and Dusky Robin. All but one of the 12 Tasmanian endemics can be found in the Park, particularly around any accommodation. The odd one out is Forty-spotted Pardalote.

Cradle Mountain Village

Over 30 bird species can be seen just in the Cradle Mountain Village. From our bush cabin window, we could observe with delight numerous Scrubtits, Tasmanian Scrubwrens, Tasmanian Thornbills, Silvereyes and other small bush birds foraging in dense shrubbery. Under our pole-mounted cabin we saw Bassian Thrush, Olive Whistler and also some wallabies with the little ones peeking out of their mothers' pouches. Put a sliced apple or cucumber out on the patio and you will have a possum show the whole night. Black Currawongs and Forest Ravens are very tame and can be seen everywhere in the Village. One pesky currawong robbed a child of his sandwich just in front of us!

Honeyeaters are very common, particularly Crescent Honeyeater whose distinctive "Eee-gypt" call can be heard from the treetops all over the area. You will also see Yellow-throated Honeyeater, Strong-billed Honeyeater, New Holland Honeyeater, Eastern Spinebill, Yellow Wattlebird and occasionally Little Wattlebird. Green Rosellas are common and other parrots such as Blue-winged Parrot, Yellow-tailed Black-Cockatoo and Sulphur-crested Cockatoo can also be found.

Surprising numbers of wallabies, echidnas, wombats, possums and kangaroos live around the people in the Village. You will see them every time you go for a walk, especially on a rainy/overcast day. Lucky ones may even catch a glimpse of the platypus in a pond near the Cradle Mountain Lodge.

The magical atmosphere of the Enchanted Walk

The 1km-long Enchanted Walk stars just opposite the Visitor Centre. You will walk under a canopy of gnarled ancient beech trees and towering pencil pines with soft curtains of water-dripping mosses hanging from every branch. The walk is the best place in the Park for Pink Robin and Scrubtit that are very visible and unafraid of the passing people.

Dove Lake Loop Track

This 6km track starts from the Dove Lake carpark and takes you first through the heath and then through the stunning rainforest growing on the slopes of Cradle Mountain. Tasmanian Thornbill and Tasmanian Scrubwren can be seen everywhere along the track.

The breathtaking panorama of Cradle Mountain from the Lake Dove Loop Track

In the heath, plenty of Olive Whistlers live. There will also be plenty of Striated Fieldwrens and Superb Fairy-wrens, even Beautiful Firetails can be seen. Watch out for robins on the track and road edges – you'll see Pink Robin, Dusky Robin, Flame Robin and Scarlett Robin. Blue-winged Parrot may also pop out on the track in front of you. We visited in summer and observed large flocks of White-throated Needletails, Tree Martins and Welcome Swallows flying over the lake. A pair of Wedge-tailed Eagles were soaring in the sky against the background of jagged edges of the Cradle Mountain.

While walking in the forest, look for Green Rosella, Scrubtit, Strong-billed Honeyeater, Crescent Honeyeater and Yellow Wattlebird.

Ronny Creek

A track along the Ronny Creek will take you through low ferns and grasses full of grazing wombats. Be on a lookout for the platypus or Tasmanian devil. From the occasional stands of trees, you'll hear a constant "Eee-gypt" call of Crescent Honeyeaters. Olive Whistler, Striated Fieldwren and Australasian Pipit are common here. Families of Tasmanian Native-hens will often run in front of you. Yellow-tailed Black-Cockatoos will fly in pairs over your head on their way from one patch of bush to the next.

Other species in the Ronny Creek area include Scrubtit, Tasmanian Thornbill, Flame Robin, Pink Robin, Green Rosella and Eurasian Skylark.

Waldheim Cabins are located in this area. Tawny Frogmouth often perches around the cabins. Look also for Bassian Thrush. At night you may hear Tasmanian Morepork calling.

Lake St Clair Section

Lake St Clair is located in the southern part of the Park. It is situated at an altitude at least 200m lower than the Cradle Mountain section, resulting in markedly different habitats and wildlife. Lake St Clair is the deepest lake in Australia (160m deep) and is the headwater for River Derwent. Vegetation around the lake is mostly dry and wet eucalyptus forest, temperate rainforest and a large are of buttongrass moorland.

This section of the National Park is accessed from the town of Derwent Bridge off Lyell Hwy (A10). Derwent Bridge is located 175km northwest of Hobart and 85km east of Queenstown. The entrance to the Park is 5km from Derwent Bridge on Lake St Clair Rd (C193). The route to Derwent Bridge winds through the mountains and sadly there is plenty of roadkill. If coming from Launceston, access is via Deloraine where you take Highland Lakes Rd (A5), turning right into Marlborough Rd (B11) then right again to Lyell Hwy (A10) to get to Derwent Bridge.

This major Park is equipped with a wide range of good facilities including a Visitor Centre, picnic area, restaurant and shop, campground, ferry service on the lake and a network of good walking tracks. The famous Overland Tk from Cradle Mountain finishes here at Cynthia Bay. No pdf map seems to be currently available online, but two good maps can be printed out from here:
http://www.parks.tas.gov.au/indeX.aspX?base=3478.

Over 80 species are on the site's birdlist. **Key species** are Scrubtit, Olive Whistler and Yellow-throated Honeyeater. Other birds of interest include Tasmanian Morepork, Tasmanian Thornbill, Tasmanian Scrubwren, Pink Robin, Dusky Robin, Satin Flycatcher and Black Currawong. Among the rarities are Lewin's Rail, Ground Parrot and Pacific Golden Plover.

Visitor Centre and Campground

The most common bird around the Visitor Centre and the camping area is Black Currawong, tame and friendly with the visitors. Other birds visible in the campground include Olive Whistler, Dusky Robin and Superb Fairy-wren. The most distinguishable sound during the day is the "Eee-gypt" call of Crescent Honeyeater. At night, Tasmanian Morepork calls frequently. While looking for Moreporks, you may come face to face with a Tasmanian devil – they like to sneak into the camp during the night.

Strong-billed Honeyeaters, Yellow-throated Honeyeaters and Tasmanian Thornbills are numerous in the trees around the camping area. Small flocks of Swift Parrots regularly visit the flowering gum trees in summer. Look also for Sating Flycatcher, Pink Robin, Flame Robin, Scarlet Robin, Scrubtit and Yellow Wattlebird.

Watersmeet Track

This 3.5km return track is a good birding site. It passes through several vegetation types where there is a chance to spot Blue-winged Parrot, Olive Whistler, Bassian Thrush, Scrubtit, Tasmanian Thornbill, Pink Robin, Dusky Robin and Tasmanian Morepork. It is a great place to look for the honeyeaters where you my get nearly all species occurring in Park.

At the north end of the track you can continue on to Platypus Bay and at the edge of the bay look for the waders including Black-fronted Dotterel, Latham's Snipe and occasionally Pacific Golden Plover.

Narcissus Bay

The bay is situated at the northern end of Lake St Clair and is connected to the St Clair village with the final leg of the Overland Tk. This area is mostly rainforest so the rainforest birds are common including Bassian Thrush, Scrubtit, Tasmanian Thornbill, Pink Robin and Tasmanian Scrubwren. Usually there are plenty of Yellow-tailed Black-Cockatoos; you'll see the evidence of their activity in the form of shredded cones and chewed small branches scattered on the ground. Whenever you pass an area of saltmarshes or freshwater swamps look for Common Greenshank, Pacific Golden Plover and Black-fronted Dotterel. Occasionally near the saltmarshes, Banded Lapwing can be found.

On the water should be some Australian Shelducks, Hoary-headed Grebes and Eurasian Coots.

Other species reported from this track include Green Rosella, Olive Whistler, Blue-winged Parrot, Southern Emu-wren and Grey Shrike-thrush.

Mt Rufus Circuit Track

The track runs from Cynthia Bay to Mt Rufus and goes back past Shadow Lake. You'll be walking in a shady rainforest filled with sassafras and tree ferns. Look here for the rainforest species such as Pink Robin, Scrubtit, Tasmanian Thornbill and Bassian Thrush.

Check the Shadow Lake for the platypus. In the tall forest around the lake you should find plenty of honeyeaters such as Black-headed Honeyeater, Strong-billed Honeyeater, Yellow-throated Honeyeater and Crescent Honeyeater. Tasmanian Native-hens can usually be found at the lake edge.

Lake Lea

The lake is located in the Vale of Belvoir Conservation Area, just 15min drive west of Cradle Mountain. If coming from Sheffield, instead of turning into Cradle Mountain Rd (still C132) past a small hamlet of Middlesex on Belvoir Rd (C132), turn right into the VDL Tk. At the T-junction, turn right and follow a good gravel track to the southern shores of the lake.

The lake is surrounded by the diverse habitats of open heathland, buttongrass, myrtle and pine forests and scrubland. The **key species** is Ground Parrot.

You can find many endemic Tasmanian and native species in the area. In the heathland, you have a good chance to flush Ground Parrot as a healthy population lives here. A good place for Ground Parrot is 100m from a locked gate on the side road. You may also encounter plenty Southern Emu-wrens and easily spot Striated Fieldwren and Blue-winged Parrot foraging in the spaces in between the buttongrass clumps.

In the forest near the lake, Pink Robin, Flame Robin and Scarlett Robin can be counted on, flickering about at the edges of the vegetation. Also, Tasmanian Scrubwrens are numerous in the bushland and woodland. Other endemics, such as Black Currawong, Tasmanian Thornbill, Yellow-throated Honeyeater and Green Rosella are all easy to find.

Around the southern shores of Lake Lea, Latham's Snipe can be found. Tasmanian Native-hens are plentiful.

Raptors regularly reported from the area include Collared Sparrowhawk, Brown Falcon, Swamp Harrier and Wedge-tailed Eagle.

Strahan and Macquarie Harbour

The small fishing town of Strahan on the west coast of Tasmania is the Australian stronghold of Ground Parrot. Getting there is a bit tedious as the western part of Tasmania is quite isolated and the roads are winding and mountainous. The long drive is rewarded by the beauty of the Macquarie Harbour and the coastal beaches.

The town is the gateway to the Franklin-Gordon Wild Rivers National Park. The popular Gordon River Cruises depart from Strahan to take you upstream of the Gordon River. For details check their website: http://www.gordonrivercruises.com.au).

A variety of habitats can be found in the area including buttongrass plains, heathland, coastal scrub, dunes, ocean beaches, rainforest, creeks and rivers. Birdlife is rich, especially the rainforest and heathland species.

Access from Hobart is via Lyell Hwy (A10 changing number to B24 in Queenstown). It is a 5hr drive. From Launceston or Devonport take Murchison Hwy (A10) and then Henty Rd (B27) from Zeehan. Alternatively, if you are a Cradle Mountain visitor, to experience the wilderness of the Strahan coast go west on Belvoir Rd (C132), then turn left onto Murchison Hwy (A10) and then take Henty Rd (B27). Roads on either route are narrow, steep and winding. Expect to take longer to get there.

There is a variety of accommodation around town but remember Strahan is very small for a popular summer destination so book your stay well in advance. Other facilities are limited to several walking tracks around the area, good for birding.

Over 100 bird species have been recorded here. **Key species** are Ground Parrot, Azure Kingfisher, Tawny-crowned Honeyeater and Southern Emu-wren. Other birds of interest include Hooded Plover, Double-banded Plover (in winter), Olive Whistler, Beautiful Firetail, Scrubtit, Swift Parrot and Brown Quail. Among the rarities are Orange-bellied Parrot, Red-kneed Dotterel, White-necked Heron, Australasian Bittern, Franklin's Gull and Australian Magpie. 11 out of 12 Tasmanian endemics can be found here. The only one missing is Forty-spotted Pardalote.

Ground Parrot is an elusive nocturnal bird, in general easier heard than seen, usually at dawn or dusk. In Strahan, they are most often found in the buttongrass plains, sedgeland or heathland located between the Strahan Airfield and the township. The areas around Ocean Beach Rd and Macquarie Heads Rd are the best sites for this bird. Other good spots include Petuna Aquaculture Tk off Macquarie Heads Rd and a short walk behind the Wilderness Lodge near Sarson Cl. The easiest way to get Ground Parrot is to select a site during the day by the edge of the buttongrass swamp and come back to it at dawn or dusk to listen to their calls which should happen within 30-40min.

Strahan Airfield

The site is located at the corner of Macquarie Heads Rd (C251) and Ocean Beach Rd (C250). The airfield is surrounded by the extensive buttongrass plains. Birding is best conducted from Macquarie Heads Rd. Besides for the Ground Parrot, this is a reliable place for Southern Emu-wren, Striated Fieldwren, Beautiful Firetail and Tawny-crowned Honeyeater. Swamp Harriers are often seen flying over the plains; they nest in the buttongrass clumps.

Scan the airfield; Latham's Snipes have been recorded many times feeding in the wet grass near the runway. Occasionally, Red-capped Plovers or Pacific Golden Plovers may be walking along the runway. Horsfield's bronze Cuckoos are common, often calling loudly from their perches on top of the buttongrass spikes.

Other birds in this area include Brush Bronzewing, Olive Whistler, Tasmanian Scrubwren, New Holland Honeyeater, Green Rosella and Tasmanian Morepork.

Orange-bellied Parrot have been occasionally reported from this site. In April 2013, Australasian Bittern was sighed in the buttongrass swamp just north of the airstrip.

Ocean Beach Road

The first section of Ocean Beach Rd (C250) near the airport features heath and buttongrass moorland and the bird selection is similar to that of Strachan Airfield described above. This is another Ground Parrot site.

Follow the road west to get to the Ocean Beach. A viewing platform is provided there for your enjoyment of a spectacle of Short-tailed Shearwaters returning to their nesting burrows at night. Waders can be found easily on the Ocean Beach, particularly around the creek mouth. A large flock (up to 300 birds) of New Zealand's Double-banded Plovers is regularly wintering in this area. Other waders here include Hooded Plover, Red-capped Plover, Pacific Golden Plover, Red-necked Stint, Australian Pied Oystercatcher and Sooty Oystercatcher. Sanderling is an occasional visitor to the area. On the dunes, look for Australasian Pipit, Striated Fieldwren and Superb Fairy-wren.

People Park

To get there, from Lyell Hwy (B24) in Strahan turn into Esplanade and then turn into the People Park where Hogarth Falls Tk starts. The track runs along the Botanical Creek to the Hogarth Falls. The 2km walk through the rainforest allows to sight Scrubtit, Pink Robin, Bassian Thrush, Tasmanian Scrubwren, Tasmanian Thornbill (very common), Golden Whistler and Green Rosella.

Green Rosella

Oliver Whistlers can be found near the upper lookout at the falls. Azure Kingfisher was recorded a few times from the creek by the track. Other birds in the park include Black Currawong, Dusky Robin, Eastern Spinebill, Black-headed Honeyeater, Fan-tailed Cuckoo and Brush Bronzewing.

Strahan Township

You may score some good findings in Strahan itself. For example, a good spot is near the bridge over Manuka River on Harvey St (C250). The swamp here is good for Little Grassbirds, calling loudly from wetland vegetation. Latham's Snipe and Sulphur-crested Cockatoos have also been found in the area.

From Strahan Backpackers YHA (in Harvey Rd past the roundabout) listen at night to Australian Owlet-nightjar, Tasmanian Morepork and Tawny Frogmouth. From the surrounding bush, Black-headed Honeyeater, Strong-billed Honeyeater and Collared Sparrowhawk have been reported.

Strahan Beach Tourist Park in Beach St off Andrew St (B27) is regularly visited by flocks of Swift Parrots. On the same trees look for a plethora of honeyeaters; most of the Tasmanian species will be there including Black-headed Honeyeater, Yellow-throated Honeyeater, Strong-billed Honeyeater, New Holland Honeyeater and Crescent Honeyeater.

Macquarie Harbour

A boat trip into the Macquarie Harbour may produce seabirds such as Arctic Jaeger, Shy Albatross, Fairy Prion, Pacific Gull, Kelp Gull, Black-faced Cormorant and White-bellied Sea-Eagle.

In winter 2016, Franklin's Gull spent a few months in the harbour on a fish farm 10km out of Strahan. This tripped a winter tourist season in Strahan which was surprised with this sudden out-of-season influx of birdwatchers in the area.

Birch's Inlet

This is a narrow cove on the southwestern side of the Macquarie Harbour, 38km south of Strahan. It is only accessible by boat. It used to be home of the second of the only two breeding populations of Orange-bellied Parrots. The birds bred here naturally until 1995 and captive-bred birds were released until 2006. The last breeding record is from 2012. The birds still use the site occasionally but now breed only at Melaleuca.

Birds likely to be found here include heathland species such as Southern Emu-wren, Striated Fieldwren, Blue-winged Parrot and Beautiful Firetail as well as Latham's Snipe.

Melaleuca

This location is important as it is a breeding stronghold of Orange-bellied Parrot, a critically endangered Australian native species. It breeds is summer in Tasmania, with Melaleuca being their last remaining breeding spot, and spends the winter on the mainland. Melaleuca is the easiest place to see these birds in Tasmania in summer but only about 50 birds remain in the wild. The Melaleuca's captive breeding population is about 320 birds. Therefore, this is one of the rarest birds on Earth. The captive population is the last hope for this species. The juveniles hatched in selected facilities are being released back from the programme to boost the genetic diversity of the remnant wild population. Supplementary feeding is provided to the released birds. A very useful bird hide is provided at the Melaleuca Lagoon where in summer you will have a chance to see the Orange-bellied Parrot at the feeders.

The majority of these birds live in the grounds of Deny King's old house at the bank of Melaleuca Inlet. Deny was a keen birdwatcher, botanist and nature observer, made a Member of Order of Australia for his services to the community. His house is now heritage-listed. His legacy still shines - a number of purpose-built hollow logs that Deny constructed are still being used by the birds to nest today.

Melaleuca is located in the southeast wilderness. It is surrounded by 440,000ha of South West National Park and Tasman Wilderness of the World Heritage Area. The mosaic of vegetation includes large areas of buttongrass (crucial for Orange-bellied Parrot and Ground Parrot), wet eucalypt forest dominated by peppermint, cool temperate rainforest, costal scrub, saltmarshes and lagoons.

Melaleuca is extremely remote and accessible only by air, boat or on foot. The easiest way is of course to fly. Try Par Avion who are providing services daily from Cambridge Airport in Hobart. The flight is 45min. Check the current schedules and prices at www.paravion.com.au. If you wish to stay overnight, basic accommodation is available in two walkers' huts (10 persons per hut) with bunk beds but you'll need to bring all supplies with you, no shops here. In case the place is full you need to take a tent and bedding to sleep in a small camping area. You cannot book a place in a hut in advance. Other site facilities are limited to a gravel airstrip, walking tracks, toilets and a Ranger's station which may or may not be staffed. You can also walk here, it takes 7 days one way on the 85km South Coast Tk, and you have to carry everything with you.

Over 110 bird species have been recorded here. The **key species** is Orange-bellied Parrot. Other birds of interest include Ground Parrot, Lewin's Rail, Southern Emu-wren, Striated Fieldwren, Hooded Plover, Olive Whistler, Tasmanian Morepork, Pink Robin and Dusky Robin. Among the rarities are Australasian Bittern and Swift Parrot. 11 out of 12 Tasmanian endemics are regularly found here. The only one out is Forty-spotted Pardalote.

The coastal heathland with buttongrass communities interspersed with tall eucalyptus stands is a stronghold of Ground Parrots which are common and easy to flush from the heath when walking. Ground Parrots are found on the track between the airstrip and the walkers' huts. They can also be seen in large numbers on Port Davey's Tk and near the boardwalk on Needwonnee Walk.

The heath also supports an abundance of Striated Fieldwrens, Yellow-throated Honeyeaters, Strong-billed Honeyeaters, New Holland Honeyeaters, Crescent Honeyeaters, Southern Emu-wrens and Beautiful Firetails. Melaleuca is probably the best place in Tasmania to see Beautiful Firetail. They visit the feeding tables at the bird hide, making use of the food prepared for the Orange-bellied Parrots.

Port Davey's Track

The start of the track is located at the end of the airstrip where you may see plenty of Striated Fieldwrens, many calling loudly from tops of small bushes. Look also for Beautiful Firetail, Australasian Pipit and Olive Whistler. Ground Parrots and families of Southern Emu-wrens can also be located in this area. Other birds on the track include Latham's Snipe, Black Currawong, Eastern Spinebill, New Holland Honeyeater, Crescent Honeyeater and Horsfield's Bronze-cuckoo.

Melaleuca Lagoon

Melaleuca Lagoon is a large water body on Elbow Creek north of the airstrip. You can usually find plenty of Black Swans and common ducks here. Australasian Bittern has been recorded in this area. White-bellied Sea-Eagles are resident. Common Greenshanks and Latham's Snipes can be found around the edges. Lewin's Rails were found in a creek emptying into the lagoon.

In the surrounding bushland look for Yellow-throated Honeyeater, Crescent Honeyeater, Strong-billed Honeyeater, Tasmanian Scrubwren, Striated Pardalote and Green Rosella.

Bird Hide and Huts

Dusky Robin

The area around the bird hide and walkers' huts is the prime place to see Orange-bellied Parrot in summer, coming to the feeders. The table also attracts Beautiful Firetails and Blue-winged Parrots. You can also see tame Dusky Robins which are plentiful around the bird hide, and occasionally Pink Robins and Flame Robins.

Bassian Thrush is quite common in the bush around the huts. While spotlighting at night you can find Tasmanian Morepork and Masked Owl or hear Australian Owlet-nightjar.

On the path to the hide look for Lewin's Rail and Latham's Snipe, often found feeding in the drainage lines nearby.

If you are lucky, you may observe Strong-billed Honeyeaters picking the fur off the wallabies' and other furry animals' pelts to line their nests.

Needwonnee Walk

Needwonnee Walk is an interpretive trail focused on the Aboriginal life story. It runs through a swamp, with part of the trail on a boardwalk. This is a fantastic spot for Ground Parrots. You may also find here Blue-winged Parrot, Latham's Snipe, Lewin's Rail, Southern Emu-wren, Beautiful Firetail, Crescent Honeyeater and Striated Fieldwren.

South West Coast Track

South West Coast Tk starts at the airstrip and runs through a dense rainforest. Expect to find Scrubtit, Bassian Thrush, Pink Robin, Black Currawong, Crescent Honeyeater, Yellow Wattlebird, Tasmanian Morepork, Olive Whistler and Yellow-tailed Black-Cockatoo here.

Outer Islands

King Island

The island, located midway between Victoria opposite Cape Otway and Tasmania opposite Cape Grim, is part of Tasmania. It is 65km long and 25km wide and covers an area of 1,100km² with the population of 1,700. The land is generally flat except for one 168m hill of Gentle Annie. The island lies in the path of Roaring Forties, with strong winds year-round. The coastline is rugged, featuring pristine beaches and lagoons and wetlands nearby.

The island is famous for its boutique cheeses. Food gourmets will also delight in local fresh seafood, organically grown meat, honey and wine.

The island has mostly been cleared of natural vegetation, only 15% of the land is covered by native forest, now protected in a few reserves. Most of this flat land is under intensive dairy farming with thousands of farm dams and small lagoons which creates a good habitat for the waterbirds. Shrubby pastures take about 20% of the farmland; these are well utilised by the introduced exotic birds. The island is fox-free which gives a chance of survival to the ground-dwelling species.

The only convenient access is by air. Regular flights are from Melbourne and Geelong in Victoria or from Launceston and Burnie in Tasmania. Accommodation on King Island ranges from hotels and motels to B&Bs, self-contained apartments, farm stays and cabins. Most of the accommodation can be found in the largest town of Currie on the western shore. Some choices also exist in Naracoopa and Grassy on the southeast side of the island where most of birding is happening.

There is no public transport or taxis on the island so the only option is to rent a car from one of the two car hire companies. King Island Tourism may help with the flights, car hire and accommodation bookings, tel. (03) 6462 1355, http://www.kingisland.org.au/. A good map can be downloaded here:
http://www.kingisland.org.au/files/King_Island_Visitor_Map.pdf.

Over 200 species are on the island's birdlist. **Key species** are Orange-bellied Parrot, Indian Peafowl, Wild Turkey, California Quail and Common Pheasant. Other birds of interest include Hooded Plover, Fairy Tern, Golden-headed Cisticola, Little Raven and the six King Island endemic subspecies. These are Green Rosella ssp. *kingi*, Yellow Wattlebird ssp. *kingi*, Black Currawong ssp. *colei*, King Island Brown Thornbill ssp. *archibaldi*, Scrubtit ssp. *greenianus* and Dusky Robin ssp. *kingi*. The list of rarities is very long and includes Australasian Bittern, White-necked Heron, Nankeen Night-Heron, Straw-necked Ibis, Royal Spoonbill, White-browed Woodswallow, Painted Button-quail, Pink-eared Duck, Red-kneed Dotterel, Swift Parrot, Lewin's Rail, Buff-banded Rail, Dusky Moorhen, Brush Cuckoo and many more.

Believe it or not but Australian birdwatchers visit King Island mainly to tick the introduced species: Indian Peafowl, Common Pheasant, Wild Turkey and California Quail. Thanks to the fox-free status of the island, these ground-nesting birds are thriving here. The first three can be quickly found, you'll see plenty walking along the road in the areas of scrubby pastures. California Quail, however, needs some effort to locate. The best place for it is Tin Mine Rd northeast of the King Island Airport in Currie. There is another species, Greylag Goose, otherwise known as the domestic goose, which breeds in the wild throughout the Island. Hundreds of them hang out around the lagoons, flying short distances over the pastures. Unfortunately, the Australian birding authority has not placed this bird on the official species list (in New Zealand they have). Other introduced species common on the island include European Goldfinch, Common Greenfinch, Common Starling, Common Blackbird, Eurasian Skylark, House Sparrow and Spotted Dove.

Emu is another introduced species, this time from the Australian mainland, derived from an emu farm escapees. There was a native subspecies, King Island Emu, but it's been extinct for a century. Emu can be found in the southwest corner of the island.

The critically endangered Orange-bellied Parrots after their breeding season in Melaleuca fly for the winter to Victoria and South Australia. On their way, they make a short stopover on King Island to feed and rest. Their favourite place is around the southern shores of Sea Elephant Estuary. They are also occasionally recorded in the saltmarshes on the western side of the island in the Yellow Rock River estuary.

King Island Brown Thornbill is the rarest of the King Island subspecies. It has large, long bill, rusty flanks and rusty undertail coverts. For years, it was believed to be extinct but in 2015 and 2016 there were a couple of sightings by experienced birders in the Pegarah State Reserve, supported by photographic evidence. The second rarest local endemic subspecies is Scrubtit; only 200 live on the island, mostly in the paperbarks in the Nook Swamp at Lavinia Nature Reserve and in the small Colliers Swamp. To locate this beautiful little bird, one has to walk through the swamp. Remember to pack your gumboots.

King Island is an important site for the migratory and local shorebirds, particularly for Ruddy Turnstone, both Oystercatchers, Hooded Plover and Fairy Tern. It hosts 10% of Tasmanian Hooded Plover population, 2% of Australian population of Australian Pied Oystercatcher and at least 1% of Australian population of Sooty Oystercatcher. There are years, when the counts for Ruddy Turnstone reach over 1,000 birds (1% of world population). Two-third of the Tasmanian Fairy Tern population breeds on King Island.

There are large colonies of Little Penguins on the island, also 700,000 pairs of Short-tailed Shearwaters breed here. The penguins can be watched when coming onshore in the Grassy Harbour. There not many vantage points to observe other seabirds on this flat land. The best places are Seal Rocks, Fitzmaurice Point and the end of Charles St in Currie. Look for Black-headed Albatross, Shy Albatross, Indian Yellow-nosed Albatross, Fluttering Shearwater, Cape Petrel, Southern Giant-Petrel and Fairy Prion.

Lavinia Nature Reserve

This 6,800ha reserve is situated on the northeast coast of King Island. It occupies much of the coastal area from Lake Martha Lavinia in the north to Cowper Point and the estuary of Sea Elephant River in the south. The whole reserve is a Ramsar site. There are swamps, long sandy beaches, saltmarshes and coastal heathland in the Reserve. It protects the largest remaining block of native vegetation on the island including swamp paperbark dry heath, scented paperbark wet heath and coastal tea tree heath. There are also large areas of bracken fern and tussock grass formed due to the frequent fires of the heathland that kill the wooded plants.

The Reserve provides the habitat for the migrating Orange-bellied Parrot in the samphire saltmarshes.

To get to the Sea Elephant estuary, from Naracoopa drive north on Fraser Rd for 3km, then make a right into Sea Elephant Rd and follow it to the Sea Elephant River mouth. Walk to the saltmarshes. Orange-bellied Parrots appear here for a few days between April and May.

The rare Scrubtit can be found in the Nook Swamp. In the bracken fern along Sea Elephant Rd look for California Quails. Fairy Terns often nest on a bare sandspit on the southern side of the Sea Elephant River mouth. Short-tailed Shearwaters are present from September to May and breed in the burrows in the dunes behind Lavinia Beach.

Waders on the beaches and in the estuary include Hooded Plover, Red-capped Plover, Double-banded Plover (in winter), Pacific Golden Plover, Australian Pied Oystercatcher, Sooty Oystercatcher, Common Greenshank, Red-necked Stint and Ruddy Turnstone. Rarer waders recorded here include Common Sandpiper and Sanderling. The estuary may also produce Musk Duck (regular appearance), Australian Shelduck, Chestnut Teal, Grey Teal and plenty of Black Swans.

Hooded Plovers frequent the beaches of the Sea Elephant River estuary

Golden-headed Cisticola is common in the marshy vegetation surrounding the estuary. This is the only population of this species in the whole Tasmania. Another species that is absent in rest of Tasmania, Little Raven, lives here in the Reserve but is difficult to identify in the mass of thousands of Forest Ravens, very common on the island. Nankeen Night-Heron is very rare in Tasmania while here it occurs erratically. It forms small colonies in the tee tree scrub then disappears for a few years.

Bushland in the Reserve may yield Tasmanian Thornbill, Tasmanian Scrubwren, Brush Bronzewing and Black Currawong.

The northern part of the Reserve can be reached via Martha Lavinia Rd. Along the road expect to find Flame Robin, Dusky Robin, Yellow-tailed Black-Cockatoo, Australasian Pipit and Brown Falcon.

A good birding spot is Pennys Lagoon. Take a walk around the lagoon through the bush. On the water, Musk Duck is regularly found along with Australian Shelduck, Black Swan and Chestnut Teal. Common Greenshank favours the lagoon edges. California Quails occur around the lagoon in large numbers. Lewin's Rail was recorded in Pennys Lagoon as well as on the south side of Sea Elephant estuary.

The bush may produce Strong-billed Honeyeater, New Holland Honeyeater, Crescent Honeyeater, Yellow Wattlebird, Tasmanian Thornbill, Tasmanian Scrubwren, Dusky Robin and Green Rosella. Large flocks of Welcome Swallows often fly over the lagoon; check if Tree Martins are among them; they are occasionally found here.

Raptors in the area include Swamp Harrier, White-bellied Sea-Eagle and Brown Goshawk.

Pegarah State Reserve

This small reserve protects the only significant remnant of eucalypt forest on the island; this forest used to cover half of the land here in the past. It is the best area for bushland birds on King Island.

To get there from Currie, drive east on Grassy Rd (B25), then take a left fork into Pegarah Rd (C203). Or, if you are in Naracoopa, drive on Pegarah Rd in the westerly direction. The entrance is on the north side of Pegarah Rd, in Blue Gum Rd which runs through the middle of the Reserve. There are also several other tracks to explore.

Common birds in the Reserve include Tasmanian Scrubwren, Tasmanian Thornbill, Olive Whistler, Strong-billed Honeyeater, Black-headed Honeyeater, Yellow-throated Honeyeater, Yellow Wattlebird, Grey Fantail, Dusky Robin, Brush Bronzewing and Green Rosella. In smaller numbers, you may find here Bassian Thrush, Pink Robin, Little Raven and Satin Flycatcher. It is much easier to observe Olive Whistlers here than anywhere else where this bird is elusive and shy. Here, it comes out into the open and forages along the road or at the edge of the bushes.

That rediscovered subspecies of Brown Thornbill was found here, in the Pegarah State Reserve. In February 2017, Scrubtit was also found here, the third site on the island. Also in February 2017, two Painted Button-quails were sighted on the track 1km from the main entrance.

If you are staying in Naracoopa, Tasmanian Morepork is often heard or seen near the Naracoopa Cottages.

Colliers Swamp

Colliers Swamp is located on the southern tip of King Island. To get there, from Grassy Rd (B25) turn into Mount Stanley Rd, then into Red Hut Rd. In Lymwood, turn into the track running in the direction of Big Lake. Colliers Swamp is not far past Lymwood. This is place where the second population of the rare Scrubtit is located.

The most common species is Crescent Honeyeater. You will also find here Bassian Thrush, Olive Whistler, Silvereye, Flame Robin, Tasmanian Thornbill, Tasmanian Scrubwren and Swamp Harrier.

Lake Flannigan

Lake Flannigan is located at the northern end of King Island. Access is via Cape Wickham Rd (B25), an extension of North Rd. Waterbirds congregate here in huge numbers. You can find here nearly all species of waterfowl that can be found on the island. Large rafts of Eurasian Coots and Black Swans often cover the water. It is a good spot for Musk Duck, Hardhead and Hoary-headed Grebe. Australasian Grebe, rare in Tasmania, was found here, too. Also, Cattle Egret, Eastern Great Egret and Royal Spoonbill have been recorded here.

Golden-headed Cisticola has been found in the marshes around the lake, the second location after the Sea Elephant estuary.

Most of the King Island exotic species are easy to find around the lake.

Wild Turkey

North of Flannigan Lake, a small Cask Lake is located on the west side of the main road. It is a good place to find Musk Duck, Blue-billed Duck and Hoary-headed Grebe.

Yellow Rock River Estuary

To get to the Yellow Rock River mouth, take North Rd (B25) from Currie, then turn west onto North Yellow Rock Rd.

In the river mouth, you may find Eastern Great Egret, Australasian Shoveler, Double-banded Plover (in winter), and Red-necked Stint. Fairy Terns breed on the beach. You may also get Australian Pied Oystercatcher, Sooty Oystercatcher, Red-capped Plover, Sanderling and Pacific Gull. In the surrounding saltmarshes look for White-fronted Chat, Latham's Snipe and sporadically Orange-bellied Parrot.

Other birds in the area include Cape Barren Goose, Purple Swamphen, Common Greenfinch, White-bellied Sea-Eagle and Brown Falcon.

Tathams Lagoon

To get there, from North Rd (B25) turn west into Bungaree Rd, the site is located just past the turnoff. GPS coordinates are 39.47.10 S and 143.53.58 E.

This is a very reliable place to find the Blue-billed Duck. Up to 24 birds have been recorded. Other species here include Musk Duck, Pink-eared Duck, Cape Barren Goose, Purple Swamphen, Hoary-headed Grebe, Dusky Robin and Swamp Harrier.

Shag Lagoon

This little lagoon is located along Heddles Rd about 1.5km east from the intersection with North Rd (B25). Site coordinates are 39.49.31 S and 143.54.06 E.

This is a very reliable place for the Latham's Snipe; they occur here in good numbers. Cape Barren Geese breed regularly on a small island on the lagoon. Huge numbers of Masked Lapwings congregate around the lagoon. Other common birds here are Australasian Shoveler, Hardhead, Chestnut Teal, Grey Teal, Hoary-headed Grebe, Tasmanian Thornbill, Australasian Pipit, White-fronted Chat and Brown Falcon.

A number of rarer species are regularly recorded here including Pink-eared Duck, Blue-billed Duck, Red-kneed Dotterel, Black-fronted Dotterel and Golden-headed Cisticola.

Tin Mine Road

From North Rd (B25) take Browns Rd east, then quickly turn left into Tin Mine Rd. This road is the most reliable place on the island for the California Quail. The birds are usually found a few hundred metres from the farm gate.

Other birds on the farmland include Cape Barren Goose, White-fronted Chat, Australasian Pipit, Forest Raven, Eurasian Skylark, Australian Shelduck, Purple Swamphen, Common Pheasant and Wild Turkey. Brush Bronzewings are everywhere.

Occasionally you may come across Olive Whistler and Bassian Thrush in the thick bush. There are plenty of Dusky Robins on the fences.

Raptors here include Nankeen Kestrel, Brown Falcon and Swamp Harrier.

Pearshape Lagoon

The site, comprising several small lagoons close together, is located at the corner of Millers Rd and South Rd in the southwest corner of the island. GPS coordinates are 40.03.31 S and 143.55.14 E.

This is another good site for the rarer waterbirds. You may come across Australasian Shoveler, Musk Duck, Blue-billed Duck, Australasian Grebe and Hoary-headed Grebe here. Cape Barren Geese breed around the lagoon. You may also find Dusky Robin, Tasmanian Thornbill, Tasmanian Scrubwren, Yellow Wattlebird, Pallid Cuckoo and Silvereye.

Dead Sea

This a small swamp located on the western side of Old Grassy Rd (C201), 6km south of the intersection with Grassy Rd (B25) which is situated about 10km east of Currie.

The site is favourite of Latham's Snipe; counts of 20 birds have been reported.

In a stand of bushes nearby look for Yellow Wattlebird, Grey Shrike-thrush and New Holland Honeyeater.

Flinders Island

Flinders Island is the biggest among the 50+ islands of the Furneaux Group. It is located 20km north of Cape Portland on the northeastern tip of Tasmania. The island is 62km long and 37km wide, with the surface of 1,330km². The resident population is 700 and declining. One-third of the island is mountainous and rugged, with granite ridges running in the southwest. The highest peak is Mount Strzelecki at 756m above the sea level. The eastern shores of the island feature a chain of large lagoons located behind the dunes. The 40° parallel runs through the island so, similarly to King Island, the strong westerly 'Roaring Forties' winds are a commonplace experience here.

Vegetation is dominated by tea tree scrub on the coast and dry sclerophyll eucalypt forest at higher elevations. There are also patches of rainforest in the gullies.

A 70km-long strip of land (187km²) along nearly the entire length of the eastern coast of Flinders Island has been identified as a Key Biodiversity Area. The area supports large numbers of Hooded Plovers and more than 1% of the world population of both oystercatchers.

Many uninhabited islands in the Furneaux Group support large breeding colonies of seabirds.

The only convenient access to the island is by air via a 1hr flight from Melbourne or 25min flight from Launceston. The flight schedule is not as frequent as that for King Island. Flinders Island Airport is located in Whitemark. There is no public transport or taxis on the island so you'll need to rent a car or a bike. Limited accommodation is available in Whitemark and Lady Barron where you can also get some supplies.

There doesn't seem to be a pdf map available online for this area. We provide a link to a map that is not downloadable but you can print it for the trip: http://flindersislandtravel.com.au/wp-content/uploads/2011/07/map50.jpg.

Over 140 bird species have been recorded on Flinders Island. However, it is not a popular birdwatching destination. **Key species** are Forty-spotted Pardalote, Hooded Plover, Fairy Tern, Indian Peafowl, Wild Turkey, Common Pheasant and White-belled Sea-Eagle. You'll also find here a good selection of seabirds, waders and waterfowl. Rare species include Stubble Quail, Painted Button-quail, Lewin's Rail, Australasian Bittern, Pink-eared Duck, Dusky Moorhen and Chukar Partridge.

Four endemic subspecies have developed on Flinders Island: Superb Fairy-wren, New Holland Honeyeater, Tasmanian Scrubwren and Black Currawong, all are common on the island. In total, 10 out of 12 Tasmanian endemics occurs on the island, with only Scrubtit and Yellow Wattlebird absent.

A small population of Forty-spotted Pardalotes still survives on Flinders Island. It was estimated in the year 2000 that 70 birds were here in three colonies. Two reserves were created to help the species: Brougham Sugarloaf Conservation Area (280ha) and Walkers Lookout (20ha) where the manna gum grows. Unfortunately, in 2002 and 2003 severe fires swept through the reserves and for the next 10 years no birds were found. In 2012, a small colony was discovered in the Strzelecki National Park in the Costers Gully - Fanning Creek area. The total size of the population was assessed to be maximum of fourteen birds. The future of this little Tassie battler is bleak as the condition of manna gums these birds rely upon is poor on the island. Old trees are dying and there is no recruitment of new trees because feral pigs consume any new seedlings.

Flinders Island has a great conservation value for the resident shorebirds and seabirds. It supports 2% of Australasian populations of Hooded Plover and Australian Pied Oystercatcher and at least 1% of the Sooty Oystercatcher population. These three species plus Red-capped Plover and Fairy Tern breed mostly on the east coast beaches. The biggest threat for them is the increasing number of 4WD vehicles tearing along the beach. There were instances when a single inconsiderate person drove through the entire 70km of the beach, driving over all breeding sites along his way. This destroys the outcome of the whole breeding season for all species. However, it is very difficult to change the attitudes of people who regard this activity and part of their lifestyles and a natural right.

Flinders Island supports at least 1% of the Australasian population of Sooty Oystercatchers

The islands of the Furneaux Group are a seabird paradise. The seabird population includes: 250,000 pairs of Little Penguins, 7.5mln pairs of Short-tailed Shearwaters, 60,000 pairs of White-faced Storm-Petrels and 2,000 pairs of Crested Terns. Many other seabird species breed here in smaller numbers. In particular a couple of small islands are the only breeding site for White-fronted Tern (3-15 nests), otherwise known to breed only in New Zealand.

Flinders Island is also an excellent place for raptors. Including the smaller islands, it holds an important breeding population of White-bellied Sea-Eagle. Several pairs raise their chicks every year. On Flinders Island the birds are nesting in Killiecrankie Bay, Patriarch Inlet and Cameron Inlet. Other birds of prey include Nankeen Kestrel, Brown Falcon, Peregrine Falcon, Brown Goshawk, Australian Hobby, Swamp Harrier and Wedge-tailed Eagle.

Fifteen migratory wader species and eight species of ducks including Blue-billed Duck and Musk Duck have been recorded on the east coast.

Australian birders mostly come to Flinders Island to tick off the exotics. The most important are Wild Turkey, Common Pheasant and Indian Peafowl which occur here in large numbers. The fourth species, Chukar Partridge, is tricky to find as it lives on scrubby hills. It is heard more often than seen. It still hasn't made it to the official Australian birdlist.

A pair of Indian Peafowls, a common sight on Flinders Island, with both male and female displaying

Some species have benefitted from the widespread land clearing. There is plenty of Cape Barren Geese, Masked Lapwings, Common Starlings and Eurasian Skylarks. Numbers of Banded Lapwings also slowly increase; the birds can be found on the paddocks in the Ranga and Memana area.

However, other species are disappearing and now can be found only in small localised area. For example, Tawny-crowned Honeyeater is only found in the Killiecrankie area where a good parcel of heathland with plenty of grass trees, stunted cabbage gums and banksias still exists.

Strzelecki National Park

This 4,200ha Park is located in the southwestern corner of Flinders Island, 20min drive south of Whitemark. It protects large areas of native woodland and a spectacular costal and mountainous landscape. The Park comprises two land sections: the larger block with the Strzelecki and Flinders peaks and a separate small coastal headland called Trousers Point. A steep track leads to the Strzelecki Peak, a trek there is a popular and challenging tourist activity. Trousers Point is also a popular destination. In this block of the National Park you'll find parking, a campground and picnic area at Fotheringate Beach and a circular walk between Trousers Point and Fotheringate Beach.

The hills are covered by the Tasmanian blue gums. Near the coast and at the mountain base you will find tea tree scrub while sassafras rainforest grows in the gullies. Trousers Point has casuarina forest, the only remnant of this habitat left on the island.

Strzelecki National Park is the best place for the bush birds on Flinders Island. At the base of the mountains you may find Tasmanian Scrubwren, Brown Thornbill, Green Rosella, Yellow-throated Honeyeater, Strong-billed Honeyeater, Tasmanian Morepork and Dusky Robin. At the top of Strzelecki Peak look for Wedge-tailed Eagles often seen gliding on thermals around the mountain.

Birds in the gullies include Pink Robin, Tasmanian Thornbill, Olive Whistler, Yellow-throated Honeyeater and Crescent Honeyeater. The last known colony of Forty-spotted Pardalote lives near Costers Gully.

Along Trousers Point Rd outside the Park and in the Park, look for New Holland Honeyeater, Australasian Pipit, Cape Barren Goose, White-fronted Chat, Black Currawong, Flame Robin, Beautiful Firetail, Superb Fairy-wren, Pacific Gull and Swamp Harrier. The rare Lewin's Rail is sporadically reported from Trousers Point.

Near the camping and picnic area at the Fotheringate Beach you'll find plenty of other wildlife including possums, pademelons, echidnas, Bennet's wallabies, wombats, etc.

Logan Lagoon Conservation Area

The lagoon, located in the southeast of Flinders Island, extends over an area of 1,000ha. The site can be reached from Lady Barron via Pot Boil Rd or Logan Lagoon Rd.

It is a Ramsar site due to its critical value to the migratory shorebirds. At the end of summer, the lagoon is nearly dry. Common waders here include Red-necked Stint (the most common species, about 1,000 birds each summer), Red-capped Plover, Masked Lapwing, Common Greenshank, Eastern Curlew and Double-banded Plover (in winter).

Since 2012, a regular seasonal influx of Banded Stilts from the mainland has been noted. 2,000-4,000 birds spend their summer in the lagoon.

Ducks and swans are plentiful. The most numerous waterbirds are Australian Shelduck, Chestnut Teal and Black Swan. Rarer species include Musk Duck, Blue-billed Duck and Australian Pelican.

In the bush around the lagoon look for Indian Peafowl, Common Pheasant, Brown Quail, Olive Whistler and Horsfield's Bronze-cuckoo. Australasian Bittern occasionally breeds in the tea tree scrub by the lagoon.

Cameron Inlet Coastal Reserve

The site is located just north of Logan Lagoon. It can be accesses via Lackrana Rd (C803), turning into Cameron Inlet Rd. On both sides of Cameron Inlet Rd, the Lackrana Wildlife Sanctuary is located, with pastures sawn for the benefit of Cape Barren Goose which is now doing well on the island. Cameron Inlet is permanent so often takes over the bird load when the Logan Lagoon dries up.

A bird hide is located at the northern side of the Inlet. From there you can walk to the mouth of the inlet and the beaches. Shorebirds found at this site include Australian Pied Oystercatcher, Sooty Oystercatcher, Red-necked Stint, Pacific Golden Plover, Red-capped Plover, Double-banded Plover (in winter), Sharp-tailed Sandpiper, Sanderling, Fairy Tern, Caspian Tern and Pacific Gull. Pectoral Sandpiper was recorded a few times.

Musk Ducks and Eastern Great Egrets are regularly found in the Inlet.

In the saltmarshes nearby look for White-fronted Chat, Australasian Pipit and Eurasian Skylark.

The scrub may produce Olive Whistler and Brush Bronzewing, both are regular findings. Olive Whistler is often found in a small, frequently nearly dry No Duck Lagoon nearby.

Sellars Lagoon

The site is located on the east coast of Flinders Island just north of Cameron Inlet. To get there, drive on Lackrana Rd (C803), then turn into Summers Rd which will take you to the lagoon. Bird composition is similar to the two previous sites but this site is very reliable for Blue-billed Duck and Musk Duck.

Memana Rd

The corner of Memana Rd and Summers Rd at 39.59.40 S and 148.04.26 E is very good for the sought-after exotics such as Common Pheasant, Wild Turkey and Indian Peafowl.

Stubble Quails were reported twice from the area. Other birds here include Cape Barren Goose, Forest Raven, Black Currawong, Green Rosella, Australasian Pipit, Olive Whistler, New Holland Honeyeater, Brown Falcon and Swamp Harrier.

Patriarch Inlet

Patriarch Inlet is situated north of the Patriarchs Conservation Area. To get there, take Memana Rd (C803) which runs all the way from Whitemark to the Patriarch Inlet.

Hooded Plover, Red-capped Plover and Fairy Tern breed on the beaches. Australian Pied Oystercatchers congregate here in large numbers. Other shorebirds include Red-necked Stint, Ruddy Turnstone, Sooty Oystercatcher and Caspian Tern. White-bellied Sea-Eagles nest in the inlet area. Eastern Great Egrets and Australian Pelicans are regularly found here. In the surrounding bush and saltmarshes look for White-fronted Chat, Tasmanian Scrubwren, Black Currawong, Olive Whistler, Green Rosella, Beautiful Firetail and Collared Sparrowhawk.

Babel Island is visible from the beach; 3mln Short-tailed Shearwaters nest there.

Settlement Point

Settlement Point is located on the northwest coast. It can be accessed from the township of Emita, located on Palana Rd (B85) 15km north of Whitemark.

A large colony of Short-tailed Shearwaters is located at Settlement Point. Birds are present from late September to early March. A viewing platform is provided in the colony. Access to the colony is possible through the Wybalenna site owned by the local Aboriginal community.

If you drive further north from Emita in the direction of Killiecrankie on Palana Rd (B85), you may find that the road is fantastic for raptors. Common species include Nankeen Kestrel, Swamp Harrier, Brown Falcon, Australian Hobby, Wedge-tailed Eagle and White-bellied Sea-Eagle. The latter breeds around the Killiecrankie Bay.

Nankeen Kestrel

The Bluff

The site is located near Whitemark. From Palana Rd (B85), take Bluff Rd and then turn into Beach Rd. Walk south along the beach. Sooty Oystercatchers can be found here in groups of up to 100 birds. It is also a reliable spot for Little Egret. Other shorebirds here include Bar-tailed Godwit, Red-necked Stint, Red-capped Plover, Australian Pied Oystercatcher and Caspian Tern.

Along Bluff Rd, look for Shining Bronze-cuckoo, Beautiful Firetail, Silvereye, Wild Turkey and Brown Quail.

Lady Barron

There should be some good birding opportunities around the town of Lady Barron, located on the south coast of the island.

On the foreshore of Adelaide Bay, expect to find Common Greenshank, Sooty Oystercatcher, Australian Pied Oystercatcher, Ruddy Turnstone, Bar-tailed Godwit, Caspian Tern and Pacific Gull. In June 2016, Great Frigatebird was observed flying near the Lady Barron wharf.

In the surrounding scrub look for Tasmanian Thornbill, Tasmanian Scrubwren, Golden Whistler, Olive Whistler, Grey Shrike-thrush, Green Rosella, New Holland Honeyeater and Brown Falcon.

Chukor Partridge is best found along Coast Rd near the Badger Corner, west of Lady Barron.

Further reading

Andrew Geering, Lindsay Agnew, Sandra Harding. *Shorebirds of Australia*. CSIRO Publishing 2007.

Birdlife. *Working List of Australian Birds* v2.1. October 2016

Dave Watts. *Field Guide to Tasmanian Birds*. New Holland Publishers, 2002.

Dave Watts, Cathie Plowman. *Where to See Wildlife in Tasmania*. Jacana Books, 2008.

Explore Australia's National Parks. 2nd Ed. Explore Australia Publishing, 2013.

Les Christidis, Walter E. Boles. *Systematics and Taxonomy of Australian Birds*. CSIRO Publishing, 2008

Lloyd Nielsen. *Birding Australia – Site Guide*. Lloyd Nielsen 2006.

Lloyd Nielsen. *Birding Australia – A Directory for Birders*. Lloyd Nielsen 2011.

Richard Thomas, Sarah Thomas. *The complete guide to finding the birds of Australia*. Frogmouth Publications, 1996.

Richard Thomas, Sarah Thomas, David Andrew, Alan McBride. *The complete guide to finding the birds of Australia*. 2nd Ed. CSIRO Publishing, 2011.

Tim Dolby Bird Trip Reports - http://tim-dolby.blogspot.com.au/.

Tim Dolby, Rohan Clarke. *Finding Australian Birds*. CSIRO Publishing, 2014.

Sue Taylor, *Best 100 Birdwatching Sites in Australia,* New South Publishing, 2013.

Bird Index

Nomenclature used in this chapter follows the *Systematics and Taxonomy of Australian Birds* by Les Christidis and Walter E. Boles, CSIRO Publishing, 2008, unless newer changes to taxonomy have been introduced (Birdlife's *Working List of Australian Birds* v2.1, October 2016).

Nomenclature of seabirds follows the *Field Guide to New Zealand Seabirds* by Brian Parkinson, New Holland Publishers, 2000.

Albatross	Antipodean Wandering Albatross	*Diomedea antipodensis*
	Black-browed Albatross	*Thalassarche melanophris*
	Buller's Albatross	*Thalassarche bulleri*
	Chatham Albatross	*Thalassarche eremita*
	Gibson's Wandering Albatross	*Diomedea gibsoni*
	Grey-headed Albatross	*Thalassarche chrysostoma*
	Indian Yellow-nosed Albatross	*Thalassarche carteri*
	Light-mantled Sooty Albatross	*Phoebetria palpebrata*
	Northern Royal Albatross	*Diomedea sanfordi*
	Salvin's Albatross	*Thalassarche salvini*
	Shy Albatross	*Thalassarche cauta*
	Snowy Wandering Albatross	*Diomeda exulans*
	Southern Royal Albatross	*Diomedea epomorpha*
Bittern	Australasian Bittern	*Botaurus poiciloptilus*
	Australian Little Bittern	*Ixobrychus dubius*
Blackbird	Common Blackbird	*Turdus merula*
Black-Cockatoo	Yellow-tailed Black-Cockatoo	*Calyptorhynchus funereus*
Booby	Brown Booby	*Sula leucogaster*
Bronze-Cuckoo	Horsfield's Bronze-Cuckoo	*Chalcites basalis*
	Shining Bronze-Cuckoo	*Chalcites lucidus*
Bronzewing	Brush Bronzewing	*Phaps elegans*
	Common Bronzewing	*Phaps chalcoptera*
Butcherbird	Grey Butcherbird	*Cracticus torquatus*
Button-quail	Painted Button-quail	*Turnix varius*
Chat	White-fronted Chat	*Epthianura albifrons*
Cisticola	Golden-headed Cisticola	*Cisticola exilis*
Cockatoo	Sulphur-crested Cockatoo	*Cacatua galerita*

Coot	Eurasian Coot	*Fulica atra*
Corella	Little Corella	*Cacatua sanguinea*
	Long-billed Corella	*Cacatua tenuirostris*
Cormorant	Black-faced Cormorant	*Phalacrocorax fuscescens*
	Great Cormorant	*Phalacrocorax carbo*
	Little Black Cormorant	*Phalacrocorax sulcirostris*
	Little Pied Cormorant	*Microcarbo melanoleucos*
Crake	Australian Spotted Crake	*Porzana fluminea*
	Baillon's Crake	*Porzana pusilla*
	Spotless Crake	*Porzana tabuensis*
Cuckoo	Brush Cuckoo	*Cacomantis variolosus*
	Fan-tailed Cuckoo	*Cacomantis flabelliformis*
	Pallid Cuckoo	*Cacomantis pallidus*
Cuckoo-shrike	Black-faced Cuckoo-shrike	*Coracina novaehollandiae*
Curlew	Eastern Curlew	*Numenius madagascariensis*
Currawong	Black Currawong	*Strepera fuliginosa*
	Grey Currawong	*Strepera versicolor*
Darter	Australasian Darter	*Anhinga novaehollandiae*
Diving-Petrel	Common Diving-Petrel	*Pelecanoides urinatrix*
Dotterel	Black-fronted Dotterel	*Elseyornis melanops*
	Red-kneed Dotterel	*Erythrogonys cinctus*
Dove	Barbary Dove	*Streptopelia roseogrisea*
	Rock Dove	*Columba livia*
	Spotted Dove	*Streptopelia chinensis*
Drongo	Spangled Drongo	*Dicrurus bracteatus*
Duck	Australian Wood Duck	*Chenonetta jubata*
	Blue-billed Duck	*Oxyura australis*
	Freckled Duck	*Stictonetta naevosa*
	Musk Duck	*Biziura lobata*
	Pacific Black Duck	*Anas supercilosa*
	Pink-eared Duck	*Malacorhynchus membranaceus*
Eagle	Wedge-tailed Eagle	*Aquila audax*
Egret	Cattle Egret	*Ardea ibis*
	Eastern Great Egret	*Ardea modesta*
	Intermediate Egret	*Ardea intermedia*
	Little Egret	*Egretta garzetta*
Emu	Emu	*Dromaius novaehollandiae*

Australian Good Birding Guide: Tasmania

Emu-wren	Southern Emu-wren	*Stipiturus malachurus*
Fairy-wren	Superb Fairy-wren	*Malurus cyaneus*
Falcon	Brown Falcon	*Falco berigora*
	Peregrine Falcon	*Falco peregrinus*
Fantail	Grey Fantail	*Rhipidura albiscapa*
Fieldwren	Striated Fieldwren	*Calamanthus fuliginosus*
Finch	Zebra Finch	*Taeniophygia guttata*
Firetail	Beautiful Firetail	*Stagonopleura bella*
Flycatcher	Satin Flycatcher	*Myiagra cyanoleuca*
Frigatebird	Great Frigatebird	*Fregata minor*
	Lesser Frigatebird	*Fregata ariel*
Frogmouth	Tawny Frogmouth	*Podargus strigoides*
Fruit-Dove	Rose-crowned Fruit-Dove	*Ptilinopus regina*
Fulmar	Southern Fulmar	*Fulmarus glacialoides*
Galah	Galah	*Eolophus roseicapilla*
Gannet	Australasian Gannet	*Morus serrator*
Giant-Petrel	Northern Giant-Petrel	*Macronectes halli*
	Southern Giant-Petrel	*Macronectes giganteus*
Godwit	Bar-tailed Godwit	*Limosa lapponica*
	Black-tailed Godwit	*Limosa limosa*
	Hudsonian Godwit	*Limosa haemastica*
Goldfinch	European Goldfinch	*Carduelis carduelis*
Goose	Cape Barren Goose	*Cereopsis novaehollandiae*
	Greylag Goose	*Anser anser*
	Magpie Goose	*Anseranas semipalmata*
Goshawk	Brown Goshawk	*Accipiter fasciatus*
	Grey Goshawk	*Accipiter novaehollandiae*
Grassbird	Little Grassbird	*Megalurus gramineus*
Grebe	Australasian Grebe	*Tachybaptus novaehollandiae*
	Great Crested Grebe	*Podiceps cristatus*
	Hoary-headed Grebe	*Poliocephalus poliocephalus*

Greenfinch	Common Greenfinch	*Chloris chloris*
Greenshank	Common Greenshank	*Tringa nebularia*
Gull	Franklin's Gull	*Leucophaeus pipixcan*
	Kelp Gull	*Larus dominicanus*
	Pacific Gull	*Larus pacificus*
	Silver Gull	*Chroicocephalus novaehollandiae*
Hardhead	Hardhead	*Aythya australis*
Harrier	Swamp Harrier	*Circus approximans*
Heron	White-faced Heron	*Egretta novaehollandiae*
	White-necked Heron	*Ardea pacifica*
Hobby	Australian Hobby	*Falco longipennis*
Honeyeater	Black-headed Honeyeater	*Melithreptus affinis*
	Crescent Honeyeater	*Phylidonyris pyrrhopterus*
	New Holland Honeyeater	*Phylidonyris novaehollandiae*
	Strong-billed Honeyeater	*Melithreptus validirostris*
	Tawny-crowned Honeyeater	*Gliciphila melanops*
	Yellow-throated Honeyeater	*Lichenostomus flavicollis*
Ibis	Straw-necked Ibis	*Threskiornis spinicollis*
Jaeger	Arctic Jaeger	*Stercorarius parasiticus*
	Long-tailed Jaeger	*Stercorarius longicaudus*
	Pomarine Jaeger	*Stercorarius pomarinus*
Kestrel	Nankeen Kestrel	*Falco cenchroides*
Kingfisher	Azure Kingfisher	*Ceyx azureus*
	Forest Kingfisher	*Todiramphus macleayii*
	Red-backed Kingfisher	*Todiramphus pyrrhopygius*
	Sacred Kingfisher	*Todiramphus sanctus*
Kite	Black-shouldered Kite	*Elanus axillaris*
	Whistling Kite	*Haliastur sphenurus*
Knot	Great Knot	*Calidris tenuirostris*
	Red Knot	*Calidris canutus*
Kookaburra	Laughing Kookaburra	*Dacelo novaeguineae*
Lapwing	Banded Lapwing	*Vanellus tricolor*
	Masked Lapwing	*Vanellus miles*
Lorikeet	Musk Lorikeet	*Glossopsitta concinna*
	Rainbow Lorikeet	*Trichoglossus haematodus*
Lyrebird	Superb Lyrebird	*Menura novaehollandiae*

Magpie	Australian Magpie	*Cracticus tibicen*
Mallard	Northern Mallard	*Anas platyrhynchos*
Martin	Tree Martin	*Petrochelidon nigricans*
Miner	Noisy Miner	*Manorina melanocephala*
Moorhen	Dusky Moorhen	*Gallinula tenebrosa*
Morepork	Tasmanian Morepork	*Ninox novaeseelandiae*
Mynah	Indian Mynah	*Acridotheres tristis*
Native-hen	Black-tailed Native-hen	*Trybonix ventralis*
	Tasmanian Native-hen	*Trybonix mortierii*
Needletail	White-throated Needletail	*Hirundapus caudacutus*
Night-Heron	Nankeen Night-Heron	*Nycticorax caledonicus*
Owl	Masked Owl	*Tyto novaehollandiae*
Owlet-nightjar	Australian Owlet-nightjar	*Aegotheles cristatus*
Oystercatcher	Australian Pied Oystercatcher	*Haematopus longirostris*
	Sooty Oystercatcher	*Haematopus fuliginosus*
Pardalote	Forty-spotted Pardalote	*Pardalotus quadragintus*
	Spotted Pardalote	*Pardalotus punctatus*
	Striated Pardalote	*Pardalotus striatus*
Parrot	Blue-winged Parrot	*Neophema chrysostoma*
	Ground Parrot	*Pezoporus wallicus*
	Orange-bellied Parrot	*Neophema chrysogaster*
	Swift Parrot	*Lathamus discolour*
Partridge	Chukar Partridge	*Alectoris chukar*
Peafowl	Indian Peafowl	*Pavo cristatus*
Pelican	Australian Pelican	*Pelecanus conspicillatus*
Penguin	Fiordland Penguin	*Eudyptes pachyrhynchus*
	Gentoo Penguin	*Pygoscelis papua*
	Little Penguin	*Eudyptula minor*
	Snares Penguin	*Eudyptes robustus*
Petrel	Black Petrel	*Procellaria parkinsoni*
	Blue Petrel	*Halobaena caerulea*
	Cape Petrel	*Daption capense*
	Cook's Petrel	*Pterodroma cookie*

	Gould's Petrel	*Pterodroma leucoptera*
	Great-winged Petrel	*Pterodroma macroptera*
	Grey Petrel	*Procellaria cinerea*
	Grey-faced Petrel	*Pterodroma macoptera*
	Kermadec Petrel	*Pterodroma neglecta*
	Mottled Petrel	*Pterodroma inexpectata*
	Providence Petrel	*Pterodroma solandri*
	Soft-plumaged Petrel	*Pterodroma mollis*
	Stejneger's Petrel	*Pterodroma longirostris*
	Westland Petrel	*Procellaria westlandica*
	White-chinned Petrel	*Procellaria aequinoctialis*
	White-headed Petrel	*Pterodroma lessonii*
	White-necked Petrel	*Pterodroma cervicalis*
Pheasant	Common (Ring-necked) Pheasant	*Phasianus colchicus*
Pigeon	White-headed Pigeon	*Columba leucomela*
Pipit	Australasian Pipit	*Anthus novaeseelandiae*
Plover	Double-banded Plover	*Charadrius bicinctus*
	Grey Plover	*Pluvialis squatarola*
	Hooded Plover	*Thinornis rubricollis*
	Lesser Sand Plover	*Charadrius mongolus*
	Little Ringed Plover	*Charadrius dubious*
	Pacific Golden Plover	*Pluvialis fulva*
	Red-capped Plover	*Charadrius ruficapillus*
Prion	Antarctic Prion	*Pachyptila desolata*
	Broad-billed Prion	*Pachyptila vittata*
	Fairy Prion	*Pachyptila turtur*
	Salvin's Prion	*Pachyptila salvini*
	Slender-billed Prion	*Pachyptila belcheri*
Quail	Brown Quail	*Coturnix ypsilophora*
	California Quail	*Callipepla callifornica*
	Stubble Quail	*Coturnix pectoralis*
Quail-thrush	Spotted Quail-thrush	*Cinclosoma punctatum*
Rail	Buff-banded Rail	*Gallirallus philippensis*
	Lewin's Rail	*Rallus pectoralis*
Raven	Forest Raven	*Corvus tasmanicus*
	Little Raven	*Corvus mellori*
Reed-Warbler	Australian Reed-Warbler	*Acrocephalus australis*
Robin	Dusky Robin	*Melanodryas vittata*
	Flame Robin	*Petroica phoenicea*
	Scarlet Robin	*Petroica boodang*
Rosella	Green Rosella	*Platycercus caledonicus*

	Eastern Rosella	*Platycercus eximius*
Ruff	Ruff	*Philomachus pugnax*
Sanderling	Sanderling	*Calidris alba*
Sandpiper	Buff-breasted Sandpiper	*Tryngites subruficollis*
	Common Sandpiper	*Actitis hypoleucos*
	Curlew Sandpiper	*Calidris ferruginea*
	Marsh Sandpiper	*Tringa stagnatilis*
	Pectoral Sandpiper	*Calidris melanotos*
	Sharp-tailed Sandpiper	*Calidris acuminata*
Scaup	New Zealand Scaup	Aythya novaeseelandiae
Scrubtit	Scrubtit	*Acanthornis magna*
Scrubwren	Tasmanian Scrubwren	*Sericornis humilis*
Sea-Eagle	White-bellied Sea-Eagle	*Haliaeetus leucogaster*
Shearwater	Buller's Shearwater	*Ardenna bulleri*
	Flesh-footed Shearwater	*Ardenna carneipses*
	Fluttering Shearwater	*Puffinus gavia*
	Great Shearwater	*Ardenna gravis*
	Hutton's Shearwater	*Puffinus huttoni*
	Little Shearwater	*Puffinus assimilis*
	Short-tailed Shearwater	*Ardenna tenuirostris*
	Sooty Shearwater	*Ardenna griseus*
	Wedge-tailed Shearwater	*Ardenna pacifica*
Shelduck	Australian Shelduck	*Tadorna tadornoides*
Shoveler	Australasian Shoveler	*Anas rhynchotis*
Shrike-thrush	Grey Shrike-thrush	*Colluricincla harmonica*
Silvereye	Silvereye	*Zosterops lateralis*
Skua	Brown Skua	*Catharacta antarcticus*
	South Polar Skua	*Stercorarius maccormicki*
Skylark	Eurasian Skylark	*Alauda arvensis*
Snipe	Latham's Snipe	*Gallinago hardwickii*
Sparrow	House Sparrow	*Passer domesticus*
Sparrowhawk	Collared Sparrowhawk	*Accipiter cirrocephalus*
Spinebill	Eastern Spinebill	*Acanthorhynchus tenuirostris*
Spoonbill	Royal Spoonbill	*Platalea regia*

Starling	Common Starling	*Sturnus vulgaris*
Stilt	Banded Stilt	*Cladorhynchus leucocephalus*
	Pied Stilt	*Himantopus leucocephalus*
		(2016 English name change from Black-winged Stilt)
Stint	Little Stint	*Calidris minuta*
	Red-necked Stint	*Calidris ruficollis*
Storm-Petrel	Black-bellied Storm-Petrel	*Fregetta tropica*
	European Storm-Petrel	*Hydrobates pelagicus*
	Grey-backed Storm-Petrel	*Garrodia nereis*
	White-faced Storm-Petrel	*Pelagodroma marina*
	Wilson's Storm-Petrel	*Oceanites oceanicus*
Swallow	Welcome Swallow	*Hirundo neoxena*
Swamphen	Purple Swamphen	*Porphyrio porphyrio*
Swan	Black Swan	*Cygnus atratus*
Swift	Fork-tailed Swift	*Apus pacificus*
Tattler	Grey-tailed Tattler	*Tringa brevipes*
Teal	Chestnut Teal	*Anas castanea*
	Grey Teal	*Anas gracilis*
Tern	Antarctic Tern	*Sterna vittata*
	Arctic Tern	*Sterna paradisaea*
	Caspian Tern	*Hydroprogne caspia*
	Crested Tern	*Thallaseus bergii*
	Fairy Tern	*Sternula nereis*
	Little Tern	*Sternula albifrons*
	White-fronted Tern	*Sterna striata*
Thornbill	Brown Thornbill	*Acanthiza pusilla*
	Tasmanian Thornbill	*Acanthiza ewingii*
	Yellow-rumped Thornbill	*Acanthiza chrysorrhoa*
Thrush	Bassian Thrush	*Zoothera lunulata*
Treecreeper	White-throated Treecreeper	*Cormobates leucophaeus*
Triller	White-winged Triller	*Lalage sueurii*
Turkey	Wild Turkey	*Meleagris gallopavo*
Turnstone	Ruddy Turnstone	*Arenaria interpres*
Wagtail	Willie Wagtail	*Rhipidura leucophrys*

Wattlebird	Little Wattlebird	*Anthochaera chrysoptera*
	Yellow Wattlebird	*Anthochaera paradoxa*
Whimbrel	Whimbrel	*Numenius phaeopus*
Whistler	Golden Whistler	*Pachycephala pectoralis*
	Olive Whistler	*Pachycephala olivacea*
Whistling-Duck	Wandering Whistling-Duck	*Dendrocygna arcuata*
Woodswallow	Dusky Woodswallow	*Artamus cyanopterus*
	White-browed Woodswallow	*Artamus superciliosus*

Site Index

www.ingramcontent.com/pod-product-compliance
Lightning Source LLC
Chambersburg PA
CBHW050804270326
41926CB00025B/4538